They Call Me Coach

John Wooden

WITH JACK TOBIN

CB

CONTEMPORARY BOOKS

Library of Congress Cataloging-in-Publication Data

Wooden, John R.
    They call me coach / John Wooden with Jack Tobin : foreword by
Denny Crum.
        p.   cm.
    Includes index.
    ISBN 0-8092-4591-4
    1. Wooden, John R.   2. Basketball—United States—Coaches—
Biography.   3. University of California, Los Angeles—Basketball.
I. Tobin, Jack.   II. Title.
GV884.W66A3   1988
796.32'3'0924—dc19   88-16157
                                                                  CIP

Grateful acknowledgment is made for permission to reprint the following
copyrighted material: "How to Be a Champion" and "The Great Competitor" by
Grantland Rice, reprinted by permission of A. S. Barnes & Co., Inc., Cranbury,
New Jersey; "They Ask Me Why I Teach" by Glennice L. Harmon, *NEA Journal*,
September 1948, reprinted by permission of *NEA Journal*, Washington, D.C.

Unless otherwise indicated, photographs are by courtesy ASUCLA Photographic
Department, staff photographers Stan Troutman and Norm Schindler.

Cover photograph by Charles Bush

Published by Contemporary Books
A division of NTC/Contemporary Publishing Group, Inc.
4255 West Touhy Avenue, Lincolnwood (Chicago), Illinois 60712-1975 U.S.A.
Copyright © 1988 by John Wooden and Jack Tobin
Printed in the United States of America
International Standard Book Number: 0-8092-4591-4
99 00 01 02 03 04 QP 34 33 32 31 30 29 28 27 26 25 24 23 22 21 20 19 18

Foreword

IT'S BEEN 17 years since I last sat beside Coach John Wooden in Houston's Astrodome, during our 68–62 Final Four victory over Villanova in 1971. And every day since, something in my life brings back fond memories of my years with this great man.

Our relationship had a rather strange beginning. I had always dreamed about going to UCLA while growing up in San Fernando. One day our president at Pierce College, John Shepherd, invited Coach Wooden over to a game. I didn't know he was there; in fact, I didn't know anything about it until he called me up and asked if I'd like to come to a UCLA game. I did go, and I never forgot that game. It was played at the Pan Pacific Auditorium on Beverly Boulevard, in Los Angeles.

The next week he called and invited me to a practice. Afterward, we walked over to Kerckhoff Hall to eat at the training table. It was a memorable walk—not for what he said, but because he took me in through the kitchen past the long row of garbage cans.

After I ate dinner with him and longtime UCLA trainer Ducky Drake, Coach asked me point blank, "Well, are you coming or aren't you?" That's the Coach. He enjoyed meeting and talking with prospects but never liked recruiting. "Yeah," I answered, "I guess I am."

That was my first experience with the man I'll always call Coach.

I learned a tremendous amount from him as a player, but the exposure that helped me most was the two years I worked with him, Jerry Norman, and the UCLA freshman team while doing graduate work for my teaching credentials. For the first time I saw the other side of John Wooden and his methods, his organization, and his practice format.

Later at Pierce College—first as an assistant, then as head coach—I began to use all that Coach taught me. I felt pretty good there, but when Jerry Norman decided to go into the brokerage business, and Coach Wooden asked me if I would come back and be his assistant coach, I immediately said yes, even though the move meant I had to take a $3,000 salary cut, a lot of money in those days.

During those years I realized that what separated Coach Wooden from so many other coaches was his ability and willingness to utilize everyone involved in the coaching program at UCLA. Here I was, a junior-college coach working for the greatest coach ever, making suggestions to him at our daily practice planning sessions. We all had input; after thinking it through Coach would say, "Let's try it in practice."

If it worked, we'd put it in the game; if not, we'd either work with it or eliminate it. Coach never gave the impression that he knew everything; he was always open to changing and moving forward. It was his greatest strength as a coach, and that's why he had such phenomenal success over the years with his teams and with individual players.

I remember how we prepared for those practice sessions. We used to spend more than an hour each morning just to plan that day's practice. We'd evaluate what had happened the day before, and then set down the practice schedule in fine detail—nothing was left to chance. At no time was any member of the squad simply watching. They were *doing*: if they weren't in a three-man drill, then they'd be shooting free throws.

Coach repeated time and time again that if you prepared thoroughly in practice, the games would take care of themselves. In later years, however, that rule wasn't quite as true. Opponents started doing so many different things and made so many changes that you had to match up against them, move for move, during the course of the game.

The chess match. I think that's the aspect of basketball Coach enjoyed most. Watching him work a game from the bench was a study in coaching mastery: he could successfully anticipate the movement and flow before it happened.

Coach and I met twice in the Final Four, the first time in the 1971–72 season. I pitted my first team at Louisville against Coach's Bruins in the semifinals at the Memorial Sports Arena in Los Angeles. The fact that we lost 96–77 hurt at the time, but today I have fond memories of coaching against the master in my first season as head coach.

We met one other time in the Final Four, in the 1975 semifinals in San Diego. I remember learning a short time after we had exchanged post-game best wishes that Coach had announced his retirement from a career that ended with his tenth NCAA championship, a 92–85 victory over Kentucky.

It's funny how these numbers and years stay with me, (as I find they do with Coach's other disciples, former teammates, and friends), but the Coach has been a powerful influence in my career and in my life. He generates great respect from everyone who has had the privilege to cross his path, especially those of us who had the rare opportunity to play for him and, those of us, a mere handful, who coached beside him.

He's touched the lives of those around him and inspired countless people to emulate his wonderful qualities: his love and dedication to his family, his appreciation of all who played for him, his honesty, his patience, and his modesty. He could teach, imparting his thoughts in a way that never alienated anyone, and he could understand the frustration of a player who wanted to play better so badly he could taste it. He controlled the most stressful situations with the ease and demeanor of a gentleman, and, most important, he knew how to listen.

It still amazes me how much of the Coach rubs off on you. You don't really think much about it until one day you realize something you do every day is something he did. Like my rolled-up program with the current stats inside. That program was the Coach's signature card. He opened up an entire way of life to us all. We all just fell in line behind him, trying to do what he did.

Whenever I speak publicly, which is often, I credit John Wooden for the success we've had here at Louisville. Most of what I know about basketball I learned at his side.

This is why I'll always call him Coach.

Denny Crum, UCLA '59
Head Basketball Coach
University of Louisville

Preface

Life is a united effort of many. My life has been inspired from my youthful days in high school, through university, and into my coaching career by one person—my late wife, Nellie. Together we survived many trials, many misunderstandings, many separations; together for over 52 years, we weathered the Great Depression of the '30s with few material possessions and shared in the innumerable joys, fears, such as World War II, and disappointments that cross every life. Whatever problems arose—and there were many in the life of a teacher/coach—Nellie was always beside me, providing encouragement in times of adversity and humbly accepting the accolades that came our way in our late years together.

Of nearly equal comfort and contentment have been my children—Nan, my daughter, and Jim, my son—and their families, whose lives have become so tightly entwined with my career. They are as much a part of my team as the many gifted players who have made possible our success in the eyes of the world.

In any attempt to recite one's life, it is not a case of carefully recording every incident whether good or bad, but of attempting to touch on those that now appear to loom large on the wide screen of life. In so doing, many hundreds of people, places, and things have been put aside—each with great consternation because everyone and everything that has crossed my life in the years since my birth October 14, 1910, has played a vital role. Every player with whom I have been associated, whether as a teammate or an opponent, has left a mark of value in my life span. Again, no single volume can properly record all the hours in a man's life.

May I thank each and every one of you who played for me over the years at Dayton High School, South Bend Central High

School, Indiana State University, and UCLA for the great memories; for the association that has been so beneficial to my memories; for the great effort you expended in pursuit of success on the basketball court; for the love and happiness each of you has showered on me by your tremendous personal effort.

To all who have assisted me in the coaching, care, and consideration of all my teams—secretaries, assistant and fellow coaches, trainers, managers, athletic directors, personal friends, and all the fans over all the years—my thanks.

No doubt all who have crossed my path in these years will recall or remember some event or episode and wonder why it was not included. There are hundreds that I recall and have set aside, for one reason or another. Some of the deletions resulted from advice given me by my late father, to whom I owe so much. "If you can't say something good about a man," he repeatedly told me, "it is best to say nothing."

Life is not all good nor is it all bad. What mortal man can separate the many gray areas into good and bad?

Hopefully, in these pages you will get some insight into the wonderful people who have walked with me. Hopefully, things will come to life that will enable you to participate in the way young America makes our way of life so marvelous.

May I just add one other thought:

> "O Lord, if I seem to lose my faith in Thee,
> do not Thou lose Thy faith in me."

July 1988   JOHN WOODEN

1

Who can ask more of a man
than giving all within his span?
Giving all, it seems to me,
is not so far from victory. *

As I TURNED away from the post-game press conference and headed down that long corridor in Kansas City toward the dressing room, my feet and spirits dragged. For while I looked forward to congratulating the team on their victory, my thoughts were also on Fred Slaughter. What was he feeling at this moment?

Throughout the entire season, Fred had started every game. He had a brilliant year. Fred was a totally unselfish player with great team devotion and was frequently asked to do things for which a player receives little public attention. Even though he was short for a college center, barely 6 feet 5 inches tall, Fred was the blocker, screener, and rebounder—things seldom seen and appreciated by the crowd. But in this final game for the championship with Duke he had gotten off to a bad start. As the game moved along, it got worse instead of better. Finally, a change had to be made, so I pulled Fred and put in Doug McIntosh. And Doug did such a fine job that I left him in until the game was ours.

While I walked along toward the dressing room, George Moriarty's words were ringing in my mind, "Who can ask more of a man than giving all within his span? Giving all, it seems to me, is not so far from victory." And yet I knew that Fred was not alone in his disappointment. Having grown up not too far away in Topeka, Kansas, where he had attended high school,

---

* George Moriarty, "The Road Ahead of the Road Behind."

11

he was well aware that the crowd had been pretty well sprinkled with Slaughter relatives and fans.

Pushing open the dressing room door, I ran right into Fred. He had evidently been waiting for me. "Coach," he said, "before someone gets the wrong impression, I want you to know that I understand. You had to leave Doug in there because he played so well, and I didn't. I wanted to play in the worst way, but I do understand, and if anyone says I was upset, it's not true. Disappointed, yes, but upset, no. And I was very happy for Doug."

You know, there are a lot of peaks and valleys in every coach's life. But this was *the* peak—the ultimate. We had won our first, and my first, NCAA title by whipping Duke 98 to 83 and closed out the 1964 season with a perfect 30 and 0 record. But my concern for Fred had damaged all of that until this moment. Now I felt really great!

You get very close to the boys who play for you. Despite all efforts to the contrary a coach becomes attached to them—at times, thinking about a player as if he were his own son. And you become very concerned about their feelings and disappointments. Fred Slaughter and the other boys on that 1964 team made me feel that way. They had done everything I asked of them. And they had done it my way in spite of the fact that at times they may have questioned it. As a team, they were impressive, but never more so than in coming from behind late in the game to beat Kansas State 90 to 84 in the semifinals and recovering from a poor start to overwhelm Duke for the championship.

Interestingly, back in January of 1963 I had predicted that the 1964 team could be champions. Each year it was my practice to write a little message to myself on how I expected the team to do before the basketball season began and to seal it in an envelope. On this occasion, however, I added something extra. Pete Blackman, who had played forward on our team before going in the service, was stationed in Hawaii. In reply to a poetic letter he had written me, I sent him a free verse letter dated January 17, 1963. The last stanza predicted what could happen.

Dear Pete—

This legal pad, my friend, must do,
To convey my remarks to you,
For I shall speak of many things,
Of players who would all be kings,
Of boys who work and boys who don't,
Of boys who will and boys who won't,
Of many things, I'm sure that you
May wonder at, but know are true.

At Washington we lost a pair,
We were quite cold, as was the air,
Not one could hit and Fred was flat,
And played more like "Sir Fred of Fat."
Too many boys just want to start,
If not, they don't want any part,
And then at times some have a flair,
That makes one wonder if they care.

One forward seems to think that he
Surpasses all at comedy,
Another does not like to run,
But is involved in endless fun.
A mother thinks her son should start,
Or from the team he should depart,
From these remarks it's plain to see
It's more than simple rivalry.

One boy has drawn some other's ire,
Because he never seems to tire.
He gives his best throughout the day,
He only knows that way to play;
A starting spot some others seek,
By partial effort through the week,
They wonder why my eyes shoot fire,
When they question drills that I require.

Sir Mil of Wee now feels that he
A starter evermore should be,

But young soph Gail of fingers long,
Cannot agree, he knows that's wrong;
Some care not if we win or lose,
Their interest is in whom I use,
When the ball is tossed by the referee,
A starter's spot is all they see.

Our problems still remain the same,
A fact you've heard me oft proclaim,
We first must think just of the team,
And sacrifice the selfish dream;
But know that if the team does well,
In every way each must excel,
It matters not who is to blame,
Each one must truly play the game.

Now is the time when some show nerve,
To hope their profs won't use the curve;
Final exams began this week,
The grades of some we soon must seek,
And I will feel a bit of shame,
When some boys will professors blame,
And feel, of course, the profs should swerve,
And give them not what they deserve.

Sir Fred just called to say that he
And Gail at practice could not be;
In the morn at eight they have an exam,
For which today they wish to cram,
They know for this I can't say "no,"
And I'd be wrong if I did so;
Miss practice—for study! I'll always agree,
But they've had no exams in the past days—three!!

It was expected and it came,
Jack's knee is sore, in fact he's lame,
He cannot practice on this day,
But is sure this weekend he can play,
He called along with Chuck and Keith,

From practice they all seek relief,
No—that remark I should not claim,
They really like to play the game.

However, Pete, there's optimism
Beneath my valid criticism,
I want to say—yes, I'll foretell,
Eventually this team will jell,
And when they do, they will be great,
A championship could be their fate,
With every starter coming back,
Yes, Walt and Gail and Keith and Jack
And Fred and Freddie and some more,
We could be champs in sixty-four.

Actually, each team I ever coached had its own particular character. But while I have never said that any one of them was better than another, I guess I'll have to admit to having a special feeling for my first NCAA champions. It was a team of tremendous courage and poise that met every challenge. While it was a short team, they played tall in style and determination and were never rattled when we were behind. There was never a show of panic or any inclination to abandon the game plan. In fact there were times when I may have teetered on the verge of a change of tactic, but they held steady and were confident. Above all, each player believed firmly in our pressing defense. They were confident that it would produce the results we wanted.

Some fans and sportswriters have said that I used the press for the first time with the 1964 team, but this wasn't the case. Years before I had used it with my high school teams, and in 1963 it was introduced as the basic defense with our UCLA squad. And toward the end of that season it really began to pay off.

In short, their defense was aggressive, and they were a fine passing team with tremendous hustle, drive, and determination. I'm certain that thoughts of defeat never entered their minds.

Each of the five starters and two backup men were strong-willed and strong-minded athletes. They were individuals who melded together on the basketball court with superb precision.

WALT HAZZARD: Walt, a senior in 1964, was a fine team leader and an outstanding passer. But most important, he thoroughly understood what I wanted to accomplish. He was my kind of a guard.

Philadelphia had been home for Walt; his father was a minister there. And through a rather complex and at times confusing set of circumstances, he ended up at UCLA as a sophomore.

Willie Naulls, the first of my players to make it in the National Basketball Association, was playing with the New York Knickerbockers at the time. He and his cousin, Woody Sauldsberry of the Philadelphia Warriors, were impressed with Walt's ability as a high school player. It was worked out for Walt to come west, but, unfortunately, his grades were substandard as far as the high requirements at UCLA were concerned, so he enrolled for a year at Santa Monica City College. Being from out of state, he was ineligible to play at Santa Monica. So we arranged for him to play that season with the old Broadway Savings team in the local AAU league, coached by the late John Moore, one of my former players.

Up to that time I hadn't seen Walt in action, but it only took one game to convince me that he had it. "Walter," I told him after that first game, "you don't have to worry about making the team when you get to UCLA next season. And, you've got a scholarship all the way." I felt certain that other coaches would soon be after him, and I wanted to reassure him of my interest.

So, with no freshman experience and no familiarity with our system, he became the starting guard and floor leader on my 1961–62 team and did a fine job after we got off to a slow start.

The next year, however, Walt reverted to his one bad habit. When he came to us he had a tendency toward fancy play and did a lot of behind-the-back and blind passing and fancy dribbling. He had found out during his sophomore year that I did not permit this type of play, but somehow, perhaps because of his success as a sophomore, he began to revert to his old habits.

Our first road trip game that year was with the University of Colorado at Boulder. Walter got carried away and was too fancy for me so I pulled him out, and he sat the rest of the game out on the bench. We lost and it was tough to take because our chances of winning had been greatly diminished with him on the bench. They beat us rather handily, however, and his presence might not have made any difference.

The next night we played at Colorado State. Again I had Walt on the bench at the start and for much of the game. We lost this one, too, by one point in a double overtime.

Shortly after, I had a call from Rev. Walter R. Hazzard in Philadelphia. It seems that Walt had called him and said he was going to quit because I wouldn't let him play basketball the way he knew best. But Mr. Hazzard said, "I'm on your side, Coach Wooden. I told Walter not to come home if he quits—there would be no place for him here." Of course, he did not mean it that strongly, but he wanted his son to stand up to adversity.

Walter stayed on and had three great years.

FRED SLAUGHTER: While lacking in height as a center, Fred had other attributes which made him the hub around which we all revolved. He was quick and did a marvelous job of setting up the others and of rebounding. As a former high school track man, he had a keen sense of anticipation. But above all, he, like the others, was innately very intelligent.

Slaughter came to us from Topeka, Kansas, although his mother lived in Los Angeles where Fred had gone through grade school. Our scouting reports indicated that he was probably even a better track man, with decathlon potential, than a basketball player. So he came to us on a half basketball, half track scholarship. If he had made good in only one sport, that sport would take over his scholarship grant. He was not a spectacular player, but was a fine team player, and, after overcoming a problem or two, accepted his role and filled it admirably.

KEITH ERICKSON: At forward, Keith was a fiery, fearless player, and the tougher the opponent, the better he played. Keith led our defense both by example and voice. As the safety man in our pressing defense, he was the only man with a full view of the floor and was in command of what was developing.

At times Erickson's fiery personality became really inflamed. And when Keith was upset because he wasn't given the opportunity to score or felt he was not being properly appreciated by the others, he let everyone in sight know exactly how he felt.

We took Erickson when no one else wanted him and put him on a basketball scholarship for a year with baseball to take over if he did not measure up in basketball. One of my early UCLA boys, George Stanich, coached Keith at El Camino Junior College, but he didn't recommend him highly. Although George felt that Keith was a fine athlete and might even become great if he could get his emotions under control, he had some reservations about his ability to do that.

In looking back on it I guess I was challenged with the idea of trying to control and direct that spirit. And I became convinced that I could work with him and help him develop into a truly great player. I was always fond of this highly spirited young man and became very proud of him both on and off the court. He played the game at both ends of the floor in a highly competitive way.

JACK HIRSCH: Probably the best way to describe Jack is to share an early confrontation we had. The team was at training table one night having dinner. Jack didn't like the menu, so he pushed his plate back and said, "I'm not going to eat this slop."

I didn't like that and promptly told him so. "You're right, Jack. You are not going to eat it. Get out, and if you still feel that way about it, just don't come back to training table."

"I can eat better than this at home," he told me.

"I know you can, Jack. You can have steak every night if you want it. You can also drive a Grand Prix while the rest of us drive some little car. We understand that, but you don't eat here anymore until your attitude changes."

He said he didn't care and stalked out. I guess he was off training table for a couple of weeks. Then one day there was a knock on my office door. The door was open, and when I looked up, I saw it was Hirsch. It was out of character for Jack to knock; usually he just barged right in.

"Coach, I'm sorry."

"Sorry about what, Jack?"

"What do you want me to do, coach? Get down on my knees and beg? You know what I'm sorry about."

At that moment I came to know the real Jack Hirsch. Not too many people liked him at that time, and when I told him so, he said he just didn't care.

Actually, Jack lacked confidence at that time and tried to bull his way with roughness. In my opinion he was so afraid of not being accepted that he made sure people had a reason not to like him.

Hirsch came to us after two years at Valley Junior College. The coach from San Fernando Valley State had talked with him, but the only scholarship offer he had was from UCLA. Although he was short for a forward, only 6 feet 3 inches, he played a great deal bigger because of his jumping skill, his long arms, and fine timing. One of our unsung heroes—Jack wasn't spectacular, but he was a great team man who played the game every inch from end line to end line. Although he seemed to lack seriousness at times, he had it when it was needed and, like Keith, often made the big play for us.

I've had a lot of favorites over the years, and Jack is one of them. I'm still very fond of him.

GAIL GOODRICH: Goodrich teamed with Walt Hazzard at guard. He was inherently a very confident player, wanting the ball and resenting it if he thought Walt was monopolizing it. Gail felt certain that he could do more with the ball, but he finally came to realize that if he worked hard and got into the open, Hazzard would see to it that he got it. This made Goodrich, in my opinion, a much better basketball player, and I believe it has been borne out by his play in the pros. Of course, his intense competitive spirit and determination were necessary as well.

Of all the boys who made up that first championship team,

Gail Goodrich's background is the most unique. It was during his junior year in high school at the Los Angeles City championships that Gail first attracted my attention. I was sitting in the Sports Arena with Paul Neal, a friend from my church. We had come to watch a couple of other boys whose names I've now forgotten. Pointing toward the floor, I said, "That little guy with Poly is the smartest player on the floor. He's only a junior. I haven't heard much about him, but I'm going to watch him another year. If he grows a little and shows normal improvement, he may be the best prospect out there."

A few minutes later a man sitting behind us tapped me on the shoulder. "Coach Wooden, you don't know us, but did you really mean what you said about that small guard out there?"

"Yes, I do."

"Well, we're his parents."

The next week Mr. or Mrs. Goodrich called and asked if they could bring Gail over with his transcripts. Jerry Norman, my assistant, and I went over them carefully and discovered that Gail would be a mid-year graduate the following school year. And unlike most other school systems, the basketball season in Los Angeles would be completed by the time of his graduation.

Gail's final high school season was tremendous. He was the star of the city tournament, and by this time everybody wanted to talk to him. Bobby Kolf, Forrest Twogood's assistant at the University of Southern California, worked hard to persuade Gail to go to USC where his father had been a basketball star and captain of the team. But that chance remark of mine the year before and our continued interest throughout his final semester paid off. Gail enrolled in UCLA in February.

KENNY WASHINGTON: It was during the summer of 1963 that Walt Hazzard called from Philadelphia and told me about Washington. "He's from Booker T. Washington High in Beaufort, South Carolina. He's 6 feet 5 inches tall, a greater shooter than Gary Cunningham (one of my former players and later my assistant), as good a ball handler as I am, and weighs about one ninety to two hundred." It seems that Walt had met Kenny when he was visiting friends in Philadelphia and was impressed by him.

After checking we learned that Washington had the grades so we admitted him on a one year "make good" scholarship. He came west on a Greyhound bus. Jerry Norman met him at the station, and he looked scared to death. Evidently he had ridden all the way from Beaufort in the back end of the bus. I guess he figured he couldn't sit anywhere else. Instead of being 6 feet 5 inches and 200, he was 6 feet 3 inches, weighed about 160, and was extremely shy. Apparently, Walt had wanted to make certain that we would be impressed.

One day at freshman practice I saw Kenny standing over to one side with tears streaming down his cheeks. "What's the matter, Kenny?" I asked.

"It's going to be 160 days until I get back to Beaufort."

"No, Kenny, it's not," I responded. "I don't know how long it took you to get out here, but it will take you just that long to get back. If you don't shape up, you can ship out tomorrow on the first Greyhound."

I'm convinced that this remark helped him grow up a little and get his feet on the ground. He and I have laughed about that many times since. Actually, he's another great favorite of mine because of the way he developed and became one of the great "sixth men" in basketball.

DOUG MCINTOSH: Although the "seventh man" on our 1964 team, Doug's big moment came when he stepped in for Fred Slaughter in the championship game with Duke and played so well for most of the rest of the game.

Doug came to us from Lily, Kentucky, on a "make good" scholarship. His freshman year wasn't the least bit impressive, and we debated about extending the scholarship. Believe me, I'm happy it all worked out, and he stayed on.

In all, this was a remarkable group of men. Erickson, Hazzard, and Goodrich went on to successful careers in professional basketball. Fred Slaughter graduated from Columbia Law School and went on to be an assistant dean in the UCLA Law School.

Today he is a practicing attorney in L.A. Jack Hirsch, long a successful businessman, is now an assistant to Walt Hazzard at UCLA. Kenny Washington went to law school at Loyola in Los Angeles and is now in business in L.A. And Doug McIntosh went to theological school and has a pastorate in the Atlanta, Georgia, area.

Sometimes I wonder if the good Lord isn't almost as much the coach as I am. He certainly has smiled on me and truly moves in mysterious ways His wonders to perform.

2

A careful man I want to be,
A little fellow follows me;
I do not dare to go astray,
For fear he'll go the self-same way.

ONCE AGAIN I was faced with an agonizing decision. It was 1965—just one year after that first championship—and we were now fighting it out in the Portland Coliseum with Michigan. The NCAA championship would be ours again if we won this game.

Doug McIntosh, whose spectacular substitution for Slaughter in the 1964 championship game contributed so much to that win, was our regular starting center. He'd had a good year, but he didn't get off to a good start in this decisive Michigan game. And just as with Slaughter the year before, I had to pull Doug and substitute Mike Lynn, a sophomore. Mike did well, and I played him almost all the rest of the game.

And so, as I headed toward the dressing room, my feelings matched those of 1964. But, like Fred, Doug understood and told me that I had no choice. There wasn't even a hint of resentment, and Doug was happy that the team had done so well.

Remembering these two incidents, along with many others that occurred during my many years as a teacher and coach, has caused me to realize just how great the so-called father-son relationship is between a coach and his players. And this takes me back to the early and formative years of my own life.

My roots are deep in Indiana soil, for on October 14, 1910, I was born in a little place called Hall where my father worked as a tenant farmer for a man named Cash Ludlow. But a couple of years later my family moved three or four miles away to Monrovia, Indiana, where dad took a job as a rural mail carrier in addition to working a small farm. It is here that my earliest memories came into focus. One of them is dad's horse and buggy, and how I loved to go with him on his mail route. My love for a horse and buggy never ceased. I had but one dream, to own a buggy with red wheels and a little black mare to pull it. A cousin of mine had such a rig. Once in a while he would let me drive it to White Lick, a stream that was a tributary to the White River. I'd drive it out on a gravel bar and wash and shine it until it sparkled. Monrovia was just a small community, perhaps five hundred people in those days, and the people were all so friendly. Anyway, between the mail route and our small farm I thought we had a wonderful life.

About the time I was to begin my second year of grade school my mother inherited from her father a sixty-acre farm near Centerton, Indiana. Those were truly the rural farm days. We had no electricity, no inside plumbing, and we got our water from a hand pump. In addition to corn, wheat, and alfalfa, we grew watermelons and tomatoes.

Farming was a family affair. Even though I was pretty small, I was good at milking cows and cranking the milk separator. Actually, I came to love most everything we had to do on the farm with the possible exception of weeding and bugging potatoes and worming the tomatoes. Then, too, picking tomatoes was backbreaking work. I guess this is why I always have a great feeling of empathy for those stooped workers laboring out in the hot sun in the fields of the Central California San Joaquin Valley.

Dad believed in work, and he saw to it that my brothers— Maurice, or Cat as we called him most of the time, Daniel, and Billy—and I were kept busy. But as with all brothers we had our disagreements, although none of them was very serious. However, I do remember one incident that happened when I was in the sixth or seventh grade that has had a great bearing on my entire life. We were all in the barn cleaning out the horses' stalls, and Cat flipped a pitch fork of manure over and it hit me in the face.

I went right after him and called him an s.o.b. Dad heard me and immediately stopped the ruckus. After listening to both sides of the story, he gave me a good thrashing for what I said.

My brother Cat got a whipping too, but I still think his wasn't as hard as mine.

Dad certainly didn't condone what Cat had done, but neither would he put up with my loss of control or swearing. I think this one incident—little though it may seem to be—taught me a lesson that has kept me from using profanity through the years.

Actually, my father had a profound influence on my life. Both my philosophy of life and of coaching came largely from him. Even as a small boy I always had great respect for him because I knew he would always be fair with me and had my best interests at heart. And I soon learned that if he couldn't say something good about another person, he wouldn't say anything at all—a philosophy I've tried to follow.

A truly gentle man, dad read the Bible daily; he wanted us to read it, and we did. That is probably why I keep a copy on my desk today. It's not a decoration, but is well marked and read. The fact that I never heard dad swear, along with the incident in the barn, surely accounts for the fact that even today when I get mad, the strongest thing I can say is "goodness gracious sakes alive."

I remember so well what dad gave me for graduation from that little country grade school in Centerton. It was a piece of paper on which he had written a creed that he suggested I try to live by. It read:

1. Be true to yourself.
2. Make each day your masterpiece.
3. Help others.
4. Drink deeply from good books, especially the Bible.
5. Make friendship a fine art.
6. Build a shelter against a rainy day.
7. Pray for guidance, count and give thanks for your blessings every day.

I carried dad's handwritten original of that in my wallet for many years until it wore out. Then I had copies made, and I keep one in my wallet today along with another little quotation which further exemplifies my father's spirit.

> Four things a man must learn to do
> If he would make his life more true:
> To think without confusion more clearly,
> To love his fellow-man sincerely,
> To act from honest motives purely,
> To trust in God and heaven securely.

I wish I could say that I have always lived by that creed and quotation. I can't, but I have tried.

My dad did love his fellow-man sincerely. He was honest to the nth degree and had a great trust and faith in the Lord. And he taught us many lessons in integrity and honesty which we never forgot. Even though he was never able financially to help his sons through college, he is undoubtedly responsible for the fact that all of us graduated from college, got advanced degrees, and entered the teaching profession.

One such unforgettable lesson occurred while we were at Centerton. Parker's and Breedlove's were the two general stores in town. And whenever we could scrape together a nickel, we would ask Mr. Parker to mix up an assortment of candy. We'd get a handful each of licorice, jelly beans, peppermint and chocolate—probably as much as a dollar would buy today.

But, on this particular hot and humid Indiana day I'd walked into town to see my friend Freddy Gooch. His parents had a charge account at Breedlove's, so when we went in there he charged a bottle of pop. I was thirsty and finally weakened, charging a bottle of cream soda on my parents' account. It was good, but I was scared to death as I walked home later because I knew my parents hadn't given me permission to buy the pop, and they really couldn't afford it.

Finally, after I had been home a while I confessed what I had done, expecting a real hard whipping. But dad and mother understood my being tempted, and they just explained firmly why my actions were wrong. Believe me, that made a big impression on me, and I never did that again.

While money was hard to come by in those days, we always ate well. All farmers did. We had a big garden, grew all our own vegetables, had a lot of fruit trees, grew all kinds of berries and, of course, if one farmer had peaches and another pears, they'd trade.

We had a big cellar where we'd store potatoes, pumpkins, things that would keep. Then we had a smokehouse where we'd smoke meat for the winter. Of course, mom spent hours and hours canning. All the boys had to help. We'd pick the fruit, help cut it up, and then seal the jars either with paraffin or those glass lids that were made by the Ball Company in Muncie, Indiana.

One of the jobs we boys had was picking wild berries. In those days in Indiana you could find all kinds of wild blackberries, raspberries, and strawberries. Mom would make jams or jellies and also can them whole so she could make them into cobblers. We had a lot of cobblers because we all were especially fond of them.

I still contend that while we couldn't go out and buy a lot of the things the way we do today, we ate well. And mom was a cook that was appreciated.

Dad always made sure we had some fun mixed with our work, so it was during these early days on the farm that my love for sports emerged. I was probably around eight years old when I first learned something about basketball. Dad made a basket for us out of an old tomato basket with the bottom knocked out and nailed it up on a wall at one end of the hay loft in the barn. Our basketball was made out of old rags stuffed inside a pair of mother's black cotton hose. She would sew it up, by hand, into as round a form as possible. It's hard to imagine now but I still think we were able to dribble that thing.

Then when I was in the third or fourth grade, dad got a forge, and one of the first things he did was make a ring out of iron for a basket. That iron ring was pretty close to regulation. It went up in the loft and we made sure we used hay from that end up first so we could play basketball.

Even in those early years my dreams were entwined with school, basketball, baseball, and college. I don't think I really knew what going to college meant but Earl Warriner, our teacher, principal, and coach often talked about it, especially at basketball practice.

One of the essentials of every school day was what Mr. Warriner called the "morning sing." I was a terrible singer. So were the others on the basketball team, but we'd mouth the words. Finally, he had enough. One day, he stopped the sing and took us one at a time to the front of the class.

"Will you sing?" he asked me when my turn came.

"No." I was stubborn, so he laid it on me with a special willow switch he had cut for the job.

"Now will you sing?" he asked after a few cracks.

"I'll try." But just to make sure he hit me a couple more licks.

"Will you sing?"

"I'll sing."

I've never forgotten that. A year or so after that whipping, I got a card in the mail with a picture of an opera singer and it read, "You must remember this one thing, In opera you have to sing."

It was signed anonymously. I always believed Mr. Warriner sent the card, but never could prove it.

One of our favorite times in grade school was Halloween. We pulled all the usual tricks. One of the best, however, was what we called "ticktacking." That's where you grooved an empty spool of thread, put it on someone's door and spun it by pulling the string from thirty or forty feet away. It made an awful racket. There was one person in town who seemed to be quite a crank, so naturally one year we decided to ticktack him. I drew the short straw and had to creep up on the porch to place it on the door. Just as I did he came around the corner, shotgun in hand.

"What are you doing?" he yelled.

I took off, leaped his three-foot-high fence, and just as I hit the ground he blasted the shotgun, and I was hit in the back with a barrage of pellets. I ran for a block or two before diving into a bush to hide. Carefully I felt my backside for blood but couldn't find any.

A little later when I sneaked back to where the gang was hanging out, I found the imagined crank and the rest of the boys really laughing it up. I'd been duped, and they were all in on it. The pellets I felt when the gun went off were pebbles the gang had thrown. It was quite a while before I would forgive my friends or even play ball with them. But that didn't last long because basketball and baseball came close to being my first loves.

But during those early days baseball was really my favorite. All of the boys loved it so dad leveled off one end of a field and made a baseball diamond for us. Our ball was usually a makeshift affair, although occasionally we could save up and get a real one. And our bats were whittled out of a tree limb that had a nice, straight grain. It would take all winter to whittle a good bat with knife, file, and a plane. Our field was pretty crude and we didn't have a backstop. Some of our games were almost funny, but we loved it and learned to play well.

By the time I was thirteen or fourteen I was good enough to play on the Centerton town team even though several of the players were in their twenties. I always played shortstop, and that ball really used to come humming at me off of those homemade bats. But I always dug in and went after it. I knew if I didn't, somebody other than John Wooden would be in that lineup. There was a lot of competition, but I hung in there, became a farm boy sportsman, and dreamed big dreams about the future. My older brother Cat was always a great help to me as were by mother and dad. Cat helped me from a technical point of view, while mother and dad furnished great patience and understanding.

3

Worm or beetle—drought or tempest
—on a farmer's land may fall,
Each is loaded full o'ruin,
But a mortgage beats 'em all. *

MY DAD was born to be a farmer. He seemed to have a way with both land and animals, which can probably best be explained by telling about our two teams of mules—Jack and Kate and Betz and Hanna. Kate was a balky animal, especially with children. When we boys worked the fields with them, Kate would balk and lie down. Dad might be a half mile away, but all he had to do was just start walking across the field and Kate would get right up. She would never lie down for him, but she sure gave us a bad time.

I don't know how he did it, but I do know that he never resorted to force with any animal. There was a gentle way about him that they seemed to understand.

Farming came to an end for dad and us in 1924. There was a depression, probably not as severe as the one later in the thirties, but we sure thought it was bad.

There was a mortgage on the farm and things weren't going well, so dad decided to raise hogs. He borrowed the money, bought the feed and vaccine for the cholera shots which all hogs must have. But instead of protecting them, the vaccine gave them cholera and they all died.

Since another investment had turned out to be with a fraudulent company, dad couldn't repay the loan so we lost the farm and moved into Martinsville. I had started to Martinsville High the year before as a freshman and had been commuting on

---

* Will Carleton, "The Tramp's Story."

the interurban. It was eight miles from the Centerton stop to the terminal in Martinsville and we'd catch it out in front of Breedlove's general store.

Martinsville was the county seat and had a population then of about 5,000. There was a town square with the courthouse in center. Everything revolved around that square. There were hitching racks and watering troughs on each corner. A few of the people had cars then, and they'd drive in early every Saturday evening and try to be first to get the prime parking place in front of Riley's Cafe or Shireman's Ice Cream Parlor.

The Blackstone, our favorite pool hall, was next to Shireman's, and just on down the north side of the square was Riley's Cafe where once in a great while dad would take us all to dinner. Little did I realize then what an expense one of those dinners was to mom and dad. I knew we weren't wealthy, but I wasn't fully aware at that age of just how hard pressed we were for the money to take care of the normal day-to-day essentials.

Dad got a job at Homelawn Sanitarium where he worked in the bath house and gave massages. Because there were artesian wells in Martinsville, it had become a resort where a lot of people from Chicago, Indianapolis, Detroit, Cleveland, and other mid-western cities came for baths. Evidently the baths were helpful to people who had arthritis and rheumatism. I guess you could compare Martinsville to Hot Springs, Arkansas, or White Sulphur Springs, West Virginia, but I doubt if it was as plush.

Dad was really good at his job at Homelawn. He always had compassion for others, especially those who were infirm. There were people who came to Homelawn and my dad for all the years he worked there, and that was more than 25 years.

While dad received a salary—and I have no idea what it was now—a good deal of our income was based on the tips he'd receive each day. We always had one of those large calendars on the kitchen wall where mom would keep track of the tips. We'd be able to compare them to a year, two years, or even three years before. There were a few people who might give dad a five-dollar tip, and if one of these didn't come back the next year or the next time they were expected, we'd know it from the calendar.

While we never returned to the farm—dad worked at the sanitarium until he died in 1950—we often had a garden and grew many of our vegetables. And mom still canned the fruit and made jellies and jam. Actually, we never got the farm life out of our systems, except we never missed doing the chores. While we hadn't objected to them as kids, we much preferred life in Martinsville where baseball and basketball came next to study, at least a part of the time.

Martinsville has a very special place for another very important reason, however. It was there at a carnival the summer of my freshman year in high school that I met the girl I was to marry. Nellie Riley was a pert, vivacious, captivating girl with a very vibrant personality.

By contrast, I was terribly shy—painfully so, in fact. I recall vividly one summer day when I was out plowing on the farm in Centerton, and Nellie and some other kids who lived in Martinsville drove out in a car to see me. They parked on the knoll where they could see me, but I just kept right on plowing. Nellie thought I had no time for her. Little did she know that much as I wanted to stop and talk with her, I was just too bashful.

When I look back on those early days, I know just how fortunate I am that Nellie Riley was a patient and determined young lady. It wasn't that I was so hard to catch, but I was very ill at ease with girls.

Even after we became better acquainted and were going together, we had a problem. Nellie's house backed right up to where Glenn Curtis lived. Curtis, the basketball coach at Martinsville High, had a rule that you couldn't date during basketball season and you had to be home by 8:00 p.m.

In a little town like Martinsville it was pretty hard to do anything which the whole town didn't know about. From my sophomore year on there was no doubt in Nellie's mind or mine that we were in love, and I always felt that Curtis would peek in the window of the Riley house to see if I was there. And I was there pretty often.

It had to be pretty tough on a popular girl like Nellie not to go out on dates during basketball season—a rather long time, in those days. Our season began right after school started and lasted until the end of February or early March.

Now while Nellie enjoyed basketball, she also liked to dance, go to the movies and just have fun. But dancing was something I never really liked, although I enjoyed watching other people dance. I felt like I had two left feet and never could keep time with the music. Nellie had trouble believing that, especially after watching me run some of the intricate play patterns Curtis designed and never botch them up.

So between the no dates and the no dancing, we'd have spats from time to time, and Nellie would have dates with other people. We always managed to make up, of course. I think I had a date a time or two during one of our spats but Nellie was the only girl I ever really went with.

One little intimacy that we maintained throughout my career began in the first game I ever played at Martinsville High. Wanting to get Nellie's attention before the center jump that first game, I looked over at the band where she was playing the cornet, and winked at her. She took her thumb and index finger to form an "O"—meaning good luck, everything is okay. I waved back. Later I just waved my rolled-up program.

Hundreds and maybe thousands of fans over the years must have wondered what in the world John Wooden was doing making that little sign just before a UCLA basketball team took the floor. Sometimes—at the Houston Astrodome, for instance— we had to do a bit of searching. In fact, in the NCAA championships there in 1971, Nellie had to stand up and wave her arms like a Navy signalman before I could see her.

Nellie's inspiration and push—more than anything else—have contributed to what success I've enjoyed in life. She never let me get discouraged, even during the darkest hour. Many times during my college days at Purdue when I wanted to quit, she kept my spirits up, encouraging me to stay and work for my degree, even though most of the time it was by telephone from Martinsville to West Lafayette.

Coach Curtis had been fearful we would get married after I graduated from high school. I remember his going to Nellie's mother and talking to her about the situation. He explained that while I might earn eighteen or twenty dollars a week, I would make far more later on if I went to college and got my degree. We have often laughed about this because at that time

Mrs. Riley felt she would be marvelously happy if I could ever earn that much.

Our families, like many families in Martinsville, were quite close. We belonged to the same church, attended the same socials, visited the same friends and of course shopped in the same stores. While Martinsville was a little place and you could walk almost anywhere in the town in five or ten minutes, both of our families had telephones and I'm sure our parents wondered how we could talk so long on the phone when we had just separated a few minutes before.

There was a little park in Martinsville where they held band concerts on Saturday nights and we'd often go there. Once in a while we'd just take a walk out in the country or a lot of us would get together, pack lunches and go out on a hayride on a team and wagon that belonged to someone in high school who still lived on a farm. And there were tennis courts at the high school where we'd play occasionally. I wasn't much of a tennis player and Nellie never had much trouble beating me. Whether I won or lost playing Nellie didn't much concern me because just being with her was the important thing.

4

Stubbornness we deprecate,
Firmness we condone.
The former is our neighbor's trait,
The latter is our own.

MARTINSVILLE, like so many small Indiana communities, lived, breathed, and died basketball. The gymnasium could hold more people than there were residents in the city. This was true in many Indiana towns, even back in those days, because the surrounding populace were avid fans.

One year the sectional tournament was held in Martinsville. Paragon, a little place two or three miles south of Martinsville, was in the first round early Saturday morning. During the game, the Paragon bank was robbed. It was claimed the robbers were successful because all the people were at the game in Martinsville, even the police.

Robbing banks was a common occurrence in Indiana in those days. John Dillinger, probably the most notorious bank robber of the time, was from Mooresville, which was about seven miles north of Centerton. Dillinger received his first jail sentence, as I recall, from Judge Williams in Martinsville. One of the judge's sons was in school with me and later became an admiral in the U.S. Navy. I remember after the judge had imposed sentence that Dillinger threatened to kill him when he got out of jail.

While basketball was vital to life in Martinsville, there were a few other things such as weekly band concerts, carnivals, Saturday gatherings, family reunions, square and round dances, county fairs and so on that provided a bit of spice.

For years, Martinsville had done very well in Indiana basketball, primarily because of a fine coach, Glenn Curtis. He had a great deal of influence in my coaching career at Indiana State

35

and UCLA. In fact, I succeeded Curtis as coach at Indiana State. That was rather ironic because at one point my basketball career almost ended because of him.

Actually, in my sophomore season it did end—for two weeks. I didn't like Glenn Curtis then as a person, but I respected his basketball ability. My dislike stemmed from problems my older brother, Cat, had with Curtis. Curtis always used him as the sixth man. Cat was a fine player and often came in as the sixth man to win many games. He went on to Franklin College in Indiana where he did very well, but he was always a sixth man with Curtis.

I felt then, and I still do, that Curtis never gave Cat the opportunity he merited based on his ability in comparison with the other players. I learned long ago that the best players don't necessarily make the best team, and I believe Cat would have made Martinsville a better team.

Early in my sophomore year another player, who was considered a Curtis pet, and I tangled. I didn't lack in courage in those days. This fellow might be able to whip me, but he didn't scare me. Curtis took his side. I knew he was wrong, and the rest of the squad knew it, but Curtis was firm.

"Well," I said, "you're not going to get the chance to give me the treatment you gave my brother." With that I stalked off the floor—there would be no more basketball for me. I stayed away for two weeks. Curtis talked to me several times. Even though I was very upset, he was persistent, and I finally agreed to come back.

I was stubborn and stood up for what I felt was right. I'm sure this incident accounts for the fact that throughout my coaching career I tried to understand the young men who stood up to me. That's why I listened to their side, and why I almost always took back a boy who had walked off the team.

While we look upon college players today as young men because of their size, they are really still boys in maturity. You have to bend. They have to bend. When both bend within proper bounds, you become a solid unit.

Curtis's greatest strength was working with the young, immature players—the obstinate ones like me. I never doubted Curtis's coaching ability, even when I stalked out. He was an excellent teacher; later he became principal and superintendent of schools in Martinsville before moving to Indiana State. After a short career as a pro coach, he returned to Martinsville in the same positions.

One of his coaching concepts I never could accept was trying to fire a team up emotionally for a game. I never believed in it, and I still don't. But Curtis could make you tingle before an important game.

However, we did have one great common bond. He often quoted poetry at practice to illustrate a point. I have always been a lover of poetry, and I believe this influenced me to accept him and his ideas. He was a solid teacher of fundamental basketball, and a strong, firm disciplinarian. And even though I was unhappy over my brother's problems, I chose to go to Martinsville because of Curtis.

Martinsville had won its first Indiana state championship two years before, and those whom I respected claimed it was because of Curtis. Basketball was big in Martinsville. In fact, it was *the* sport. We didn't play football because it had been abolished some years before when a player was killed. And we didn't play baseball, but there was a meager track program, and I would run the dashes and broad jump once in a while, but I was no 10-flat sprinter.

Basketball dominated the life of the state and of our town. They used to say when a game was on in Martinsville, "Don't try to buy anything because everyone's at the game."

We played about twenty games in our regular season, and then we would go into the state tournament. The tournament was made up of sixty-four sectionals with sixteen teams each. Next came sixteen regionals, and then the final round of sixteen. There were no classes based on school size or player skills. The smallest or the largest school could end up champion. We were in the final championship game all of my three years at Martinsville and won the title in 1927.

The championship series can be a severe physical test. You could play four full games within a 25-hour period. For three years straight we drew the last game Friday night, the last game

Saturday morning, the last game Saturday afternoon, and the championship in the final game Saturday night. It sounds horrifying, but actually, it wasn't. In those days we had the center jump rather than the end-line-in-bound pass after every basket. This gave us the opportunity to catch our breath before the jump.

I jumped center once at Martinsville in the state finals during my sophomore season. Curtis put me in for the tip against Charles (Stretch) Murphy of Marion—a big man who stood 6 feet 7 inches tall. I believe he could play today with any man of comparable size. We later played together at Purdue. My job this time was to force as tight a jump as possible so our center could block off against Murphy. The theory may have been correct but Murphy was too much. We lost to the Marion "Giants," 30–23.

During my junior year we won the state title by beating Muncie Central, 26–23. I remember that not so much for the victory but for the beautiful silver Hamilton pocket watch that the people of Martinsville gave to each of us on the team. It's a fine watch, and I keep it at home now under a little glass bell. It runs as well as it did the day I got it.

Usually you would think that the championship would be the important memory of my high school career. But actually, it is the defeat in the championship during my senior year that takes the honor. Again we were playing Muncie Central. With moments to go, we were ahead, 12–11. A Muncie player turned his ankle and called time out. Since they had used their allowed three times out, it was a technical foul. We had the ball when time was called. When you shot the technical, the ball went back to the center jump if you made it. I was captain and elected to refuse the shot, thereby keeping the ball. Curtis leaped off the bench yelling, "We'll shoot it. We'll shoot it."

I argued, because under the rules then, we had the ball. And by keeping it I knew that Muncie could not get it back before time ran out. I could keep it on the dribble alone and we'd win, 12–11, for back-to-back championships.

Curtis prevailed. I shot and missed, and the ball went back to the center jump. In those days, the center could tip to himself.

Charlie Secrist, the Muncie center, tipped the ball behind him, grabbed it and in a wild, sweeping underhand motion arched the ball toward the basket. To this day, it is the highest arched shot I have ever seen. It seemed to go into the rafters and came straight down the middle of the basket, hardly fluttering the net.

Indiana basketball buffs still talk about that game. They'll tell you that it ended just as the ball dropped through the basket. I have personally heard the story from more people than Butler Fieldhouse could ever hold. Actually, what happened was that I called time as the ball came through the basket. Knowing Muncie would look for me to shoot, Curtis set up a play with me as the decoy. The center tipped to me, a forward screened for the center who got wide open, I faked a shot and passed to him underneath the basket, and he laid the ball up on the board. In doing so, he gave it a little English—it went around and around and around and then out. A forward was right there, but he was so confident the ball was in that he was jumping up and down in jubilation and wasn't positioned to rebound. When he saw it spin out, all he could do was bat it back up, but it didn't go in. It seemed like a disastrous turn of events at the time but by summer vacation the hurt had worn off a bit.

Hustling jobs was always a never ending task for me. Another fellow, Lloyd Whitlow, and I worked every Tuesday night at the Martinsville Elks Club. That was their dinner meeting night. We served the meal, washed the dishes, and cleaned up the kitchen. There was no guarantee, so it meant that we were dependent on tips. In passing the tray, we learned early to start with a big tipper. Usually he'd drop a dollar bill on the tray. That meant then that the others might give us a dime or a quarter instead of just a nickel or dime.

On Saturdays, I'd often box groceries at either the A & P or Kroger grocery store. I remember one Saturday night. It was just past closing time and there were a lot of loose bananas in the bin. Some of the other box boys egged me on to try and eat a dozen bananas without stopping. I ate the dozen, and instead of making me sick, it increased my appetite for them.

Even today I frequently buy a banana for dessert at lunch in the Student Union.

I can't say the same about another of my eating feats. I was about six or seven and really loved my mother's coconut cream pie. I had been begging her to let me eat a whole pie. One day she did, and I haven't touched coconut pie since.

Food wasn't too expensive in those days. For five dollars you could fill the back seat of your car or wagon. But it was tough for a kid to find a job that might earn him a dollar a day.

Over the years in Martinsville, I had some fun jobs and some unusual jobs. Once I worked in the canning plant packing tomatoes and peas. Another time I worked on high tension lines planting poles in that Indiana limestone that was so soft you had to blow out the holes constantly and pop the pole in quick. I also worked on road gangs graveling county roads, using a team to haul the gravel from the pits that dot the Indiana countryside.

One of the jobs I enjoyed the most was in the Collier Brothers' Creamery. I worked with Speedy Collier on the receiving dock. We unloaded the milk, weighed each can, lifted them chest high, and poured the milk into the vat. Each full can weighed about eighty-five pounds. When you were through you were ready for a break.

In the afternoon we might work the bottling line, stack cases of bottled milk in the cooling room, or work in the ice cream plant. I remember when Eskimo Pies first came out, they were like our ice cream bars now but with no stick. We wrapped them in bright silver tinfoil.

People had always told me that when you worked in a candy store or an ice cream plant, you got tired of eating it real quick. I never did. Collier's made the greatest fresh fruit ice creams ever in the summers—strawberry, peach, blueberry, all the fresh fruit flavors. You could eat all you wanted, and in those days John Wooden didn't worry about calories or weight. He needed a lot of both.

I couldn't find any kind of a job during the summer vacation between my junior and senior years at Martinsville High. So Carl Holler, a high school friend, and I decided to hitchhike to Kansas and other midwestern states to work at harvesting wheat. Hitchhiking was tough in those days. There weren't too many cars. Most of the roads were gravel, although a few were oiled and one was bricked or paved with cement.

Everything we owned was in one suitcase. We wore our red and blue lettermen's sweater with a block "M" and stripes for years on the varsity. I had been asked by a Kansas alumnus to stop and see the late Phog Allen, then the head coach who wanted me to go to Kansas to play basketball. Then we worked two days on the KU stadium and pushed on to work the wheat harvest.

We worked fourteen to fifteen hours a day, sometimes longer, but made as much as eight dollars per day, a huge sum compared to the dollar a day we were used to in Martinsville. During the course of the summer we worked our way into the Dakotas almost to the Canadian border before heading home.

The next year, after graduating from Martinsville High, I went to work on a garbage truck in Muncie. Ball State Teachers College wanted me to go there and play basketball so they got me the job. About the second day of work, while going down a narrow alley, the truck ran over two little puppies.

"Scoop them up and throw them on," the driver told me.

"No," I said.

"If you don't throw them on, you're fired."

"I'm fired," I said. I went back to the YMCA, packed my stuff, and went down to Anderson where I got a job in the Delco-Remy factory as a buffer. On my application, the man wrote "expert buffer" under qualifications. I had never seen a buffing machine before. But there was nothing to it, and in a few days, I could do more than men who had been working there for twenty years. Then I got the word: we were paid by the hour but we also received a bonus by the piece. If we did ten pieces an hour today, they expected fifteen tomorrow and then more the next day. One day the man beside me let one of the bronze plates we were buffing slip. It sailed by his head and severed his ear. He reached down, picked up the ear and raced to the first aid station. Years later I heard they had sewed it back on and you couldn't tell the difference.

That summer also I played ball for Anderson's town team. It was here that I had one or two offers to sign a pro baseball contract. Donnie Bush, who at different times over the years managed the Senators, Pirates, White Sox, and Reds, was running the Indianapolis club in the American Association. He talked to me and so did one of his scouts. They thought I was a prospect as a shortstop, but after I hurt my arm I never could handle the deep throw from short and I was not a really good hitter. They felt I could become a good hitter, however, and that my arm would come back.

For a while I thought about signing because I enjoyed baseball so much, and the money was important, although it wasn't much by today's standards. Believe me, it was a lot more than the dollar a day I could earn in Martinsville at the creamery, and besides, it was fun.

Money was always dear to me. I worked hard for it and took great care where and how I spent it. One of the things that money was needed for, especially if you were on the basketball team, was a haircut. I always kept mine extremely short. Today you would call it a GI or a crew cut. I wore my hair that way for two reasons: it didn't have to be cut as often so you saved money, and during basketball season it never got in my eyes. It was clipped almost down to the skin, but not quite. I liked it that way, but few others did. Nellie and my mother didn't like it especially. Maybe I was just trying to assert myself; I really don't know. I'm told that there are still barbershops in Indiana where you can see the sign: "Johnny Wooden Haircuts."

5

Learn as if you were to live forever;
Live as if you were to die tomorrow.

EARLY IN LIFE, my father convinced me that the only road to success was through education. And during my junior year at Martinsville High I became aware of the fact that basketball could be the means of achieving a college education. I was always a fairly good student, and I believe I have mom and dad to thank for that.

They encouraged us to read, to study, and to learn. My lifelong interest in poetry comes from my father. He read poetry every night either before or after reading the Bible. Frequently, he read aloud to all of us. These are some of the happiest memories of my childhood.

When I was at Martinsville High there were no athletic scholarships as we know them today. About all a college or university could do for an athlete was get him a job hashing—waiting tables—in a fraternity house and some kind of a weekend job to cover his tuition with a little left over for spending money.

I had four or five offers to go to college. I'd been All-State for three years, and by today's standards I was what we call a "sought-after athlete." Everett Dean, who later coached at Stanford, was then at Indiana, and he talked to me about going there. I visited Butler, where the state basketball tournament was held in Indianapolis, and talked to Tony Hinkle about playing basketball for him. George Keogan, then the basketball coach at Notre Dame came to see me, but I never visited the campus.

I had never visited Purdue or even been in West Lafayette until I entered school there in the fall of 1928. In those years,

Purdue was the power in Big Ten basketball. Ward (Piggie) Lambert, who was the coach, was an impressive man and a gifted teacher but probably more important to me, he played the kind of basketball I thought I would like to play—fast break.

Coach Lambert had promised me a job waiting tables and washing dishes in the Beta house. He also thought he could get me a job on the weekends working in the athletic department handing out equipment or taping athletes in the training room. That paid thirty-five cents an hour—big money to me in those days.

With all my belongings in one suitcase and a dollar or two in my pocket, some friends drove me to West Lafayette where I hoped to be good enough to play basketball and smart enough to get my degree.

That first semester, I discovered that if a student made the Dean's list he got free tuition for the spring semester. From then on, I worked especially hard to make honor roll. As I recall, tuition was about seventy-five dollars a semester. And when you divide that by thirty-five cents an hour, it meant putting in a lot of hours just to pay tuition.

During basketball season, I only worked breakfast and lunch in the fraternity house because I was at practice during the dinner hour. I had to eat later and then clean off the table, do the dishes, and police up the kitchen. Then I could begin to study for the grades to keep me on the free tuition roster.

I think I had more jobs in my four years at Purdue than anyone could possibly imagine.

Stretch Murphy, the great Purdue center, "willed" to me the program concession for the basketball games. I got the starting line-ups and numerical roster for both teams and had them mimeographed with the up-to-date statistics of the teams and players. Then I'd get some high school kids in West Lafayette to sell them at the game for a dime apiece. They made a nickel, and I made a nickel. I don't recall how much I'd clear, but it was only a few dollars.

Now, football programs were different. I sold them for four years. Early on a Friday morning I would get five hundred programs checked out to me, and I'd make the hotels and restaurants where the alumni were hanging out. I soon learned to time myself so as to catch them when they were feeling pretty good from an over-exposure to bootleg liquor. If they were especially "happy," instead of getting a dime for a program, my take could range all the way from a quarter to a dollar. Selling football programs helped me accumulate a little money for books and supplies and a date with Nellie when I could get back to Martinsville.

It was always a scramble to try to figure out ways to make a little more money. One of the most unusual was my "walk to Chicago." I bought the concession rights on the special football train that ran on the Monon Railroad from Lafayette to Chicago. One of the Big Ten's most famous rivalries then was between Purdue and Chicago. Amos Alonzo Stagg was the head coach of Chicago, and, next to Knute Rockne, he was probably the most famous name in football.

I hired a couple of my frat brothers to work with me, and we would walk up and down the aisles hawking our wares as the train rolled toward Chicago and onto a special siding near the university. We'd sell sandwiches, candy, cigarettes, chewing gum, apples, oranges, and soft drinks. It was hard work walking up and down those aisles, and it took a lot of hustling to get things together to sell that would make a profit.

Coach Lambert believed an athlete should work for his education. Then it would be appreciated more. I remember during my sophomore year he called me into his office. It was near the start of the season for my first year of varsity competition. Coach Lambert told me that there was a doctor in Lafayette who had taken a liking to me and wanted to pay my way through Purdue so I wouldn't have to work so hard. "He'll pay your fraternity house bill, your fees, tuition, and anything else you may need."

"That's wonderful, coach," I told him.

"Are you going to take it, John?"

"What do you mean?"

"I just wonder how you're going to pay him back."

"Coach," I said, "I thought you just told me that he wanted to do it."

"That is right, John, he does. Remember, though, that I told you when you came to Purdue, you would work hard but would get through and wouldn't owe me or anyone else a cent. You will have earned your way.

"Now if you accept this doctor's offer, even though he doesn't expect to be repaid, I think you're the kind of person who wouldn't feel right about it unless you did.

"Think about it, John," he said, "and in a day or two I'll talk to you again."

A couple of days later, I went by to see him. "I decided not to accept the doctor's offer."

"I really didn't think you would, John," he said, "after you thought about it."

Later on he called me in again and said that the same doctor would like to give me a suit and a topcoat. Coach Lambert felt I should accept this, and I did. It was the second suit I ever owned. I got my first suit for my graduation from high school, and I had never owned a topcoat.

My last year at Purdue was the most dedicated of all. I worked at every possible job, at the same time studying hard to make the Dean's list. There was little time for anything but basketball, books, work and, once in a while, pool, which I'd learned to play pretty well in Martinsville.

Nellie and I had seemed destined for each other from our first meeting. Even in high school we were sure that we would one day marry, but Nellie insisted that I go to Purdue and that she would wait those long years. Thus, it came as a shock to her during the summer between my junior and senior years that I had an offer to leave Purdue and accept an appointment to the United States Military Academy at West Point.

Back in those years, West Point was allowed to recruit as cadets proficient athletes who had graduated from college and play them another four years. One of Purdue's great football players, a fullback named Elmer Oliphant, went to West Point after graduating. Another great Army back, Chris Cagle, had done the same thing.

A uniform must have had some allure for me since in high school I had joined an infantry unit of the local National Guard.

But when I told Nellie about the offer there was what you would call a confrontation.

"I agreed to wait these four years," she told me. "You go, but I'll wait no longer."

That ended my consideration of West Point and began our planning to be married upon my graduation from Purdue. It was a big step for us, the biggest of our lives. It required advance planning and a forced saving program as neither of our parents had the means to provide financial assistance. However, they gave us the kind of love and guidance for which we consider ourselves to be very fortunate.

After the close of the Big Ten season and a second championship, I received an offer from George Halas, the man who created and coached the Chicago Bears football team for so many years. Halas, who also owned a basketball team then, hired me to come to Chicago and play three games for a hundred dollars each, the most money I had ever had in one lump sum in my life. There probably was considerable interest in my playing since Purdue had won the Big Ten title, and I had made All-American for the third year, in the process breaking Stretch Murphy's conference scoring record with 154 points in the twelve games. In addition I had been selected as College Player of the Year.

In Chicago, I met Frank Kautsky for whom I later played pro basketball on weekends and in the summers during many years of my coaching career in Indiana.

At the same time a representative of the original New York Celtics approached me about joining the team to barnstorm around the country. They offered me five thousand dollars for the year, an unheard-of figure to me, as some teachers who also coached were making as little as nine hundred dollars a year. Eighteen hundred dollars was considered a fine salary.

The Celtic offer seemed tremendous. Once again, I went to Piggie Lambert about it.

"What did you come to Purdue for?" he asked, after hearing me out.

"To get an education," I told him.

"Did you get one?"

"I think so."

"You're not going to use it?" he asked.

"I hope to."

"Well, you won't be using it barnstorming around the country playing basketball. You're not that type of person."

Purdue had offered me a teaching fellowship in English upon graduation. I weighed that quite carefully but Coach Lambert, in his way, had convinced me that coaching was the best direction to take. By the time the spring semester of my senior year was ended, Nellie and I had set our wedding date, and I had a job at Dayton, Kentucky, as athletic director, coach, and teacher.

We were going to be married August 8, 1932. That was a Sunday. I had saved 909 dollars and a nickel from barnstorming games around Indiana, Illinois, Ohio, and Kentucky during the spring and summer after the end of my senior season. We had ordered a brand new Plymouth sedan and would take delivery on Saturday.

That morning when I went to the First Bank and Trust Company to withdraw a part of the $909.05, it wasn't open. The bank had gone broke.

Immediately, we canceled the order for the Plymouth and the wedding. We had planned to be married in Indianapolis in a quiet little church ceremony because Nellie's father wasn't well and couldn't afford a large wedding. Furthermore, the minister in Indianapolis had married Nellie's only brother, Emil, to her sister-in-law, Julia.

To say we were despondent that Saturday hardly expresses our feelings—we were totally depressed. That $909.05 seemed like our lives that day. Even so, we knew we were more fortunate than many elderly people who had lost their life savings. We were young and could bounce back.

When the word of the bank failure and our wedding plans got to the father of Nellie's best friend, Mary Schnaiter, he called me immediately. Mr. Schnaiter, who owned a large grain mill in Martinsville, offered to lend me two hundred dollars to be paid back when I could so Nellie and I could be married. Though it was and still is against my principles to borrow from anyone, we did accept the loan. My brother Cat and his wife-to-be drove us to Indianapolis and stood up for us.

After the little ceremony, we went to dinner at the Bamboo Inn in Indianapolis and to the Circle theater to hear the Mills Brothers. We have kidded about that show for years. The Mills Brothers answered encore after encore and they have remained my favorite singing group.

The next morning we had to get up early. Coach Lambert was giving a basketball clinic in Vincennes, a city in southern Indiana, and was driving by Martinsville to pick me up. I was going to get $25—a very vital $25 since the loss of the $909.05—for being part of that week-long clinic.

At 6:00 A.M. we caught the bus out of Indianapolis back to Martinsville where I left Nellie for that first week while I participated in the clinic. We were probably one of very few couples to have spent their first week of marriage apart.

6

The true athlete should have
character, not be a character.

A GREAT MANY people are responsible for my success in basketball, both as a player and a coach. Nellie, who waited through the Purdue years so we could marry, was the most important person spiritually and mentally. She kept me going during many dark hours.

From a technician's viewpoint, however, Coach Piggie Lambert had the greatest influence on my career both from the viewpoint of playing as well as coaching.

There has never been any doubt in my mind that Lambert was definitely way ahead of his time. A comparatively small man, Lambert was a fine athlete. He had gone to Wabash College in Indiana, was a quarterback on its football team in a historic game with Notre Dame, played professional baseball, and was a thorough student of basketball.

A dynamic, fiery individual, Lambert was known throughout the Midwest as a brilliant, free-lance strategist whose teams were always prepared mentally and physically.

It was from Lambert that I first realized the value of a controlled offense with free-lance aspects. In other words, Lambert believed in building a platform or a base from which the offense would start. He wanted movement by design but not by precise, repeated pattern.

There was always someone going in, going out, and crossing over. Within this platform he would design little improvised changes that capitalized on the individual abilities of his team. When he had Stretch Murphy playing center during my sophomore year, we did it a little differently than when Dutch Fehring, who once coached the line at UCLA and baseball at Stanford.

Lambert was not set in his ways. If the guards seemed superior he might utilize them more. He always went to the strength of the individuals after studying each of us closely. Lambert was a great psychologist, accomplishing more with words than any coach I've ever known. I think it is one of my attributes that can definitely be traced to him. He was not one for team meetings; I'm not either.

Every day in practice, he might stop you several times and point out that you are going too much to your right or too much to your left. He always had options, as he never wanted to take away a man's initiative; he merely wanted to direct it within the bounds of his attack.

Coach Lambert never gave you a demand route. He might say, "The first two times you hit the center, fake right and go left. The third time, reverse it. You must outthink, outmaneuver, and outcondition your opponent."

Players had tremendous respect for him. He worked hard and expected you to work hard. It is because of his theory on condition that I have based my entire coaching career on a similar thesis. Lambert brought this point home early in my years with him.

On one occasion we were to play Indiana. Everett Dean, one of the fine coaches, was then at Indiana. But Coach Lambert told us we could beat them.

"We'll beat them because Mr. Dean is too nice a person. He will not work his players hard enough for them to stay with us. We'll wear them down in the first three quarters of the game and beat them in the last quarter. You see, we're prepared to run the whole game, but Indiana isn't."

If any one premise typifies my teams in all the years I've coached, it is this concept. Often as a player, I'd tell myself, "I may play someone better than I am, but I'll never run against one who is going to be in better condition." And I never played against a man in my life I felt was in better shape, and Lambert often cited me as an example of top conditioning.

But there is considerable difference between Lambert's theory on conditioning a team and mine. He believed in continual full court, up and down, work. He might scrimmage a team an hour the day before a game, but I never do. Also, he scrimmaged five on five a lot more than I do. It seems to me that I achieve the same conditioning with a lot more two-on-two, three-on-three drills, and five-on-five half-court situations.

While I try to achieve my aims through these drills, Lambert accomplished a similar purpose within a full court, five-on-five scrimmage. Basically, our coaching concept sought the same result; we just went down different streets.

Lambert constantly urged us not to worry about our opponent—just play our own game and force him to follow it. We were made to believe that those of us playing for him at Purdue were the best in basketball. Confidence was a virtue he attempted to exploit at all times.

In all probability Coach Walter "Doc" Meanwell of Wisconsin was one of the finest pattern basketball coaches in the country. He used a weave offense almost continuously. When we played them, we would press the ball at what would now be the mid-court line. We'd press them tight, and when they were through running their weave, instead of being under the basket, we had forced them to finish up twenty or twenty-five feet out. Lambert insisted that they would never deviate, never change, but I worried constantly about Wisconsin going to reverses on us and coming back to our weak side.

As the only starter back in my junior year and captain of the team, and thoroughly indoctrinated into all the Lambert principles, I felt that I could speak up.

"Mr. Lambert," I asked, "don't you think we're leaving ourselves vulnerable to reverses by pressing so tight against Wisconsin?"

"Yes, we are," he responded, "but Meanwell has his players drilled and coached so well in his offense that they'll never try to reverse." His method was to force them out of what they wanted to do, and then they'd break down. It worked all the time. Wisconsin never really hurt us with reverses, even though we were very vulnerable.

In the years following our great success at UCLA, I often

overheard people say that I originated the pressing defense. Not at all. I played the press at Purdue under Lambert. It wasn't a zone press, but it was a pressing defense with zone principles. At that time I didn't know of any other coach using it.

The press works in so naturally with the fast break offense. The foremost exponent of fast break basketball was Piggie Lambert. He believed in speed, and that the team which made the most mistakes would probably win. Now, that statement takes a bit of analyzing. What he was trying to get across was that the doer makes mistakes, but the doer usually wins because he gets more shots and controls the game more.

Actually, if there was an originator of fast break basketball, it was Lambert. He demanded movement and action. I admonish my boys with a different verb—move, move. I want movement. In the end we both want the same.

Lambert was also a very precise man. Known as a man who thought of everything, he was meticulous, thorough, and well organized. And while conditioning and organization were two of Lambert's demands, one thing he couldn't control was accidents. I probably had more accidents in my four years of college than anyone. Just before the Christmas holidays of my freshman year, I came down with scarlet fever and spent three weeks in isolation.

Then, in my sophomore season we were leaving to play Butler in Indianapolis. Andrew Thomas, whose nickname was "Prune," and I were waiting for the trolley that ran between West Lafayette and Lafayette. After a time we discovered that the trolley couldn't make it to where we were because of ice on the track. So when a fellow we knew came by driving a small truck and motioned us to climb into the back end, we jumped at the chance. I was carrying my basketball gear and a Christmas present for Nellie. Prune climbed up ahead of me, and I tossed our gear up to him and was trying to pull myself up with one hand while holding Nellie's gift with the other.

"Watch out," yelled Prune.

I whirled around just in time to see a truck bearing down on us. It couldn't stop because of the ice. I tried to swing out of the way, but it was too late. I was caught between the two trucks, and a rod protruding from one of the trucks jammed right through my thigh. Nellie's present—a little vanity case—was shattered, and I spent that Christmas in the hospital.

The next year, just before the holidays, I was at practice and cut sharply on a drive off the post man. Slipping on a loose plank, I crashed to the floor and gouged out a hunk of flesh. Blood was spurting all over the place, and I was rushed to the hospital again for what I thought would be just a day or two. However, infection set in, and I spent another Christmas in the hospital.

To make it all complete, in my senior year Lambert was disturbed because I kept getting an infected throat. Just before the holidays, it cleared up and he suggested I have a tonsillectomy. Another Christmas—four in a row—in the hospital.

In all probability, however, it was the injury during my sophomore year that was the most damaging. Not only did it shatter Nellie's gift but Lambert always insisted that we would have remained unbeaten if I hadn't tried to hop that truck. He claimed that my being out caused the team to lose its tempo even though Murphy and the rest were in the game.

Today, only the real basketball buffs who lived in the Midwest are aware of just how great Stretch Murphy was. He's in the Hall of Fame. In my opinion, he was an all-time great player. Stretch was the first really big man to play basketball with coordination and skill. He was quick and could jump. His timing was flawless, and he was a great rebounder and shooter. In addition, Stretch was a great team player.

There is no doubt that it was Murphy who started me on my way to being an outstanding player. I might not have become so well known if I hadn't played with him as a sophomore. His presence and Lambert's coaching insured our having a great team.

We both made All-American during my sophomore year. And I've always contended that if you make it as a sophomore, it's not as hard to make it again as a junior and senior, as I did. It was during my senior year that I broke Stretch's Big Ten scoring record.

Over the years since I graduated, I've wondered how we would have done in an NCAA tournament as it is constituted now. Those tournaments are packed with pressure. It's sudden death, and there's little room for a mistake. Lambert was a man who made a fetish out of stressing little details, and I am sure that if we'd had the opportunity, we would have done well.

I think most of us have a superstition or a fetish that becomes part of life. I had one as a player, although I don't believe I'm a superstitious person. But if you look at any photograph taken of me at Purdue, you will notice a key tied into the lace on my left shoe.

Why?

At first it served a very practical purpose. We didn't have combination locks then, and there were no pockets in basketball uniforms. So, I just ran the lace through the hole in the key to my locker, then double tied the lace. After a time some sports writer noticed it and called it a "good luck" piece. Actually, it had nothing to do with luck but was merely a handy place to keep the key.

During my senior year, I was pretty close to Lambert. Since I was the only senior and had started for three years, I knew what he wanted done on the floor, and by then I was reasonably certain that I wanted to become a coach. I had achieved the closeness that exists between player and coach, although at the time I wasn't truly aware of it.

We had a fine team my senior season, losing only one game all year, and that was to Illinois. There was a bit of irony in that defeat. We were driving to Champaign-Urbana for the game in Lambert's car. On an icy stretch of highway outside of Champaign we rolled over. Glass broke and I cut my right hand rather deeply.

I played despite the cuts but really couldn't do too much. Whether we would have won if we hadn't had the accident we'll never know. But I did lead the Big Ten in scoring that year, and in that game I was well below my average.

It just seemed, looking back, that I must have been accident-prone, especially where cars and trucks were involved.

7

Do not let what you cannot do interfere with what you can do.

MY FIRST coaching assignment at Dayton High was filled with foreboding. Nellie's sister, Audrey, and her husband, Ray, drove us down from Martinsville. We didn't have a car because my money was still tied up in the bank foreclosure, and it appeared we were never going to see a penny of it again. Everything we owned was either in the trunk or on the back seat of their car.

We had no place to live, no furniture and no personal things except for our clothes and a few wedding gifts. The superintendent of schools, Olin W. Davis, hired me for $1800 per year, a fine salary for those days. He helped us find an apartment and arranged for us to buy furniture on time. The people who lived in the apartment below us, Melvin and Dorothybell Wuest, are still dear friends.

The assignment in Dayton was rather horrifying when I look back on it. My precise duties included athletic director, head football coach, head basketball coach, head baseball coach, head track coach, supervisor of the total physical education curriculum from the first through the twelfth grade, plus teaching English.

Only football worried me. Since Martinsville didn't have a team, I had never played the game. And I hadn't tried it at Purdue, even as a freshman. During the summer before school started I had spent many hours with Purdue's head coach, Noble Kizer, and his assistant, Mal Elward. Both were fine technicians and knew the game, but you don't learn football with talks and diagrams. It was obvious at the outset that it was unfair to the

Dayton players for John Wooden to continue something for which he was not qualified.

After explaining this to Mr. Davis, I asked to be relieved and suggested that Willard Bass, who had been football coach prior to my acceptance, should resume the assignment, and I would help where I could. Davis agreed, and Bass took over. We had a good season, losing only one game, and some record books still list John Wooden as head football coach.

It has been said over the years that I never had a losing season as a basketball coach, but that isn't so. I can't recall the figures, but we lost more than we won during my first season. Things picked up in my second year, and we had a fine team, closing out the season with only three or four defeats.

On weekends I played pro basketball for the Kautsky Athletic Club. We played thirty to forty games a year throughout the Midwest. I got fifty dollars a game plus an expense allowance for travel. Frank Kautsky was a marvelous man, a true basketball buff, and when we won or had a good game, he would see that we got a little bonus in our envelope after the game.

In all I played pro ball, primarily for Kautsky, for about six years. It was during my last year that the center jump was abolished. I've always thought that it would have been great to have played my entire career under those new rules. The year after the center jump was eliminated I scored twice as much as I had ever scored before even though I had slipped some because of a leg injury. The game without the center jump was right up my alley.

I remember one year when I was playing for Kautsky that I made 100 consecutive free throws. When the 100th dropped through the basket, Kautsky stopped the game and gave me a hundred dollar bill. It was the first time I had ever seen a hundred dollar bill. Believe me, Nellie grabbed that in a hurry.

There wasn't a pro basketball league at that time, so we played in places like Indianapolis, Ft. Wayne, Sheboygan, Oshkosh, Chicago, Detroit, and Akron. Usually the teams were sponsored by a large plant such as Goodyear or Firestone or by someone like Frank Kautsky.

One of the great teams we played those years was the New

York Rens. I guess you could call them the forerunners of the Harlem Globetrotters. The greatest pure shooter I ever faced was one of their players, Bill Yancey. Fats Jenkins, a guard who also played outfield with the New York Black Yankees, was another gifted player and a fine person. And their center, Wee Willie Smith, was the toughest, meanest basketball player I ever faced. He wasn't dirty, just tough and mean. We met again years later at the basketball Hall of Fame. I always contended that Willie could have whipped Joe Louis, who was heavyweight champion then, if he had been a boxer. He weighed about 220, had a beautiful build, was quick, with lightning reflexes, had great balance, and was truly a superb athlete.

Pro basketball in those days was hectic and harrowing. Even the stories that are told about the early years of the NBA couldn't compare to my years when we carried our own gear, liniment, tape, bandages, and basketball. It was a life all its own and was certainly different from the life of an average Indiana school teacher.

Midway during my second year in Dayton, I was offered a position in the South Bend, Indiana, school system. It meant returning to my home state, being in a larger school, and living in a bigger city. And in addition, South Bend was the home of Notre Dame. I had enjoyed Dayton, the people, the school, the kids, and especially O. W. Davis, the superintendent, who had hired me. Also, our daughter, Nancy, had been born in nearby Covington. So, we had many attachments to the Dayton area, but now, in the summer of 1934, it was back to Indiana. This time we moved in our own Plymouth, plus a moving van. We'd acquired a few more possessions as well as a daughter.

Nellie was more content back in Indiana. And South Bend Central High presented a tremendous challenge to a young coach in one of the toughest high school conferences in the country.

I was the athletic director, basketball and baseball coach, the tennis coach, taught some English classes, and later on was comptroller of the school. This was rather ironic. I am not too good a numbers man, and I certainly don't claim to be a professional businessman. It was a good thing that I had such fine assistants as Mrs. Clara McClary, C. L. Kuhn, and Walt Kindy.

Being the comptroller meant I was responsible for the book store, the cafeteria, and the ticket sales to all school events, athletic or otherwise. I'll always remember what happened one time after our annual football game with Mishawaka, the next town just east of South Bend. That game was played in the Notre Dame stadium. We almost filled it a time or two, and, if I'm not mistaken, student tickets were a quarter, advance adult tickets were fifty cents, and all gate sale tickets were a dollar.

There were many places around South Bend that sold advance tickets. After the game was over on Saturday, I'd make my rounds with my little black satchel and pick up the unsold tickets and the money for those that had been sold in advance.

Looking back on those collection rounds, I can see that it was foolish to handle it that way. I could easily have been robbed or have misplaced a collection or two and then I would have been in bad trouble.

I was bonded, and insured, of course, but probably would have resisted any hold-up attempt. One time I was in my office balancing out the collections. Everything was in and tabulated carefully, but I was twenty dollars short. I went back over all my addition and checked the beginning and ending number on all the ticket rolls, but I was still short.

Usually when this happened, I would go over it with greater care and find where I had made my error, but this time I found no error. I knew it had to be something simple because it was an even amount. By this time I had been through the brown envelopes at least two or three times. But once again, I fingered through the envelopes and there in the one from Clark's Restaurant was a twenty dollar bill. The glue in the bottom of the envelope had become wet and the bill had stuck to it.

There never seemed to be a dull day at Central. I enjoyed the school, the city, the people, and the players. Central did well in both basketball and baseball during my years. We won the conference many times but never took the state championship. We didn't have much luck in the state tournament or in any one-game, sudden death tournament, such as the NCAA.

We had some happy years in South Bend. Our son, Jim, was born there. And I believe to this day that if World War II hadn't come along to take me away in 1943, that I would still be at Central High. We weren't getting wealthy, but we had a wonderful life, a fine school, great associates, and I always felt I was cut out for the high school level. I loved to teach, and I lived for it. Furthermore, a teacher could not ask for a finer principal under whom to work than Mr. P. D. Pointer.

As a matter of fact, I'm frequently asked why I chose coaching as a career and then stayed with it. Amos Alonzo Stagg, who coached football at Chicago when I used to make my annual "walk to Chicago," best sums up my feelings on the subject. Stagg, who worked with youth and coached well into his nineties, when asked why he coached once said, "It was because of a promise I made to God."

As a young man, Stagg planned to become a minister and attended Yale Theological School. One day after talking with God through prayer he decided he could best serve Him on the athletic field rather than from the pulpit. He once wrote, "I have made the young men of America my ministry. I have tried to bring out the best in the boys that I have coached. I truly believe that many of them have become better Christians and citizens because of what they have learned on the athletic field.

"You must love your boys to get the most out of them and do the most for them. I have worked with boys whom I haven't admired, but I have loved them just the same. Love has dominated my coaching career as I am sure it has and always will that of many other coaches and teachers."

I feel that my love for young people is the main reason I have stayed in coaching and have refused positions that would have been far more lucrative.

A poem by Glennice L. Harmon that ran many years ago in the *NEA Journal* typifies my deep feelings on the subject: *

---

* "They Ask Me Why I Teach," by Glennice L. Harmon, in *NEA Journal* 37, no. 1 (September 1948): 375.

THEY ASK ME WHY I TEACH

They ask me why I teach,
And I reply,
Where could I find more splendid company?
There sits a statesman,
Strong, unbiased, wise,
Another later Webster,
Silver-tongued.
And there a doctor
Whose quick, steady hand
Can mend a bone,
Or stem the lifeblood's flow.
A builder sits beside him—
Upward rise
The arches of a church he builds, wherein
That minister will speak the word of God,
And lead a stumbling soul to touch the Christ.

And all about
A lesser gathering
Of farmers, merchants, teachers,
Laborers, men
Who work and vote and build
And plan and pray
Into a great tomorrow.
And I say,
"I may not see the church,
Or hear the word,
Or eat the food their hands will grow."
And yet—I may.
And later I may say,
"I knew the lad,
And he was strong,
Or weak, or kind, or proud,
Or bold, or gay.
I knew him once,
But then he was a boy."
They ask me why I teach, and I reply,
"Where could I find more splendid company?"

8

*You cannot live a perfect day
without doing something for someone
Who will never be able to repay you.*

I OFTEN TOLD my players that, next to my own flesh and blood, they were the closest to me. They were my children. I got wrapped up in them, their lives, and their problems.

Sometimes this concern for my players became so dominant that it quite possibly may have influenced decisions I had to make in regard to personnel. I always tried to be fair and give each player the treatment he earned and deserved, but I realize I may have been subconsciously influenced at times.

Although I strove constantly to avoid this, one instance stands out in my memory. It was at South Bend Central. I had a fine second baseman on my baseball team who was also a guard on the basketball team, but he had never done well in basketball practice and it's always been my premise to give the ones who do best in practice the vast majority of the playing time in the games.

On this particular weekend during his junior year at Central, we were playing Emerson of Gary on Friday, and the next night we were to play Fort Wayne Central. We edged Emerson by a point or two and were driving back to South Bend from Gary. We had stopped in a restaurant to eat, and everyone was sitting together in the luxury of a big win when I noticed Eddie Pawelski all alone in a corner.

"What's the matter, Eddie?" I asked.

"I don't get to play, coach, so I'm thinking about quitting."

"You know, Eddie, I don't like quitters. You shouldn't quit. You should stick it out." My advice might well have been based on the fact that I didn't want to lose him for basketball because I might also lose him for baseball, and I expected a lot from him for the next two baseball seasons.

"Coach," he said, "I know I can play ball if I just had a chance. If I could just get in there with Eddie Ehlers, Jimmy Powers, Warren Seaborg, and the other players, I know I can do well playing with them."

I thought that I'd just shut him up real quick. "All right, Eddie," I said, "I'll give you a chance. I'll start you against Fort Wayne Central tomorrow night."

Suddenly I wondered where those words came from. Three of us were locked in a battle for No. 1 in Indiana. We had just beaten Emerson and tomorrow we faced powerful Fort Wayne Central. Murray Mendenhall, who later coached in the original NBA, was at Fort Wayne, and his team was built around Bill Armstrong who later became an All-American at Indiana University and was truly a great player.

Eddie hadn't played in the Emerson game. In fact, he hadn't played much in any game because he looked so bad. Yet, here I was going into a crucial game and I'd just told him he could start when he wasn't even a number two guard—actually I think he was number five.

As we drove home to South Bend, I told Nellie that I'd made a horrible mistake. "I told Eddie Pawelski I'd start him tomorrow night, and now I have to go through with it."

To this day I've never figured out why I did that. I do not believe appeasement is best for either party. I try never to compromise my judgment because of my affection for a boy. Decisions must be based on reason, not emotion.

"Well," Nellie replied, "you never said how long you'd play him, did you?"

"No, I didn't. I just said I'd start him."

The next night I started Eddie against Fort Wayne. I figured I'd shut him up within a minute or two because I just knew he'd play up to his practice performance and that would be so embarrassing for him before a large crowd that he would be happy when I replaced him.

I put Eddie on Armstrong, the toughest player in the state.

Eddie literally took him apart. Armstrong got the lowest point total of his career, Eddie scored 12, and our team showed the best balance of all season. Actually, I don't think Eddie had ever scored 12 points total in his entire career. But in addition to his scoring, his defense, rebounding, and play-making were excellent.

Eddie never sat on the bench again except to rest. He started every game and was named the most valuable player that year and again the following year as a senior. He went on to Indiana University and I warned Coach Branch McCracken that he'd be the poorest practice player he ever had but he could be a great game player if given the opportunity.

Indiana never got to see Eddie play. World War II broke out and he enlisted in the service. Ultimately, he came with me to Indiana State. Because of an injury he couldn't play and became my assistant and later came to UCLA with me. By then he had changed his name to Eddie Powell. After a couple years at UCLA he became head coach at Loyola of Los Angeles, then moved into city government work and became city manager of Placentia, a suburb of Los Angeles. Eddie just recently retired from that job and is now doing consultant work to city governments in the area.

Why I ever said I would start him is still a mystery to me. I had other kids come to me many times after that and ask the same question, but I never appeased another one—at least in that respect. Perhaps there was another Eddie Powell among those kids. I'll never know.

Every once in a while, though, I think back to that restaurant in Indiana and that brief exchange with Eddie. He was one of my favorites, there is no doubt about it. Perhaps unknowingly I had compromised my better judgment because of my personal feelings, or perhaps because I wanted him happy for the baseball season, a sport of which I am very fond.

There was another youngster at Central of whom I was also very fond and who, in his way, got to me. That was Harvey Martens, a kid from the wrong side of the tracks, a tough competitor, and a fine ball player, but he constantly caused problems.

For several days at practice, Harvey had created a disturbance by arguing with another player, Wayne Thompson. Wayne's father was a professor of law at Notre Dame. Harvey seemed to think that Wayne was a sissy. It is true that Wayne was not hard-nosed like Harvey, but he still could handle things pretty well.

On this particular day, Harvey was interrupting practice by badgering Wayne. I had talked to both of their fathers about the problem and had told them my proposed solution. The fathers supported my proposal and I decided to try it.

The idea was to put them into the boxing ring one day right during practice. At the time we worked out at the YMCA in South Bend and the ring was on the way up to the basketball floor.

"We're going to settle this once and for all," I told both of them as I stopped practice.

"We're going to put you two in the ring with the old-fashioned rules—no three-minute round, no bell. If someone goes down, we'll stop things to see if he wants to continue. If you don't go down, I don't want any running around. Mix it up and get it over with."

Harvey was in his glory. He was a rough, tough street fighter, but in the ring it was a different story. Wayne could hold his own. Harvey came rushing out of his corner and drew back to throw one from the bleacher seats.

Wayne just slipped the punch and popped a left in his face and Harvey sat down hard. He wasn't hurt, but he was stunned and surprised. A trickle of blood came from his nose, but he hopped right up ready to go, obviously embarrassed.

Harvey rushed bull fashion at Wayne again, but this time he was more cautious. Wayne faked a shot, and Harvey covered his face with both hands. Thompson crossed with his right to the pit of Harvey's stomach.

This time Harvey went down hard, rolling around and gasping for breath. I gave him some smelling salts and said, "Are you satisfied?"

"Naw, I'd like one more chance."

Once more he barged in. Wayne set him up with a fake or two and dropped him again. When I went over to check him, he rolled over and breathed deeply of the smelling salts.

"Are you convinced, Harvey?" I asked.

"Yep, I barked up the wrong tree."

It wasn't until later that Harvey found out that Wayne's father had boxed at the University of Michigan and that Wayne was a proficient boxer. After that Harvey would always warn a potential problem-maker with, "You'd better behave. I'll get Wayne after you."

They became good friends, and while I have never done that before or since, it solved the problem once and for all.

One of the real pleasures of coaching is the association you build up with kids like this. You follow a good many of them the rest of your life, and their joys and disappointments become your joys and disappointments. You love to see them excel in whatever profession they pursue.

There's a community leader by the name of Eddie Ehlers in South Bend today who played for me at Central and who fits that mold. He was probably as gifted an all-around athlete as I have ever seen.

He was so skilled as a Purdue fullback that he was a high draft pick of the Chicago Bears. Eddie was also selected by the Boston Celtics in the NBA, but the New York Yankees signed him to a fine bonus contract. However, he also played some with the Boston Celtics.

My introduction to Ehlers came one spring when baseball practice was rained out, and we were in the gym playing pick-up basketball. The junior high basketball prospects who were entering Central the next year would always show up when it rained in the spring because they knew that I would call off baseball practice and have basketball practice.

Eddie was a tremendous prospect. It was only a question of which sport—football, basketball, track, or baseball. On this particular day during a break Eddie came up to me and said, "Coach, every time I make a basket I look over at you and you're shaking your head no at me. My junior high coach would always nod his head and smile when I scored."

"Eddie," I said, "why are you looking at me after a basket? Don't you have someone to guard? I don't want you looking at me, and I don't want you looking up at the stands. You can be sure that I'll always shake my head as long as you're playing for the plaudits of the coach and the crowd."

He looked at me kind of hurt, but he never turned his eyes toward me again in the years he played for me at Central. He was always looking to pick up his man. However, he did draw many a smile and many a pat on the back from me.

Years later, Eddie stopped by Terre Haute to see me one day. By now he was in the Yankee chain playing for Quincy, Illinois, in the Three-Eye-League. Eddie was all confidence. He was a handsome young man, intelligent, and a great athlete. After talking for a few minutes, he said, "Coach, do you mind if I call you John?"

"No, Eddie, I think that would be fine."

A gleam of accomplishment crossed his eye. I could see he was pleased.

"Well, John, it's like this," he continued, "I'm doing pretty well, John. I've signed for a big baseball bonus, John. I got a good salary, John, with the Celtics last winter, and you probably think I'm on a Three-Eye-League salary.

"I'm not. I probably make more money than you do, John. That's why I think I should call you John. Don't you think so, John? Don't you agree, John?"

During the next five minutes he called me John a dozen times. Then suddenly he stopped. "I can't do it," he said. "I've tried. It's going to have to be coach."

9

*Be more concerned with your character
than with your reputation,
Because your character is what you
really are
While your reputation is merely
what others think you are.*

WHEN PEARL HARBOR was attacked on December 7, 1941, I had been at South Bend Central about seven years. I tried immediately to get into service and finally enlisted in 1942. However, I wasn't called to active duty until February of 1943. Induction into an officer's training program was to take me away from South Bend, coaching, and my other duties until 1946.

My first assignment as a lieutenant, junior grade, was at the University of North Carolina in Chapel Hill. There I found myself surrounded by a large group of men who had all been connected with athletics as coaches or players. We were to undergo a 30-day period of indoctrination to prepare us for the Naval Air Corps V-5 physical fitness program.

One of my roommates was the late Paul Christman, the former Missouri All-American and pro quarterback with the Chicago Cardinals. Most people probably remember him from his career as a commentator on pro football telecasts. Paul, a delightful man, was so far advanced in naval training that he made the rest of us look like apprentice seamen. He owed his superiority to having gone through basic training as a seaman at Great Lakes Naval Training Station prior to being assigned to officer's training.

Our group also included Bud Wilkinson, who later became one of the great coaches at Oklahoma and a TV commentator for college football; the late Jim Tatum, who gained coaching fame at North Carolina and Maryland after the war; and Don Faurot, who developed Paul Christman at Missouri. That's also where I met the late Red Sanders, who did so much to develop UCLA into a major national football power before his death.

Following the thirty days at Chapel Hill, I was assigned to Iowa Pre-Flight on the campus of the University of Iowa at Iowa City. Within less than ninety days, I received orders to report to the U.S.S. Franklin, somewhere in the South Pacific, as a fitness officer.

After a short leave—which I spent in South Bend—I was enroute back to Iowa City to close out my affairs when I became quite ill. Stubbornly ignoring the severe pains in my side, I pushed on into Iowa City and the Navy residence area at the university. The doctor who checked me over at sick bay told me I had a red-hot appendix and they would have to operate right away.

Since Navy regulations say you can't go to sea for a minimum of thirty days after certain types of surgery, my orders to the Franklin were rewritten. I was reassigned to Iowa Pre-Flight, and a friend of mine from Purdue, Freddie Stalcup, replaced me on the Franklin. Perhaps it was coincidence that Freddie, a Purdue fraternity brother and football player, and I were look-alikes. His battle station on the Franklin was the gun position that was hit by a kamikaze, resulting in the terrible fire that virtually destroyed the Franklin. But for the emergency appendectomy that seemed so unfortunate when it happened, John Wooden's name rather than Freddie Stalcup's would probably have been on the casualty list of dead.

A series of assignments followed, including one at St. Simons Island, Georgia, where ironically, since I don't drink, I had the responsibility for the officers' wine mess. Counting cases of bourbon, scotch, and gin bore only remote resemblance to the football and basketball tickets I had handled as comptroller at South Bend Central.

All of my players, at some point in their college careers, heard my lecture on the subject of drinking. I would explain the problems it could create for them, the university and for me. I said I hoped they would have sufficient pride in our program that they would refrain for the few months of basketball. There was a time in my coaching career when drinking or smoking meant automatic dismissal. But in my later years of coaching I used a different approach. I realized that liquor is so often present in the home today that you must use reason with regulations. So I'd tell them that, because they were in the public eye and were seen wherever they went and whatever they did, they should feel obligated to set a good example for admiring youngsters.

Probably the peak of excitement in my entire naval career came only weeks before my final discharge. Japan had surrendered and combat carriers were now going to become transports for planes and pilots who were land based in the Pacific. I was just about to report to an overseas assignment when I received deferred orders to the U.S.S. Sable. I had never heard of it. It wasn't listed among the ships of register, and, of all places, I was to report to the Great Lakes Naval Training Station, hardly where you would expect to pick up a combat ship of any kind.

The explanation turned out to be simple. Sable and her sister ship the U.S.S. Wolverine were being used to train young pilots in how to land and take off from a carrier. If a pilot made a mistake or became shy of hitting the deck, he could easily return to the nearby air station and land safely.

When I reported to the executive officer of the Sable, he turned ash white, as if he had seen a ghost. Shocked, he explained that he had been aboard the Franklin and was the last person to speak to Freddie Stalcup and his gun crew before the Japanese kamikaze hit.

The Sable was full of greenhorns like me, getting ready to go overseas and handle patrol duties or whatever tasks remained to bring all the forces home. Of course, having been in the Navy long enough to accumulate sufficient points for separation, I was hoping to be out before my 90-day delay was up. I certainly didn't want to get stuck out in the Pacific for several months.

Time passed all too rapidly until one night shortly before I was to leave. The captain and executive officer having gone ashore, I was the senior officer aboard the ship when a squall came up on Lake Michigan. It was a lulu. The captain had warned me that it might blow up big and ordered three anchors put out. We got the two other anchors out but now the storm was really on when the watch officer called me to the bridge.

A short distance away, an LST (Landing Ship Tank used in

amphibious landings) dragging its anchor was heading right at us. There was no way we could get underway; no way, in my mind, to avoid a collision. I could see myself standing before a court martial. I ran back to my quarters to see if the Watch Officer's Guide would tell me what to do. It didn't.

There was nothing we could do but wait. The LST finally blew past our bow. It missed by maybe a hundred feet, but in ships this size that was too close. I was still shaking when the captain came aboard. He agreed that our wait-and-pray solution may not have been good seamanship, but at least there was a ship for the captain to come back to.

It was just after this, thanks to the skipper, and his phone calls to Washington, D.C., that my orders for separation came through. Great Lakes, which was handling separation for anyone living in the Midwest, seemed almost literally in perpetual chaos. The lines were huge, and there seemed to be no end to how long all the red tape would take. As I waited in line with my sheaf of papers it was some comfort to encounter an old friend, the great Notre Dame coach Frank Leahy, also a Naval officer, who was being processed at the same time. We talked so long I was beginning to feel embarrassed about monopolizing him while admirals were waiting to get his attention.

After being separated from the Navy just before Christmas of 1945, I returned to South Bend and to Central High the Monday after New Year's Day in 1946. Another man had been coaching basketball, but he had been replaced and I picked the team up in midseason.

Some of the other coaches who had also gone into service were not so fortunate. Their old positions were not made available to them when they returned. I felt this was wrong. A man who had served his country should be given back his same job. It was obvious that although Central was physically the same, and P. D. Pointer was still the principal, my school and the whole South Bend system, for that matter, had changed. And I didn't like the new attitude I found there.

On top of that, we found a change in the city too when we tried to buy back our old home. We had had to let it go when the individual to whom we had leased it didn't pay the rent.

We couldn't keep up rent at our service locations and the house in South Bend, too, so we lost it.

Now, less than three years after we had bought it for $6,000, it had a price tag far beyond our reach, and we could not find a satisfactory rental within our means.

All these things, but especially the way some of my friends were being treated about regaining their pre-war positions, made me decide to leave. In the spring of the year several job offers seemed to come to me all at once. There were some opportunities in public relations, another with a fine book publishing company, and some college and good high school coaching offers. Instead I decided to accept a position at Indiana State University in Terre Haute. This seemed a good time to try the college level.

On July 1, 1946, we moved to Indiana State. It was a pretty, little school, with about 2,500 students, although today it has an enrollment of around 15,000. I was athletic director, head basketball and baseball coach and taught those two sports in the physical education department.

After eleven years of high school basketball at Dayton and South Bend, this was a new challenge. My record in high school, while lacking in a state title, was very good. We had won 218 games, lost 42, for a percentage of .839.

It was obvious, however, from the first day that things were going to be different at Indiana State. Almost all the candidates were veterans, many of them married. Most were on the G.I. Bill, but some needed extra work to support their families.

Ironically, a lot of my former South Bend Central players were enrolled as well as some other players from the South Bend school system against whom my Central team had participated prior to World War II. Eddie Pawelski enrolled, but because of an injury, not lack of talent, he was not able to participate.

One of our starting guards, Lennie Rzeszewski, was from Central. When he graduated from high school he was 5 feet 7 inches and perhaps 145. When he turned out for fall practice, he was 6 feet 3 inches and was around 185. He had grown eight inches in the four or so years he was in service.

On that first varsity at Indiana State, I kept fifteen players, fourteen of them freshmen. Bobby Royer, a sophomore guard, was the only starter who was not a veteran. One of the reserves on that first club, Jimmy Powers, later became the basketball coach at Central in South Bend where he developed Mike Warren, who made All-American for us at UCLA.

After winning our conference with an 18 and 7 record that first year, we were invited to the National Association of Intercollegiate Athletics (NAIA) tournament in Kansas City. I refused the invitation. They wouldn't let us bring Clarence Walker, a fine young black reserve from East Chicago, Indiana, along. While he didn't play too much compared to our starters, I felt that the whole team or no team should go.

During the second season at Indiana State, we had another fine club. With a 29 and 7 record we were again invited to the NAIA tournament. This time there was no question about Clarence playing. It was a mighty tough tournament, with Brigham Young headed by Mel Hutchins, Marshall College with Andy Tonkovitch, Hamline with Harold Haskins and Vern Mikkelsen, and Louisville, all well-schooled basketball teams. We lost to Louisville in the finals. They had an outstanding player in Jack Coleman, who played in the NBA for several years, as well as some other fine players. We might have been an even better team if we hadn't lost one of our expected starters, Freddy Stelow, who had been killed in an auto accident the previous summer.

This year was also unique because it marked the first time I had ever been to Madison Square Garden as either a player or a coach. Piggie Lambert never would take Purdue and was even upset at my taking Indiana State. While I have always preferred to play on a college campus and firmly believe that is where all intercollegiate competition, except for post-season tournament play, should be held, I have always gone to public arenas when necessary or desirable and still do.

After two successful seasons at Indiana State, I began to receive offers to move. One large Big Ten school talked to me indirectly but I didn't appreciate the kind of offer they made. They stated that if I'd stay at Indiana State another year I would be offered the head coaching position. That, to me, meant that the man coaching then was going to be fired and they would like to keep me in the bank to take his position. That didn't set well with me. Apparently, they did not want their present coach, but did not want to pay off his contract.

In a matter of days other offers came my way. My feeling was that it was more in keeping with my philosophy and character to move to a new job on my terms and on my concepts than to be a court appointee in waiting.

10

Things turn out best for those who make the best of the way things turn out.

WITH MY DEPARTURE from South Bend Central, my goal was to move gradually into a coaching position at a major institution. Needless to say, I hoped it would be in the Big Ten where I had played.

It was shortly after our return from Kansas City and our runner-up finish in the NAIA that a number of offers came in. Two, in particular, interested me—the University of Minnesota and the University of California at Los Angeles. I actually favored Minnesota.

Frank McCormick, who was then the athletic director at Minnesota and later became the supervisor of officials in the Pacific Coast Conference, was well acquainted with me from my years as a player at Purdue and in coaching in Indiana. I didn't know how Wilbur Johns of UCLA knew about me until I found out that an old friend, Bob Kelley, formerly a broadcaster of football and basketball games in Indiana and later with the Los Angeles Rams, had first suggested my name to him.

After visiting both Minnesota and UCLA, I had promised to give Frank and Wilbur my answer on an agreed-upon evening. I had decided to take the Minnesota job except for one problem—the retention of Dave McMillan, the man whom I would be replacing, as my assistant. Even though I liked Mr. McMillan, I wanted my own man, Eddie Powell.

Minnesota had to get approval from its board that was meeting this particular day for me to bring Powell and not keep McMillan. As it was set up, McCormick was to call me for my answer at

75

6:00 P.M. and Johns would call at 7:00. There was a snow storm raging in Minneapolis that day and Frank got snowed in and couldn't get to a phone on time.

I didn't know of the problem so when Mr. Johns called, right on time, I accepted the UCLA job. When McCormick finally reached me about an hour later, he told me everything was "all set."

"It's too late," I told him. "I have already accepted the job at UCLA."

Frank wanted me to call Wilbur back and try to get off the hook, but I refused. I had accepted; UCLA was committed, and had already released the news of my appointment to the press in Los Angeles.

My first impression of UCLA, on my visit, had not been good. I was appalled at the facilities. That was probably the reason I preferred Minnesota. They had a huge fieldhouse while UCLA had a tiny gym that later became known as the "B.O. Barn" when we began to fill it to the ceiling.

While UCLA lacked the major facility, I was led to believe that one was on the drawing boards and was expected within three years. Also the Southern California climate was lovely. I enjoyed playing golf and could do it the year round.

Immediately after accepting the position, I arranged to take a week off from Indiana State and go to Los Angeles to conduct spring basketball practice which was then permitted. On my previous visit I had been all over the campus, visited various administrators and officials, but had not met a one of the basketball players.

When I went up on the floor for the first time in the spring of 1948 and put them through that first practice, I was very disappointed. I felt that my Indiana State team could have named the score against them. I was shattered. Had I known how to abort the agreement in an honorable manner, I would have done so and gone to Minnesota, or if that was impossible, stayed on at Indiana State.

However, that would be contrary to my creed. I don't believe in quitting, so I resolved to work hard, try to develop the talent on hand, and recruit like mad for the next year.

While the talent disturbed me during the five days I worked with them, the discovery that I was not working for the university but rather for the Associated Students really upset me. That meant the student body president was my boss. I had not known, or, didn't understand that when I first looked at the job or I would never have considered it in the first place.

These two factors really contributed toward a harrowing week. It was necessary for me to return to Terre Haute and leave spring practice in the hands of two hold-over assistants from Mr. Johns' staff, Bill Putnam and Don Ashen. But before leaving, I began to delve into just how the junior college system worked in California. Because we had so few junior colleges in the Midwest, I wasn't particularly familiar with them. But I found it hard to believe the junior colleges could help much. Nevertheless I was desperate for help and reviewed some films of jaycee games in which there were some players Putnam and Ashen thought might help.

After the close of school at Indiana State, I moved my family to Los Angeles, realizing that I had a tremendous job ahead to turn things around. By the time regular practice started, the press had already tabbed us to finish last in the old Pacific Coast Conference. The year before, UCLA won 12 and lost 13, and as far as I could determine the three best players—Don Barksdale, Davage Minor, and John Stanich—were gone.

It was like starting from scratch. Almost all of the early practice sessions were devoted to fundamentals, drills, conditioning, and trying to put my philosophy over. Within a few weeks things didn't look quite as dark.

Alan Sawyer, who had not been at practice in the spring, looked very good at forward. We had obtained Carl Kraushaar from Compton Junior College, and he played center. George Stanich looked like a fine guard, but he, too, had not been out in the spring since he was also a fine high jumper and baseball pitcher. Then there was a little sophomore guard, Eddie Sheldrake, who I knew would do the job. He was cut out of the kind of cloth I like guards made from. And Chuck Clustka was a rugged, hard-driving forward who complemented the fine shooting but poor driving Sawyer.

Ronnie Pearson, who was elected captain; Paul Saunders, another junior college transfer; and the rest developed rapidly, seeming to pick up what I wanted.

We turned things around almost instantly and won the Southern Division title with a 10 and 2 record. However, we lost to Oregon State in Corvallis in the conference playoffs—2 games to 1. In all, we won 22 and lost 7 for the full season—the most wins any UCLA team had ever compiled in history.

We won many of our games that year and in ensuing years more on condition than we did on ability although we rapidly gained more than our share of ability. We were prepared physically to play fast-break, pressure basketball from end line to end line the entire game.

The second year, 1949–50, we were a much better ball club. We had more depth, and the boys had a more thorough understanding of my philosophy of basketball. Again we took the Southern Division, but this time we won the conference title in two close games with Washington State. The Cougars were a very fine club led by Gene Conley, who later played with the Boston Celtics in the NBA and the Boston Braves as a pitcher, and Bob Gambold, who played in the NFL.

We won that first game in the play-off 60–58, but our playing wasn't all that good. With little time left to play, we had a six to eight point lead, but every time we would go down the floor, Ralph Joeckel, one of our forwards, took a shot he had no business trying. He missed every one of them. Then Washington State would go down and hit and keep closing in, but I couldn't get Joeckel out.

Finally, after another of his wayward shots, Washington State missed, and Ralph got the rebound with the score tied. Ralph dribbled on down the floor to about the center line. Photographs show that he took off with a high arching jump shot just back of the center line in our back court and came down just about the same distance the other side. The ball seemed to go up among the rafters in the old barn, banked off the backboard, and came down through the net just as the gun sounded.

Bedlam broke out when the shot went in. You couldn't see Joeckel in the crowd that poured onto the floor. Finally they carried him off the court and down the winding stairs to the dressing room.

When I finally reached the dressing room, Ralph was at the door. "I sure tried to throw that ball game away, didn't I, coach?"

"You sure did," I responded and resolved then and there to reemphasize to all my players the importance of taking only high percentage shots when protecting a lead.

That shot and the 52–49 win the next night put us in the National Collegiate Athletic Association playoffs for the first time. As we prepared to go east, I thought we had an excellent chance of winning the NCAA. We played Bradley in the first round at Kansas City and had the game won if we just stayed with our style. With less than three minutes to go we had a five or six point lead but fell into a rash of horrible mistakes. It was just a classic example of how to lose a basketball game you had won. I had not properly prepared my players and had no one to blame but myself.

Despite the fact that the first two years had been fairly successful, I was not totally enthralled with UCLA. And it was about this time that various representatives from Purdue were talking to me about going back to West Lafayette. They made a tremendous offer—a lot better financially than the $6,000 I got to come to UCLA. In addition I was to have a perpetual five-year contract with built-in increases that I could renegotiate annually. There were also a number of other amenities, including a family membership in country clubs, a new car every year, a very nice home on campus at a nominal rent, a large insurance policy, and several other so-called fringe benefits.

I agreed to accept the Purdue offer if I could gracefully get out of the final year of my three-year contract at UCLA and arranged for a meeting with Wilbur Johns and Bill Ackerman, then graduate manager of the Associated Students. I fully expected they would decide to release me.

But Wilbur and Bill surprised me. They pointed out that I was the one who had insisted on a three-year contract and felt that I should honor it. They made me feel like a heel for even considering leaving. I was irritated to say the least. Although I understood their position, at the time I felt it was unfair. They offered to amend my contract with an increase in salary for the final year.

"No," I told them, "I signed for three years, and I'll continue for three years."

I was peeved and a bit stubborn. Wilbur later told me he was afraid I would leave for sure when my third year was up, particularly since he saw no hope of a new place to play in the foreseeable future.

But after the third year I decided that it would take a most unusual and unlikely offer to get me to leave, and even then it would be a question. The children had fallen in love with California, and they fought every discussion of moving. I am also one who believes that things always turn out for the best and, even though I could not foresee ever having a team of mine play in our own building on campus, UCLA was a fine school. Furthermore, I could see the caliber of basketball improving every year. This, plus the rapid population growth of the Los Angeles area and the ideal climate, seemed to offer hope for realizing a few of my dreams.

11

Full many a gem of purest ray serene,
the deep unfathom'd caves of ocean bear:
Full many a flower is born to blush unseen
*and waste its sweetness on the desert air.**

THOSE WORDS do not apply to Los Angeles. Here you are going to be seen. And there are few places in the world that you are going to be seen as much. I suddenly realized that during my third year in Los Angeles, as I became aware that if we could get a suitable place to play, we would have a plethora of talent available to us as basketball progressed in Southern California.

Here in what is now the second largest city in the nation, there have been, at one time or another, several dominant college basketball forces, including California State at Long Beach, Pepperdine, USC, and UCLA. There is no state in the nation, let alone a city, that can present such powers. This in itself creates a natural rivalry that provides a tremendous incentive to coaches and players to succeed. Then when you take in the state and include California, Stanford, Santa Clara, University of the Pacific, and schools like that, it is easy to understand why basketball has boomed.

We must also give due credit to the influx of professional basketball in the state. But when I was coaching I usually preferred that my boys not watch pro basketball too much, because of the emphasis on individual play, the type of hand checking defense that is illegal for college play, and the bad habits they could pick up. Of course, I knew they would also see many things that could be helpful. But from my point of view the primary value of the pro game has been to develop interest, not to show college players how to play.

---

* Thomas Gray, *Elegy Written in a Country Churchyard.*

The intense competition between the large number of schools in Southern California certainly accounts for the fantastic interest in basketball. Obviously this calls for enormous reservoirs of talent, but happily it is pouring out of the high schools year after year. No one wins without talent, and when you are in the heart of it with an attractive, successful program, you attract the quality needed to contend nationally. Couple these factors with the construction of several fine playing facilities—the Los Angeles Sports Arena, the Forum, the Long Beach Arena, the Anaheim Arena, and Pauley Pavilion at UCLA—and it is easy to understand the strides made in basketball in the almost forty years I have been in Los Angeles.

One of the things that truly solidified our program at UCLA was moving into Pauley Pavilion on the UCLA campus in 1966. It seemed to give us a little more incentive. I know I worked just as hard in the years we were playing in everything from the B.O. Barn to the Sports Arena, but I didn't work with the same deep-seated purpose that is inspired by playing in your own facility.

Possibly a frequent comment of mine describes the difference. "Don't mistake activity for achievement."

There is a very fine line between the champion and the runner-up. Six or seven of my teams, in my opinion, had the potential to win the NCAA championships before the 1964 team succeeded. Each might have been good enough to win but the "if" always arose . . . if we had done this or if we had done that, it might have been different. That line between the champion and near champion is something no one can properly define. I can't and I've tried. But I do know that with the first NCAA championship, the dedication of Pauley Pavilion, the appointment of the late J. D. Morgan as athletic director, the acquisition of two full-time assistants, the transfer to Morgan of schedule-making, and the freedom of not having to prepare a basketball budget, all my efforts became concentrated on one thing—teaching basketball.

It seems to me, too, that the sports climate of Los Angeles contributes to the keenness of competition and the striving toward success. I'm sure that the presence of the Dodgers, the

Rams, the Lakers, and the intense cross-town rivalry with USC gives UCLA an incentive to succeed and do well that it might not have in a South Bend or a Colorado Springs or an Iowa City. Here we have to hustle to stay up with the success of our peers.

It is essential that we look forward constantly. Looking back could well cause us to stumble and fall.

Still another contributor to the intensity and success of the basketball climate in California is the community college program. Community colleges have provided UCLA—and for that matter all the schools in the West—with some excellent talent.

Shortly before I retired I compiled a rather interesting set of statistics which pointed out the route by which all of my lettermen had come to UCLA. Up through the 1959–60 team 62.1 percent had come in from junior colleges. And from 1960 to the time of my survey, 56.6 percent had picked up some credits from junior college before being admitted to UCLA.

Another factor that makes the California area so fertile for basketball is the overall athletic program. Every sport receives great emphasis, and there is tremendous competition in what many people call minor sports, such as golf, tennis, swimming, soccer, rugby, cross-country, volleyball, water polo, etc.

But I think a key factor is something many states do not have—the classification teams. Most high schools in the area have not only a varsity basketball team but others known as Class B, Class C, and in some cases Class D teams. These teams are formed by boys based on what they call exponents—height, weight, age, etc.—and they play a regular schedule.

Occasionally a young man who is small and slender and playing on the Class B team suddenly blossoms out, grows a few inches, and moves up to the varsity where he will star. Gail Goodrich, who twice made All-American at UCLA and did amazingly well in the NBA, is one of those little fellows who grew up to become an outstanding player.

There was one factor which I opposed that some believe played an important role in the development of basketball here. It was the so-called "summer leagues" that have since been banned by the NCAA.

Those leagues got completely out of hand. People were "sponsoring" teams made up of California, Stanford, USC, or UCLA players. They might play two or three nights a week around the area. It was way out of bounds and I was very thankful when the NCAA stopped such programs.

Basketball is a great game, and I probably appreciate it as much as the next man, but I always felt that playing competitively during the summer takes away some of the edge when it comes time to play the regular college schedule. Furthermore, I did not want my players to miss the value of other things. I wanted them well rounded.

Now, let's face it: many basketball players are going to play or practice the year around. I even knew some of my kids to play pick-up games when I gave them a day off because I felt they needed a rest. This was fine as long as it was of their own volition.

That merely typifies the intensity of the competitive athlete. Throughout the entire summer, pick-up games are being played practically every day at a dozen places. And there is nothing wrong with that kind of play. The only admonishment I used to make to my boys was that they police the play, not allow it to get too rough, and try to avoid careless fouls and ball handling, because they might carry those bad habits into our games and it could hurt them.

It has always been my contention that controls must be placed on the boys, and controls must govern every facet of the program. Perhaps a better word than control would be organization. Without organization and leadership toward a realistic goal there is no chance of realizing more than a small percentage of your full potential. Every effort should be made, in the proper manner and keeping everything in proper perspective, toward maximum development of both the individual and the group as a whole. Too much emphasis in the off-season can, in my opinion, deprive the players of many other worthwhile activities, and may also cause some to grow stale during your own season.

12

*Success is peace of mind
which is a direct result of
Self-satisfaction in knowing you
did your best to become the
Best you are capable of becoming.*

DEFINITIONS OF SUCCESS VARY. And everyone has a different degree of acceptance of success. My own quest for an acceptable definition began when I was in Martinsville High School. One of our teachers, Lawrence Schidler, gave the class an assignment—to define success. He had tried to point out to us that success didn't necessarily mean the accumulation of material possessions or a position of power or prestige.

That started me thinking about just what a proper definition of success would be for John Wooden. Through my years in high school and college I thought about it many times but never really had the time to delve into it deeply. While I was at South Bend Central, in the middle to late '30s, I again became concerned over what success really was or should be.

Perhaps it was a selfish concern, I don't know. But a part of my concern was due to the fact that many parents judged teachers by the marks their children received in class. If the grades were good, the teacher was good, and if the grades were poor, it was the teacher's fault.

I began to try to develop a paper that would help my students to understand how to judge success. I had seen various ladders of success so I began using blocks with key words followed by an expanded definition.

Over the next few years, and after hundreds of hours effort, I developed what is now known as John Wooden's Pyramid of Success. My definition is at the top of the pyramid. Only one person can judge it—you. You can fool everyone else, but in the final analysis only you know whether you goofed off or not. You know if you took the shortcut, the easy way out, or cheated. No one else does. I know that I look back with regret on some things that seemed to be success to others.

Over the years, I have given out literally thousands of copies of the pyramid. Once a year on my Los Angeles television show, we used to offer the pyramid to those who wrote and asked for it. Each year we sent out several thousand. A couple of years ago, Leonard Le Sourd wrote an article about it in *Guideposts* magazine and mentioned that I would send a copy to all who wrote for it. This got completely out of hand. After mailing out several thousand, we started bundling up the requests and sending them to *Guideposts* for distribution. That article brought requests for some fifteen thousand.

At the beginning of every season and of all my summer camps, I used to discuss the pyramid in detail and give each person a copy of it. I firmly believe it can be a base for anyone to build upon.

No building is better than its structural foundation, and no man is better than his mental foundation. Therefore, my original cornerstones are still the same—*industriousness* and *enthusiasm*. There is no substitute for work. And to really work hard at something you must enjoy it. If you're not enthusiastic, you can't work up to your maximum ability.

One of the late Grantland Rice's writings epitomizes my feelings on the role industriousness plays in success, especially athletic success.

> You wonder how they do it and you look to
>   see the knack,
> You watch the foot in action, or the
>   shoulder, or the back,
> But when you spot the answer where the
>   higher glamours lurk,
> You'll find in moving higher up the
>   laurel covered spire,
> That the most of it is practice and the
>   rest of it is work.*

---

* Grantland Rice, "How to Be a Champion."

Then three attributes that I placed in the base between the cornerstones are *friendship, cooperation,* and *loyalty.* They are all similar and help illustrate that it takes united effort to tie in the cornerstones.

The anchor blocks of the second tier of the pyramid are *self-control* and *intentness.* If you lose self-control everything will fall. You cannot function physically or mentally or in any other way unless your emotions are under control. That's why I prefer my team to maintain a constant, slightly increasing level of achievement rather than hitting a number of peaks. I believe that there is a corresponding valley for every peak, just as there is a disappointment for every joy. The important thing is that we recognize the good things and not get lost in self-pity over misfortunes.

For an athlete to function properly he must be intent. There has to be a definite purpose and goal if you are to progress. If you are not intent about what you are doing, you aren't able to resist the temptation to do something else that might be more fun at the moment.

Alertness and *initiative* are within the second tier. You've got to be constantly alive and alert and looking for ways to improve. This is especially true in basketball. You must be alert to take advantage of an opponent's error or weakness. Coupled with this must be the individual initiative to act alone. You must have the courage to make decisions.

Now at the heart of the pyramid is *condition.* I stressed this point with my players. I don't mean physical condition only. You cannot attain and maintain physical condition unless you are morally and mentally conditioned. And it is impossible to be in moral condition unless you are spiritually conditioned. I always told my players that our team condition depended on two factors—how hard they worked on the floor during practice and how well they behaved between practices. You can neither attain nor maintain proper condition without working at both.

At the very center—the heart of the structure—is *skill.* Skill, as it pertains to basketball, is the knowledge and the ability quickly and properly to execute the fundamentals. Being able to do them is not enough. They must be done quickly. And being able to do them quickly isn't enough either. They must

**THE PYRAMID
OF SUCCESS**
*John R. Wooden
Head Basketball Coach
UCLA*

SUC

FAITH
Through prayer

COMPETITIVE

FIGHT
(effort and hustle)

RESOURCEFULNESS
(proper judgment)

POISE

Just being yourself. Being at ease in any situation. Never fighting yourself.

CONDITION

Mental — Moral — Physical. Rest, exercise, and diet must be considered. Moderation must be practiced. Dissipation must be eliminated.

SKILL

ADAPTABILITY
(to any situation)

SELF-CONTROL

Emotions under control. Delicate adjustment between mind and body. Keep judgment and common sense.

ALERTNESS

Be observing constantly. Be quick to spot a weakness and correct it or use it as the case may warrant.

AMBITION
(properly focused)

INDUSTRIOUSNESS

There is no substitute for work. Worthwhile things come from hard work and careful planning.

FRIENDSHIP

Comes from mutual esteem, respect, and devotion. A sincere liking for all.

LOYALTY

CESS

PATIENCE
Good things take time

RELIABILITY
(others depend upon you)

INTEGRITY
(speaks for itself)

HONESTY
(in all ways)

SINCERITY
(makes friends)

Success is peace of mind which is a direct result of self-satisfaction in knowing you did your best to become the best that you are capable of becoming.

GREATNESS
"When the going gets tough, the tough get going." Be at your best when your best is needed. Real love of a hard battle.

CONFIDENCE
Respect without fear. Confident not cocky. May come from faith in yourself in knowing that you are prepared.

A knowledge of and the ability to properly execute the fundamentals. Be prepared. Cover every detail.

TEAM SPIRIT
An eagerness to sacrifice personal interests or glory for the welfare of all. "The team comes first."

INITIATIVE
Cultivate the ability to make decisions and think alone. Desire to excel.

INTENTNESS
Ability to resist temptation and stay with your course. Concentrate on your objective and be determined to reach your goal.

To yourself and to all those dependent upon you. Keep your self-respect.

COOPERATION
With all levels of your co-workers. Help others and see the other side.

ENTHUSIASM
Your heart must be in your work. Stimulate others.

be done quickly and precisely at the right time. You must learn to react properly, almost instinctively.

Team spirit is also an important block in the heart of the structure. This is an eagerness to sacrifice personal glory for the welfare of the group as a whole. It's togetherness and consideration for others. If players are not considerate of one another, there is no way we can have the proper team play that is needed. It is not necessary for everyone to particularly like each other to play well together, but they must respect each other and subordinate selfishness to the welfare of the team. The team must come first.

Poise and *confidence* will come from condition, skill, and team spirit. To have poise and be truly confident you must be in condition, know you are fundamentally sound, and possess the proper team attitude. You must be prepared and know that you are prepared.

Near the pinnacle must be *competitive greatness*. And this cannot be attained without poise and confidence. Every block is built upon the other. One will not succeed without the other, and when all are in place, you are on the road toward success. If one crumbles, it may lead to the breakdown of all.

Grantland Rice's writing again illustrates well the role of competitive greatness in the game of life or sport in his marvelous poem, "The Great Competitor":

> Beyond the winning and the goal, beyond the
> glory and the flame,
> He feels the flame within his soul, born of
> the spirit of the game,
> And where the barriers may wait, built up
> by the opposing Gods,
> He finds a thrill in bucking fate and rid-
> ing down the endless odds.
> Where others wither in the fire or fall be-
> low some raw mishap,
> Where others lag behind or tire and break
> beneath the handicap,
> He finds a new and deeper thrill to take him
> on the uphill spin,

Because the test is greater still, and something he can revel in.

This pyramid is tied together with a number of other qualities that are essential to the ultimate definition of success. You tie them together with *ambition*, which if properly focused, can be a tremendous asset, but if it is out of focus, it can be a detriment. You must be *adaptable* to work with others and to meet the challenge of different situations. And you must display *resourcefulness* because in almost every situation good judgment is necessary.

Fight gives you the ability to do it and not be afraid of a tough battle. *Faith* must walk beside *fight* because it is essential that you believe in your objective, and you can't have faith without prayer. *Patience* must be strong because the road will be rough at times and you should not expect too much too soon. Then come *reliability, integrity, honesty,* and *sincerity.*

All of these tie the blocks together into a solid structure. When all these factors are united, you can build toward a success that is based on your own personal set of goals, not those of someone else.

Some of my skeptics, and there have been a few of my players among them, question whether the pyramid really accomplishes anything. I can't answer that. Each person has to answer that for himself. All I know is that I receive request after request from all types of organizations to speak about my pyramid. I do believe it can help everyone to some degree, and certainly can't hurt anyone.

A number of people have suggested that I copyright the pyramid and sell it, but I have refused. If in some small way this chart will help others, then that is enough for me. It was not created to be sold but to be used as a teaching tool, and it has been used just as much in the classroom as on the court.

There have been many players, especially after graduation, who would come back and ask for a few copies.

"Coach," they would tell me, "it's been a great benefit to me."

The youngsters who attended my basketball schools in the

summer were always eager to receive copies of the pyramid, and some of them would even ask for extra copies for younger brothers and sisters. I made it a policy to personally autograph each copy, and this seemed to make a great impression on the youngsters.

Even my UCLA players were youngsters until they got out and were on their own. Then they began to understand and appreciate what we were trying to instill through the pyramid. Steve Patterson, our fine center on that power line with Curtis Rowe and Sidney Wicks, came by after his first year in the NBA to tell me that now he realized what I was driving at. Today he is head basketball coach at Arizona State University.

Patterson is not unusual. I feel that similar circumstances take place every year with every coach and with every player. I am highly flattered by a comment made by Bart Starr, the famous Green Bay Packer quarterback, in his book *A Perspective on Victory* (Follett Publishing Co., 1972).

"To continue to win is the mark of a champion. Of a winner. I think John Wooden at UCLA is a good example of that.

"What he's done year in and year out over the past decade is fabulous. He continues to win because he has something going for those young men that will help sustain them for the rest of their lives. His philosophy is very much the same as Coach Vince Lombardi's was. Coach Wooden equates basketball to the game of life. He says you have to be unselfish, that you have to play for the good of the team, that you have to be disciplined and do what he wants you to do as a team, that he will tolerate no individuality within that team. He wants you to play as a unit. This is really what you end up doing in life because sooner or later you end up on a team."

That's what I always tried to get across, but I had to constantly remind myself that the Pattersons and the Wickses were young.

Sidney Wicks lectured at some of the summer basketball schools for me. He had a marvelous rapport with kids, especially the little ones. There was this huge man, towering over them by several feet, talking to them about the basics of the pyramid, and they were enthralled.

"You suddenly realize," Sidney told them, "that all those things Coach Wooden harps on all the time are true. So take it from me, pay attention, do it Coach Wooden's way. It's right."

Sidney's words pretty well typify most of the young men who left me. We gave them a foundation; it was up to them to improve the structure.

13

Remember this your lifetime through—
Tomorrow, there will be more to do . . .
And failure waits for all who stay
With some success made yesterday . . .
Tomorrow, you must try once more
And even harder than before.

It is most difficult, in my mind, to separate any success, whether it be in your profession, your family, or as in my case, in basketball, from religion.

In my profession, I must be deeply concerned with God's belief in me and be truly interested in the welfare of my fellow-man. No coach should be trusted with the tremendous responsibility of handling young men under the great mental, emotional, and physical strain to which they are subjected unless he is spiritually strong. If he does possess this inner strength, it is only because he has faith and truly loves his fellow-man. This was the belief of Amos Alonzo Stagg, who also felt the obligations, opportunities, and responsibilities in coaching are manifold. The coach who is committed to the Christlike life will be helping youngsters under his supervision to develop wholesome disciplines of body, mind, and spirit that will build character worthy of his Master's calling. He must set the proper example by work and by deed. It is not easy.

It is my belief that in one way or another we are all seeking success. And success is peace of mind, a direct result of self-satisfaction in knowing that you did your best to become the best that you are capable of becoming, and not just in a physical way. "Seek ye first His Kingdom and His righteousness and all these things will be yours as well."

I tried to get this idea across to my players, and I knew that I must practice what I preached if it were to be effective. There are many things that are essential to arriving at true peace of

94

mind, and one of the most important is faith which cannot be acquired without prayer.

Webster partially defines faith as an unquestioning belief in God with complete trust, confidence, and reliance. Faith is not just waiting, hoping, and wanting things to happen. Rather it is working hard to make things happen and realizing that there are no failures—just disappointments—when you have done your best. As someone once said, "If you do your best, angels can do no better."

I tried to convince my players that they could never be truly successful or attain peace of mind unless they had the self-satisfaction of knowing they had done their best. Although I wanted them to work to win, I tried to convince them they had always won when they had done their best.

It isn't what you do, but how you do it. No system is any good if the players are not well grounded in fundamentals. Team play comes from integrating individuals who have mastered the fundamentals into a smooth working unit. Confidence comes from being prepared.

And approval is a great motivator. I tried to follow any criticism, whenever possible, with a pat on the back, realizing that I could not antagonize and influence favorably at the same time. We attempted always to give public credit and acclaim to our play-makers, our defensive men, and those whose roles didn't leap out of the statistical chart.

I considered playing basketball for UCLA a privilege, not a right, and stressed that every player should work harmoniously with his teammates for the common good of all.

At the same time I always tried to make it clear that basketball is not the ultimate. It is of small importance in comparison to the total life we live. There is only one kind of a life that truly wins, and that is the one that places faith in the hands of the Savior. Until that is done, we are on an aimless course that runs in circles and goes nowhere. Material possessions, winning scores, and great reputations are meaningless in the eyes of the Lord, because He knows what we really are and that is all that matters.

> To have your name inscribed up there is
>   greater yet by far,
> Than all the halls of fame down here and
>   every man-made star.
> This crowd on earth, they soon forget the
>   heroes of the past,
> They cheer like mad until you fall and that's
>   how long you last.
> I tell you, friend, I would not trade my name
>   however small,
> If written there beyond the stars in that
>   celestial hall
> For any famous name on earth or glory that
>   they share,
> I'd rather be an unknown here and have my
>   name up there.*

Today we hear a lot of criticism of our young people, but one thing we cannot fault them on is their growing interest in religion. My own interest in the Lord and especially in reading the Bible comes directly from my father. I read from the Bible every day, sometimes more than once.

There's a story about the small brown New Testament that used to sit on my desk at UCLA and now sits on my desk at home. For several years, I worked at a summer basketball school at Campbell College, a small school in Buie's Creek, North Carolina. One year I went east and discovered that I had left my Bible at home. I got this small one in a book store, and since it was handy to refer to, I kept it on my desk ever since. Once in a while one of my new players would pick it up when he came in and found me busy on the phone. Some of them used to be startled when they opened it, but many of them would read a bit while I completed my call.

In addition to the New Testament, I get a great deal of help from reading the *Daily Word* and *The Upper Room*. I also carry a letter in my wallet entitled "Where to look in the Bible." It points out specific references that will be of help in time of

---

* "God's Hall of Fame," source unknown.

Joshua Hugh Wooden, Coach Wooden's father, a truly wise and gentle man.

Coach Wooden in 1930 as a sophomore at Purdue University.

John Wooden with President Edward Elliot of Purdue at his 1932 Purdue University graduation. Elliot had just presented John with the Big Ten medal for scholarship and athletics.

Coach watching the UCLA baseball practice.

Coach Wooden with his 1947-48 Indiana State Team which was the runner-up for the NAIA championship.

John and Nellie kiss the Blarney stone at a St. Patrick's Day Dance on St. Simone Island, near the end of World War II.

Coach Wooden in action on the bench.

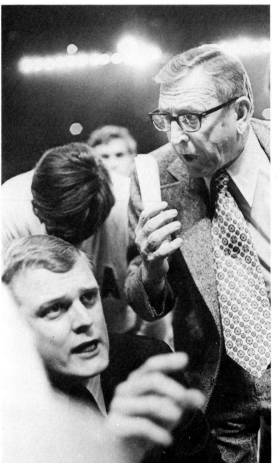

Coach and assistant coach Gary Cunningham get down to brass tacks during a time-out.

On the bench, from right: assistant coach Jerry Norman, Gail Goodrich, Fred Slaughter, Keith Erickson, Doug McIntosh, and Jack Hirsch.

Cutting the cake on his 58th birthday in 1968.

Leaving with Jesse Owens and our wives to receive the Victor Awards in Las Vegas.

John Wooden with the Victor Award Winners, 1968, which included Tom Harmon, Carl Hubbell, Johnny Weismuller, Satchel Paige, Maurice Richard, Henry Armstrong, Jesse Owen, Vicki Draves, Henri Cochet, and Gene Sarazen.

John, with Nellie, Frank Sinatra, and Mayor Tom Bradley, upon receiving the UCLA Distinguished Service Medal.

Coach Wooden with this 1970 NCAA championship team: Sidney Wicks is wearing a net, Curtis Rowe stands at the far right, Steve Patterson is behind Coach, Rick Betchley at far left, John Ecker 2nd from right, and Jon Chapman directly behind Wicks.

UCLA vs. Duke in this NCAA 1964 finals. #53 is Keith Erickson, #25 is Gail Goodrich, #23 is Kenny Washington, and #32 is Doug McIntosh.

In usual posture in his UCLA office.

Coach is looking for the goodluck sign from his wife, Nellie, at tip-off time.

Larry Farmer grabs the rebound for UCLA. Bill Walton is on the other side of the basket.

Kareem Abdul-Jabbar puts one in against USC in 1966; from left to right in white are Lucious Allen, Jim Nielsen, and Mike Warren.

Coach Wooden, overlooking the site for the new Pauley Pavilion on the UCLA campus.

John in front of the John Wooden Center on dedication day.

At the home of our dearest friends, Walt and Dorthea Kindy. Walt was my assistant during my years in South Bend and no one ever had a better friend.

John with Earl Warriner, his grade school principal and coach at Centerton, Indiana.

Coach and two long-time friends: Jim Enright, Chicago sportswriter and former Big Ten Basketball official and the late Walter Alston, manager of the L.A. Dodgers.

The only person to be elected to the basketball hall of fame as a player and as a coach.

Judge William Keane, Charles Hathaway, Coach Wooden, and Coach Gene Bartow present Marques Johnson with the first annual John R. Wooden Player of the Year Award, 1977.

John receiving the *Sporting News* Sportsman of the Year award from J. D. Morgan, UCLA Director of Athletics.

Coach Wooden giving instructions at practice.

Coach giving his farewell speech to the UCLA student body at his retirement party.

Coach relaxing during a break at his basketball camp for youngsters at California Lutheran College.

Coach Wooden with Carol Burnett at the 1985 UCLA Graduation where they received Honorary Doctorate Degrees. Coach has received a number of honorary degrees, including one from his alma mater, Purdue, Campbell College, Indiana State, and California Lutheran College.

Coach Wooden at a UCLA basketball game in January, 1987 with his daughter, Nan, his granddaughter, Caryn, and his great-granddaughter, Cori.

Coach's son, Jim Wooden, with his family. From left to right: John, Kim, Mike, Greg, Carleen, and Jim.

need: "When desiring inward peace . . . When things look blue . . . When tempted to do wrong," etc.

For many years I have been a deacon of the First Christian Church in Santa Monica. I remember the first Sunday, shortly after we moved to Los Angeles, that we went to services with the children. Much to my amazement, as we went up the walk to the entry, I read the minister's name on the bulletin board. It was Wales E. Smith. Now, I had known a Wales Smith when he was a classmate of mine at Martinsville High, but as far as I knew, he was a pastor in Kokomo, Indiana. However, when the minister walked out for the service, it was our Wales Smith. What a happy surprise! He continued to be our pastor until his recent retirement.

It seems to me that man has a great need to communicate with the Lord. For years now, I have carried a little cross in my pocket. Few people, except my immediate family, are aware of it at all. It was clutched in my hand during all of the games I coached, and I still grab on to it whenever I anticipate tension. A friend, my minister at the First Christian Church in South Bend, the late Rev. Frank E. Davidson, gave it to me just before I went into the navy in 1943, and I've carried it in my pocket ever since.

Frank E. Davidson was a most unique man. He directed the Forum Club for men which replaced regular Sunday school class. Ultimately, it involved people of all faiths—Methodist, Presbyterian, Jewish, Catholic—and became rather famous. It was just what its name implied, a forum on religion and life. One Sunday, I was to receive a button for attending 52 consecutive weeks. This was in the heart of the Indiana State basketball playoffs and two local schools—Central and Washington—were to meet for the regional championship on the previous night.

At the presentation the next morning, Dr. Davidson told a little story: "I sat there last night waiting for the game, aware that Coach Wooden was to receive his '52 button' today. As the teams went into the huddles before the tip, I looked at Coach John How, a Catholic, a member of our club, and saw his players crossing themselves in prayer. I knew John Wooden was quietly saying a little prayer, and I just couldn't help but think, 'Now isn't the Lord in a hell of a spot.' " Then he congratulated me on winning the game, and being perfect in attendance.

Perhaps there isn't an hour of a waking day that I don't think of Frank Davidson. Every time I reach in my pocket for my pocketknife or comb, my fingers touch the cross he gave me. It's been worn down quite a bit now from my clenching it in my left hand during games. I feel it definitely enabled me to better control my emotions. When I had a firm grip on it, I was reminded to take care.

This was especially true when it came to my running comments during games. I had been known to chide an official to watch "that butcher," meaning some tough, hard-nosed kid pushing one of my players around. I made that remark one time to Ken Stanley, one of USC's fine players and a boy I admired so much for his tough style. Ken became highly incensed over that remark, and rightly so. I didn't do that quite so much after that, and the little cross is partly responsible.

Another cherished friend who would prefer to remain anonymous sent me the following lines a few years ago. I feel they best describe my association with the little cross.

I carry a cross in my pocket,
A simple reminder to me of the fact
   that I am a Christian wherever I may be;
This little cross is not magic, nor is it
   a good luck charm,
It isn't meant to protect me from every
   physical harm;
It's not for identification for all the
   world to see,
It's simply an understanding between
   my Savior and me;
When I put my hand in my pocket to bring
   out a coin or a key,
The cross is there to remind me of the
   price He paid for me;
It reminds me, too, to be thankful for my
   blessings day by day, and to strive
   to serve Him better in all that I do

and say;
It is also a daily reminder of the peace
and comfort I share with all who know
my Master and give themselves to His care;
So I carry a cross in my pocket reminding
me, no one but me, that Jesus Christ is
the Lord of my life if only I will let
Him be.

We who coach have great influence on the lives of all the young men who come under our supervision, and the lives we lead will play an important role in their future. It is essential that we regard this as a sacred trust and set the example that we know is right. We must try to prevent the pressures for winning scores from causing us to swerve from moral principles.

That's why, in the years after I was given this small cross, I grasped it tightly in my hand during games to seek support in maintaining my composure and my emotions no matter how heated the game became. I believed that my being able to control myself might help my boys to control their emotions and play up to their true potential. I know that I faltered at times, but I also know that for the most part my policy of control was most helpful.

Often I have told coaches assembled at clinics throughout the world that I am somewhat like the unknown fellow who said:

I am not what I ought to be,
not what I want to be,
not what I am going to be,
But thankful that I am not what I used
to be.

14

Be a gentleman at all times.
Never criticize, nag, or razz a teammate.
Be a team player always.
Never be selfish, jealous, envious, or
* egotistical.*
Earn the right to be proud and confident.
Never expect favors, alibi or make excuses.
Never lose faith or patience.
Courtesy and politeness are a small price
* to pay for the good will and affection of*
* others.*
Acquire peace of mind by becoming the best
* that you are capable of becoming.* *

MY LIFE has been wrapped around the family structure and the church from my earliest memory. My personal family life— with my wife, my children, and my grandchildren—is merely an extension of a life-style formed in my boyhood with my mother, father, and brothers.

As long as I can remember, Sunday was set aside for the family and for the church. As a boy, this pattern was established. We would go to services, then either go home for dinner with the family and friends, or go to a friend's home for the dinner.

When Nellie and I were married, our life seemed to fall into a similar pattern. And when we moved to South Bend our own family Sunday ritual became firmly established. After Sunday school and the worship service, we would go some place to eat with the Kindys or some other friends and occasionally we drove to Benton Harbor, Michigan, to be with the Perigo family.

Walt Kindy came to Central High the same year I did and became my assistant in basketball and ultimately my assistant in all other capacities—tennis, baseball, comptroller, and athletic director. And Bill Perigo, who later coached basketball at the

---

* From Wooden's set of normal expectations.

University of Michigan, became a close friend through our play-ing pro basketball together with Kautsky's. When we moved to South Bend, Bill was coaching at Benton Harbor, Michigan, not far across the Indiana line.

When we moved to Los Angeles our life followed a similar style except for being in a new city and finding new friends. Then as the years passed, our daughter, Nan, and our son, Jim, grew up, became very involved with life, UCLA, and then mar-ried.

Nancy Ann now has three lovely daughters, Christy Ann, Caryn Audrey, and Cathleen Amy. James Hugh, who was named after my father, met Carleen Garcia from Hawaii after he was discharged from the Marine Corps. Now they have three hand-some sons—Gregory James, John Todd, and Michael Hugh— and Kim Louise, our fourth lovely granddaughter, to share our love. Our lives have truly been enriched by our children and grandchildren.

Our family makes for quite a handful for dinner after Sunday services. It's also a problem for all of us to get together. Nan lives in Reseda, quite some distance out in the San Fernando Valley, and Jimmy now lives in Irvine, near the southern end of Orange County.

We almost always are with either of our children and our grandchildren on Sunday afternoons unless we are out of the city. I recall so well the Sunday after we won the 1970 NCAA title against Jacksonville at the University of Maryland. All the family had come to the airport to meet us, and we had gone home to leave our things, freshen up a bit, and go to dinner with Nan and the girls. We were taking the family to Lawry's Prime Rib, our favorite restaurant.

We were about to go out the door when the phone rang. When I answered, the operator said, "Long distance calling." I waited and waited and waited. It seemed a long while. The grandchildren were impatient to go, Nellie was waving at me, and Cathleen was pulling me by the arm.

"Operator," I said as she came back on the line for a second, "I'm ready to take my family out to dinner. They are all waiting. If this isn't something important, I'm just going to have to leave. I can't wait any longer."

"Sir," she said, "the President of the United States is call-ing."

"In that case, I'll wait," I stammered, covering the phone with my hand and trying to explain to the children. Of course, when I told them President Nixon was calling, they really were excited.

The president explained that he had tried to call me in College Park the night we won only to learn that we had left for home right after the game. He congratulated us on our victory, said how much he enjoyed watching it and was very gracious and nice.

"Mr. President," I told him, "I have three of my granddaughters here. It would be a tremendous thrill if they could talk to the President of the United States." He talked and visited with each one of them.

One of the greatest compliments I believe I have ever received came from Christy, my oldest granddaughter and first grandchild. When she was in the third grade, one of her assignments was to write a paper entitled, "The Person I Admire Most." She wrote,

> The person I admire most is my grandfather. His name is John Robert Wooden. He is very fond of sports and coaches basketball. I am fond of his great skills in both coaching and playing. He also taught English, and I admire the way he can write rhymes. I am also very fond of the way he handles children, as he does with my little sisters and cousins. I admire all his talents and wish I could have some of them.

> Christy, Oct. 22, 1968

Occasionally Nellie and I liked to get away alone. One of the places we enjoyed so much is Welcome Inn, a Lawrence Welk enterprise located near Escondido in Southern California. They have a tricky little 18-hole par-3 golf course, a Jacuzzi pool in which I relaxed several times a day, a beautiful swimming pool, a fine restaurant, and the setting is very peaceful and restful.

I worked the crossword puzzle in the morning after breakfast, and then caught up on my reading. I don't know how many times I've read and reread the Zane Grey series, *Magnificent Obsession* and *The Robe* by Lloyd Douglas, and many books of poems. The late Paul Wellman, whose historical novels are so well done, is one of my choice authors, not only because he was a friend for most of the years we have been at UCLA, but also because his work is so appealing to me.

It was during one of these times of relaxation some years back that I made the decision to give up smoking for good. I had been a cigarette smoker since my days in the service in the Second World War. While I was never a heavy smoker, I did smoke regularly except that each year I would quit on October 14, my birthday, and not smoke again until basketball season was over.

An extra benefit of giving up smoking was that then my boys couldn't point to me as being a smoker, even though I had never smoked during the season and never in front of them. It's pretty hard to expect a boy not to do something that he knows you do. I always tried to live the life I wanted them to follow.

15

It is amazing how much can be accomplished if no one cares who gets the credit.

UNSELFISHNESS IS A TRAIT I always insisted upon. I believed that every basketball team is a unit, and I didn't separate my players as to starters and subs. I tried to make it clear that every man plays a role, including the coach, the assistants, the trainer and the managers.

My managers were always considered part of our team. They were not the team's servants. Rather, they worked for the team, and the team had to work for them. One of my demand rules had to do with the way we left our dressing room, either at Pauley Pavilion or on the road. Many building custodians across the country would tell you that UCLA left the shower and dressing room the cleanest of any team. We picked up all the tape, never threw soap on the shower floor for someone to slip on, made sure all showers were turned off and all towels were accounted for. The towels were always deposited in a receptacle, if there was one, or stacked neatly near the door.

It seems to me that this is everyone's responsibility—not just the manager's. Furthermore, I believe it is a form of discipline that should be a way of life, not to please some building custodian, but as an expression of courtesy and politeness that each of us owes to his fellow-man. These little things establish a spirit of togetherness and consideration and help unite the team into a solid unit.

In my early years as a coach, I ran a pretty taut ship. Every detail was spelled out from the cut of the player's hair to the style of dress for games. Even late in my career, I probably kept a tighter rein on my players than most coaches, although I did ease up a lot over the years. I realized there was no way I could keep a constant eye on them all of the time, and I wasn't going to sit up all night in some hotel lobby to make sure they didn't sneak out. Rather, I tried to develop a personal concern among them that my requirements were dictated only for their good and ultimate success.

I did remain very strict about being on time for practice and team meals. But I relaxed my rules on dress by no longer insisting that the team wear jackets, dress shirts, and ties in public. Sport shirts were okay, although I still preferred that a tie be worn with a dress shirt. If we were having a team meal in a private dining room, I would allow them to dress casually, but if we were in a public dining room, I wanted them to look nice, both for themselves and for the university. Politeness, cleanliness, and neatness are characteristics that should be expected, not demanded.

Over the years I have become convinced that every detail is important and that success usually accompanies attention to little details. It is this, in my judgment, that makes for the difference between champion and near champion.

One of the little things I watched closely was a player's socks. No basketball player is better than his feet. If they hurt, if his shoes don't fit, or if he has blisters, he can't play the game. It is amazing how few players know how to put on a pair of socks properly. I didn't want blisters, so each year I gave in minute detail a step-by-step demonstration as to precisely how I wanted them to put on their socks—every time. Believe it or not, there's an art to doing it right, and it makes a big difference in the way a player's feet stand the pounding of practice and the game. Wrinkles which cause blisters can be eliminated by just a little attention.

Along this same line, I attached great importance to the shoes our players wore and how they fit. When most of them came to us, they were wearing shoes a size to a size and a half too large. This seemed to be a holdover from childhood, when their feet had been growing fast. But our players' feet weren't going to grow much once they got to college, and if they did, we could refit them with new shoes. I wanted the toe of the foot to be exactly at the end of the shoe when they were standing up so that when they made a quick stop, the foot wouldn't slide.

For most of my coaching life, my teams wore Converse shoes. I had worn them in high school and at Purdue. In all probability I was among the last of the coaches to switch from black, high-top Converse to white high-tops. And I'm sure that I was among the last to go to low-cuts for those players who wanted to wear them. Then in the early seventies several players said they would like to try another make of shoe. Finally, I agreed to try them, and said that if the majority of the team voted to wear them, we would change. After that, I let the majority decide each year. A little-known fact is that some players, usually guards, are very hard on shoes and may go through a half-dozen pair a year.

Our uniforms were all alike, even at practice. That was part of my discipline. I didn't want one guy practicing in a high school shirt, another wearing a castoff football jersey, another in green shorts, and someone else in yellow. It was important to me that the team be dressed alike, with shirttails in and socks pulled up.

During my years at UCLA, we used the same type and make of practice shirt and pant I had been using since the 1930s, and our game uniforms and warm-up suits were made to measure for each boy. I designed them and had each player measured for fit. When the uniforms arrived, we had an inspection to be sure they fit. If they were not just right, they went back for revision. I wanted the players to feel proud of their appearance and be comfortable for both practice and games.

It's the little details that are vital. Little things make big things happen, and that's what I tried to get across to my players.

My talks with the players usually took place right on the floor during practice. I'm not a believer in meetings or so-called chalk talks or blackboard drills. I believe in learning by repetition to the point that everything becomes automatic. Only very rarely did I stop group action to correct one player, as I preferred to explain to an individual his specific mistakes. I do not believe in having several players stand idly by while I am talking to one. But if I did call the team together in a meeting, it was usually for the purpose of making a major change in our offense or defense or to correct a first-time mistake that I wanted all to be aware of. I felt that the basics could best be presented at one session. However, it was only common sense not to digress and take thirty minutes to explain what should take only five or ten.

We didn't have a playbook at UCLA during most of my coaching years. At one time I did issue a rather expansive playbook, but I became convinced the players didn't pay much attention to it, so it was abandoned. Then, when I did give them a sheet or two of information once in a while, I think they paid more attention to it. But basically, I tried to get my "notebook" across verbally every day, bit by bit.

The best teacher is repetition, day after day, throughout the season. I never gave my teams any kind of a written test. After all, they didn't have time in a game to sit down and write something. It had to be instant recognition and instant reaction.

I always kept personal notebooks that I updated after every game or at the end of the season. One was a statistical record of what we had done. Another was a coaching book of drills and practices. Even today, I can go back twenty-four years and tell you what we did at 3:30 P.M. on a given afternoon. The third book was really a zipper binder that I used when I was at clinics. It was a collection of diverse materials from lectures to play diagrams to poetry to speeches on various aspects of the game.

Then there were the notes to myself. These were cautions to be alert to certain things. For example, "Be more strict about being on the floor at 3:15 P.M." . . . "Organize my time-outs better" . . . "In three-man drills have the shooter take the shot from outside the lane and use the backboard" . . . "Be ready for all types of zone defenses" . . . "Emphasize team play" . . . "Prevent internal problems of any kind early."

Many of these little admonitions originated each day in planning practice. My assistant and I used to spend about two hours every morning closeted away planning a practice that might not last that long. Every entry was made on a white 3 x 5 card that I carried in my pocket. As things developed during practice that I wanted to note, I wrote them on this card. Then I transferred the schedule and my comments into my notebook.

One of my constant reminders was, "End practice on a happy note." I wanted the boys to want to come out to practice, and I wanted them to get a certain amount of pleasure out of basketball. It's a game. It should be fun. So I always tried to counterbalance any criticism in practice with a bit of praise. I wanted my players to feel that the worst punishment I could give them was to deny them the privilege of practicing. If they did not want to practice, I did not want them there.

16

*If you keep too busy learning
the tricks of the trade,
you may never learn the trade.*

MANY DIFFERENT people influence a man's life. My father had a tremendous influence on mine. So did Glenn Curtis, my high school coach, and Piggie Lambert of Purdue. Some of my dedication to organization comes from the late Frank Leahy, the former Notre Dame football coach. I often went to his practices and observed how he broke them up into periods. Then I would go home and analyze why he did things certain ways. As a player, I realized there was a great deal of time wasted. Leahy's concepts reinforced my ideas and helped in the ultimate development of what I do now.

Another man who influenced me by observation rather than association was the late Walter Alston, who for many years was the manager of the Los Angeles Dodgers. He was often called the "Quiet Man," but I believe a better description is the "Patient Man." While I was never intimately acquainted with Walter Alston, I could spot his tremendous virtues merely by watching him during a game.

I once heard Al Campanis, the Dodgers' general manager, describe Alston's ability to handle players. "Alston is like a man handling a dove. If you squeeze it too tightly, you'll smother or kill it. If you hold it too loose, it'll fly away."

That's the way I tried to work with players. They were just like doves. Some needed to be held a little tighter or they would get out of my control. Others needed a looser grip in order to play their best. There was no standard that would work for all.

The good Lord had blessed me, as a player, with tremendous

109

quickness and a driving desire to be the best conditioned player in basketball. Therefore it took me quite a while as a coach to realize that the great majority of players would not pay the price of conditioning unless they were driven. Later on I came to see that I could make them work if I kept after them and repeated things time and again. But they could never be forced to do anything by brute strength. It was like one of our old mules— you could hitch him to the wagon or the plow, but you could not make him go. I continually told my teams that the last law of learning—repetition—is the most important.

In game play it was always my philosophy that patience would win out. By that, I meant patience to follow our game plan. If we believed in it, we would wear the opposition down and would eventually get to them. If we broke away from our style, however, and played their style, we would be in trouble. And if we let our emotions, rather than our reason, command the game we would not function effectively.

I constantly cautioned our teams: "Play your game, just play your game. Eventually, if you play your game, stick to your style, class will tell in the end." This does not mean that we will always outscore our opponent, but does insure that we will not beat ourselves.

It always seemed to me that more games are lost than are won. That's why scouts had little difficulty writing a report on UCLA while I was coach. We seldom changed our attack— we seldom introduced new patterns—but we tried never to lock ourselves into doing the same thing in the same situation. We were not too concerned about opponents knowing what we were going to do as long as they didn't know when.

An important ingredient of patience is perseverance. I tried to instill in our players the desire to do everything correctly— not to give up on something but to persevere until it was mastered.

Over the years, I have been asked repeatedly which of my UCLA players I would rate as the best. Until this book, I never answered that question. I will say that I have never had any more successful players—by my definition—than Conrad Burke or Doug McIntosh. It wasn't so much because of what they did but how they did it. They weren't especially gifted physically, and they weren't particularly fast or maneuverable. But by perseverance and dedicated hard work they learned their assignments minutely and made few mistakes.

Burke was a starter for two and a half years and McIntosh for two years, although as freshmen, neither one had looked as if he ever would be a starter or even earn a letter. Yet Burke made the starting five midway through his sophomore season in 1956. McIntosh came in to play that great game in the NCAA finals in place of Fred Slaughter in 1964 and started the next two seasons. Neither did it with any tricks, fancy stuff, or brilliant talent. Patience, perseverance, and desire made them major contributors. They truly made the most of the ability they possessed. Who can do more?

It is because of the Burkes and the McIntoshes that I tried to exercise strong patience before I made the ultimate selection of a starting team. Many players begged me to start, but their practice performance didn't merit it. Only Eddie Powell ever got me to compromise and that's one I'll never understand.

There are only five starting positions. I feel two, or, maybe, three others can support them. Therefore, I felt it was important that I not predetermine those starters without giving every man on the squad the opportunity to work his way into that unit.

The older and more experienced men usually started out running on the first five when practice began. They had earned that right the year before even though I sometimes had strong feelings that a younger man, perhaps a sophomore or a junior who had come on strong toward the end of the previous season, would turn out to be the best. I experimented and tried to give them all an equal opportunity.

During preseason practice I worked different combinations and tried different units on both offense and defense so as to obtain a full evaluation of all players. And then I tried to reach a decision before our first game, or definitely by mid-December.

The starting unit was selected when I had determined their combined strength from the composite results from our set offense, our fast-break offense, our set defense, our pressing defense, and best use of first replacements. It is the sum total of the entire unit that counts, not the total of any one part. So I tried to be patient first in my evaluation and then in my selection.

This was always a very emotional time both for the players and for me. To them particularly, it was a highly charged period in their lives. Every player believed he was capable of starting— I wouldn't have wanted them if they had thought otherwise. Yet only five would start, seven to eight would see considerable playing time, and the rest would be charged with keeping our system going to produce the highest level of competition.

While these were trying times for everyone's emotions, I had a firm policy never to charge up my team on an emotional level. I believe that for every artificial peak you may create there is a valley, and I don't like valleys. Games can be lost in valleys. The ideal is an ever-mounting graph line that peaks with your final performance. There will be difficulty and adversity to overcome, but that is necessary to become stronger.

Other coaches believe in charging a team up. I never did and never will. I sought a calm assurance in our dressing room, a calm assurance warming up on the floor, and a calm assurance in my final remarks before going out to play. But once that game started, it was a different matter. I never tried to get a Walt Hazzard emotionally high, for example, before the tip. However, once we were underway, I would. I might yell something to him as he went by, or call some substitute's name to come sit beside me as Hazzard was running past. I would do anything that might work to shake loose a lethargic situation.

(I am citing Walt Hazzard only as a name, not as an individual. Walter didn't have to be charged up very much once he assimilated our philosophy. Like so many other of my players, Walter always came to play.)

There is a fine line between spirit and temperament. I always wanted spirit and derided temperament. Keith Erickson, probably one of the greatest defensive players I've ever coached, rode that line like a silver bullet. Few have balanced it like Keith did.

Keith was the kind of young man who loved to test me to see how far he could go. He was mischievous but not mean. Not bad. I believe that basketball should be fun but not funny. I don't want players doing things in practice that I don't allow in a game. When Lewis Alcindor triggered the "no-dunk" rule, I did not permit it in practice.

Erickson had great peripheral vision, and he liked to horseplay in drills. He liked to see how far or how high he could throw a ball. He'd watch me out of the corner of his eye and when I'd turn away, he'd try it. He was half hoping I'd see him and chide him. And I suspect that at the same time he was hoping I wouldn't see him, but the other players would. This way he could prove to them he wasn't falling totally into line.

Keith was just the kind of boy I looked for. He gave me fits at times, but when the chips were down and it called for the total effort Keith was ready. And he never was afraid of any other player. If I assigned him to a tough man, he played a much better game. If his man wasn't tough, Keith didn't play as well.

I'll always remember his game against Brigham Young in the 1965 NCAA regionals. He went into the game with a badly pulled groin muscle. It was hard for him to run and jumping really hurt. I gave him Kramer; he did a tremendous job on him and scored 28 points. That's the type of a player Keith was. Give him a stern assignment and he would give a super performance.

I seldom punished players at practice or in front of others. Some coaches believe in giving laps or sprints for errors. I don't think that works. I'm not sure how the body chemistry functions precisely, but I doubt that it responds properly to punishment of that type.

In every facet of basketball, we work on pressure. The opponent provides that during a game. I tried to provide it in practice with drills that recreated game conditions.

I think I thrived on pressure. It never got to me either as a player or a coach. I believe that, when a player constantly works under pressure, he will respond automatically to it. For this reason I am confident that what the team does on the weekend in a game relates 100 percent to what it does during the week.

Essentially, I was always more of a practice coach than a game coach. This is because of my conviction that a player who practices well, plays well.

17

Success is never final.
Failure is never fatal.
It's courage that counts. *

AFTER A FEW years at UCLA, I began to wonder about many
facets of my basketball philosophy. We did very well, but except
for an "if" or an "and" here and there we might have enjoyed
even greater success. I have long contended that there were
many earlier years when UCLA might have won an NCAA
title if everything had fallen in place like it did in the years
since 1964.

At least six or seven times between 1948 and our first title
in 1964 we had the talent that could have won the NCAA—
not should have, but could have. I've spent hours trying to evaluate where I fell short because the ultimate failure to win must
rest with the coach who creates the program and directs the
game plan. A lot of things could have fallen into place during
those years, but they didn't. Some we had no control over. I
had no control over Bill Russell being at the University of San
Francisco in 1956 when we had a great club led by Willie Naulls.
Russell was the first master of the defensive aspect of college
basketball, and when we couldn't match his quickness, height,
and desire, we couldn't match USF in points.

Russell later became the most dominant force in pro basketball
and was the first of the great intimidators. I'll never forget one
occasion when Willie Naulls, who later played with Bill on the
Boston Celtics, going up for a shot, had faked one way and
Bill had gone for the fake. Willie went by him, driving for

---

* Winston Churchill

the basket, obviously bent on dunking the ball with both hands.

Just as Willie began to drive the ball down for the dunk, Russell's hand went over the basket. Willie nearly dunked the ball, but Russell blocked the shot. I contended that this was goal tending, but the official insisted the ball never left Naulls' hands.

The move was incredible and surprised everyone so much that no one knew what to call. I think it really shook up our team and probably was the turning point of the game.

Four years earlier, in 1952, I believe we had the talent capable of winning, but we didn't. That was during the Korean War, and freshmen were eligible to play. Two of them, outstanding young players, made the starting five, Don Bragg and Johnny Moore. Bragg was from San Francisco and Moore came from Indiana. Bragg teamed with Jerry Norman at forward while Moore alternated with Mike Hibler at center. We had what I considered an ideal guard combination—the big one in Don Johnson and the little, quick man in Ron Livingston. Both could direct the attack well and understood my game philosophy.

We beat Washington that year for the Pacific Coast Conference title. When we reached the NCAA regionals in Corvallis, Oregon, we ran into a tough Santa Clara team in the first round and were eliminated by a score of 68–59. In the NCAA, every game is a finality. There is no second chance, no double elimination to come back up on the loser's bracket such as there is in the NCAA baseball championship. The fact that Don Bragg, one of our irreplaceables, had broken his big toe when he stumbled coming out of the shower the day before the tournament was small consolation.

You get one shot—and you sink or swim with it. I believe that's the proper system, but it also puts everything in one basket.

Don Johnson and Jerry Norman were co-captains of that 1952 team. Perhaps Norman, more than any other young man, typifies the challenge strong-willed players present to me. Jerry gave me fits. I don't believe I ever had a boy more strong-willed, more sure of himself, and more outspoken.

Jerry was at UCLA when I arrived for the 1948–49 season. Even though he did not play that year, he showed his strong will and temperament in practice. Then, the next year, even though he had been warned to reform, it was necessary for me to dismiss him for insubordination. Jerry was a rebel—very head-strong, set in his ways, and profane. I dismissed him more for profanity than anything else. That I would never tolerate. Sure, boys were going to slip during practice and say something; I understand that. But if it continued, I asked them to leave the floor for the day.

Besides having a problem with profanity, Jerry was obstinate and continued to do things—such as making cross-court passes or using the wrong hand when taking an underbasket shot—that riled me. He was an unselfish player, but I felt that his insubordination undermined the total team effort.

After missing three or four conference games that second year, Jerry came back and apologized to the team and was rein-stated. Jerry had a lot of skills and potential, and I had convinced myself that one way or the other I was going to get him to come around to my way of doing things. I was sure he was cut out for my style of basketball, and I wasn't going to let him beat me, but, more important, I didn't want him to beat himself. However, it should be mentioned that his close friend Eddie Sheldrake was very instrumental in my giving him another chance.

A strong competitor, full of fire and drive, and with a great innate basketball sense, Jerry ultimately accomplished all the goals I had set for him, and, I hope, all of the goals he had set for himself.

By the time Jerry graduated and finished his military obligation, my brother Maurice, the one we called Cat, was principal of West Covina High School in the San Gabriel Valley east of Los Angeles. Cat needed a basketball coach, and upon my recom-mendation hired Jerry. Later Jerry returned to UCLA as my freshman coach and taught in our Department of Physical Educa-tion for the 1957–58 season. And in 1963 he became head varsity assistant.

There were some who wondered about my logic in hiring Jerry, but they didn't know him as I did. He had fine basketball sense and was an excellent recruiter—something I hate doing. And it has always been my contention that anyone who whipped a problem the way Jerry did shows signs of strength. When a person overcomes obstacles, he becomes stronger, and Jerry did that. Today Jerry is a highly successful investment banker in Los Angeles who regularly attends UCLA games. And he never uses profanity anymore.

I never wanted a yes man for an assistant. In reality, I guess, I wanted a rebel—someone who would stand up to me. A man who agrees with you merely inflates your ego and can't be of much help. On the other hand, there had to be moderation. I didn't want a daily brawl with my assistants. I wanted to hear their side, their views, their ideas. Some I adopted, some I rejected, but because of them we became a better unit.

During my years, I was very fortunate with assistants. Eddie Powell, who came to UCLA with me from South Bend Central and Indiana State, probably knew me better than any of my assistants, and he knew what I wanted done. Bill Putnam, who was Wilbur Johns' aide when I came, stayed on with me until 1963, when he left to go into business. Bill was one of the most loyal, hard-working coaches who ever worked with me. He came to understand me and my ways very well, but his obligations as assistant director of athletics required much of his time.

Doug Sale, who replaced Eddie Powell, would have become outstanding had he stayed with me. He had not played for me and was just learning my ways when he left. There could be no more loyal, determined, nor harder worker than Doug.

Denny Crum, who played guard for me in 1958 and 1959 after coming to us from Pierce Junior College, was with me for three years before moving to Louisville as head coach. Like Norman, Crum was a very strong-willed, intense but highly skilled young coach. And Gary Cunningham, who played forward for me, was equally intense and was an exceptional analyst. He also had a very winning way about him. After I retired, Gary came back to have two successful seasons as UCLA head coach. Then he elected to go into administration and is now the athletic director at Fresno State University.

Frank Arnold, who joined me after Crum moved to Louisville, was my first non-player assistant since Bill Putnam and Doug Sale. He went on to coach at Brigham Young University, and assist Steve Patterson at Arizona State.

Every assistant made a contribution. Some perhaps more than others, but without them the task would have been formidable. Several such contributions stand out in my memory, but probably the most famous one came from Norman. That was in the 1967–68 NCAA championships which were played for the first time in the Sports Arena in Los Angeles. We were meeting Houston and Elvin Hayes in the semifinals. This was after we had lost to Houston in the Astrodome, 71–69, in a game in which Lew Alcindor was hardly effective due to an eye injury sustained the week before and in which Elvin Hayes had one of the finest individual performances that I have ever seen.

The Big E, as they called Elvin, believed (if you could accept the press reports) that he could again dominate Alcindor and UCLA. Jerry proposed that we use what is known as a box and one defense. That is a defense tailored to contain one very good player, such as Hayes. I didn't like that because it meant pulling Alcindor out from underneath to one side and would take away from our defensive rebounding. I did not think it wise to take Lewis away from the basket at either end of the court. Furthermore, I was convinced that there was no way that Houston could beat us with Lewis healthy again.

After considerable discussion, we changed the box and one idea to a diamond and one, and we were both pleased. That left Lewis as the point man of the diamond under our defensive basket. I had never used a diamond and one and had used a box and one only on rare occasions. But neither had I worked with a man like Alcindor before, and, to repeat, I didn't want to pull him away from either board—ever.

With the diamond and one, Lynn Shackelford became the one. His sole assignment on defense was to shadow Hayes, staying with him even if he went into the stands. Primarily noted for offensive skills, especially that huge rainbow jump shot, Shack did an absolutely amazing job on Hayes, and with support from everyone else, especially Lewis, we literally destroyed a great Houston team, 101–69. I think Shack surprised himself as well as others and followed his assignment to near perfection. Of course, Lewis was always "back there" to help.

Denny Crum helped revise our attack against the zone defense in a way that proved to be very successful. Many other little things that are difficult to isolate were also put in, thanks to the assistants, especially in the many drills we ran every day. Gary Cunningham was a very intelligent contributor and offered many worthwhile suggestions.

All the assistants over the years made one important contribution in common. On the bench they were another set of eyes, familiar with what I wanted to do and able to communicate to the players the little things that could make the difference between victory and defeat. Only one man could make the decisions, but I wanted all the evidence and information possible before making them. I continually reminded myself that I had to be open to the various ideas, not bull-headed and stubborn. Each decision had to be made through reason, not emotion. Wilfred A. Peterson best illustrates this point in his essay on leadership, "A leader," he said, "is interested in finding the best way—not in having his own way."

In the final years of the 1950s, it was obvious something was not quite right with my basketball philosophy. After we had won 22 and lost 6 in 1956, including the defeat by USF in the Far West Regionals, we went 22 and 4 in 1957, 16 and 10 in 1958, and 16 and 9 in 1959.

Then we started off the '60s by winning 14 and losing 12, the poorest record in my coaching career, except for my first year at Dayton High. A lot of those defeats—Kentucky, Oklahoma State, Purdue, Butler, West Virginia, California—were close, but we were playing basketball, not horseshoes, so close didn't count.

Something was missing. Something was wrong. Something had to be changed, but what? All progress comes through change, and I felt we were not making as much progress as we should. After that 14 and 12 season closed in 1960, I decided to make a total analysis, from recruiting to playing, of everything we did over all the years. Failure is not fatal, but failure to change might be.

18

A man may make mistakes,
but he isn't a failure
until he starts blaming someone else.

To POINT PRECISELY to any one thing or factor as "the problem" in our not going all the way to an NCAA title is impossible. I can't do it. I don't believe any coach can define to the nth degree why the team succeeded one time and didn't another.

I always contended that coaching was done during the week. I don't think basketball is any great strategy game or that it has any master strategists. Admittedly, there is an art to substitution, but there are not too many things that you can change in a game that you haven't prepared for during the week.

Three things are vital to success in basketball—condition, fundamentals, and working together as a team. I said that when I played, I said that when I first started coaching, I said that last year, and I will keep on saying it next year, the year after, and for the rest of my life.

As I tried to put my finger on that one elusive factor that had stood in our way, I went back over every statistical record I had. Only one thing seemed to stand out. Perhaps I had worked the players too hard early, and by season's end—or tournament time—they had been too worn out to survive the rigors of that level of competition. A related factor seemed equally important. Players on the so-called starting five had practiced more together, and when necessity—an injury, foul trouble, or fatigue—required a sixth, seventh, or eighth man to go into the game, the new group hadn't melded as well together as a team.

Throughout the years, I had always been aware that I should

work those top substitutes in with the starting group, but I had usually gotten so wrapped up in practice I hadn't done it properly. I wanted them in there automatically during practice so they were as familiar with the unit as the starting five.

When we began practice in the fall for the 1960–61 season, I had prepared a possible method to accomplish that ideal.

I decided to split the squad of fifteen into two units during the approximate one-third of the practice time we devote to five on five. One unit might consist of seven or eight men, depending on the personnel, the other of the remainder. In other words, if one year I felt we had an eight-man unit that appeared to be the core to play most of the games, they would be in that first group and there would be seven in the second. The next year, it might turn around.

As an example, let's suppose we had three guards like we did in 1971 when we had Henry Bibby, Terry Schofield and Kenny Booker. When we were working five on five, the other guard—let's say it is Booker—would be over on the side court shooting free throws. When Booker made ten free throws he would automatically come over and wait for play to break. When it did, he would go in for Bibby, who would make his free throws and then come in for Schofield. This procedure would be repeated throughout the practice.

Instead of going through the motions of making free throws, with this system the players tended to concentrate all the more. The quicker they made ten, the quicker they would get back into the five-on-five action which was our type of scrimmage and which they all enjoyed.

Both units and all three positions—guards, forwards, and centers—would go through the same procedure. This means that not just the starting five but all of the top seven or eight became very familiar with each other. It also cut down on the game-type contact which the players were under every day. Hopefully, this would stretch their endurance down to those rigorous days of NCAA title play when they would need more energy, drive, and desire.

Since my objective was to keep the rotation going one man

at a time, I varied the number of free throws the players were required to make. Maybe the guards would make ten, the forwards twelve, the centers seven. That way we wouldn't have two, or even three men, coming in at the same time.

Not only were the players thus more familiar with one another and with working together as a team, but they were more content. This was true not only with the first unit but the second as well. You didn't find the thirteenth, fourteenth, and fifteenth men being more or less off to themselves and isolated. I believe that this definitely helped them maintain their mental and emotional stability.

Was this rather minute change the reason for our string of successes beginning in 1964? I don't know. It is the only change I made. I know I had teams in earlier years that played better basketball, and maybe we had better material. But I believe material is relative and I believe other teams had better material, too.

Maybe it just took me a long time to mature as a coach. I don't know.

There is no doubt that a winning tradition gives players more confidence in what the coach is trying to do. They can look back and realize it was right in 1964 and 1965 and might be right now. A fine heritage can enter into the subconscious and enable players to perform to their maximum.

Contrary to what George Allen says, I don't believe they are capable of playing 110 percent or even 100 percent. But they can play closer to 100 percent if they can maintain composure, self-control, and endurance. Too much contact work—five on five—seems to take away the competitive edge. Reducing that contact with the rotation of the sixth, seventh, and eighth men in those five-on-five sessions, helped ensure that the players wouldn't tire as much in a game late in the season when condition was so vital to the group that sees most of the action.

Selecting those two groups was as difficult as selecting the five that would start the first game. Every man believed he was capable of being in that first unit. If he didn't have that kind of self-confidence, I wouldn't have wanted him on the squad.

That line between first and second unit players is fine indeed. I probably exercised more patience and took more care making those selections than in any other facet of our preparation. Though some of my players may have firmly believed I knew from day one who would be where, they could not have been farther from the truth.

The importance of that so-called sixth man cannot be overestimated. You must have a man who can come off the bench when things are going wrong to get you untracked with a quick basket or two, a sparkling steal that will get your running game going, or so much spirit that it infects the others on the floor. Probably the sixth men best known to the world have been some of the pros. Red Auerbach's Boston Celtics may have had two of the greatest in Frank Ramsey and John Havlicek. The latter also turned out to be a great starter, something you usually don't find in a true sixth man. For years, I selected a man I believed would be a good sixth man; and, in fact, have even recruited sixth men, usually someone who caught my eye for possessing just the right dynamic qualities.

The kind of man I'm talking about is almost always a highly emotional individual who gets instant adrenalin flowing as soon as you call his name. Kenny Washington, who as a freshman didn't show much promise of making the varsity, is probably the most striking example you could point to from any of the UCLA championship teams. Though he never looked good when he started, Kenny was tremendous as a sixth man. Phlegmatic in appearance to the spectators, Kenny seemed to just shuffle onto the floor, but when that ball popped into play, Kenny was off. I can't tell you how many times he came in to hit quick baskets, steal a ball or force an errant pass that resulted in a turnover.

Kenny earned quite a reputation as the sixth man at UCLA, especially when we won in 1964 and 1965, when he came off the bench to ignite us against Duke and Michigan, but he was just as capable in 1966 when we didn't make the NCAA.

Another great one was Fred Crabtree, who played for UCLA in 1956–57. Although Fred gave up basketball after his sophomore season and transferred to Cal at Berkeley, he was one of our most valuable players. He came to us with fine credentials, living up to them in fine style that one year, with 163 points in 25 games for a 6.5 average. Statistics, however, never reflect the true value of a sixth man. Fred was one of the best I ever had.

19

*It is what you learn after
you know it all that counts.*

IT SEEMED TO TAKE almost two years for things to jell with our new practice regime. I know we were better because of it in 1960–61, when we were 18 and 8 but only second in the Pacific Eight Conference. The next year, 1961–62, I feel the change really began to pay off. We won the conference with a 10 and 2 record, beat Utah State 73–62 in the first round of the NCAA Far West Regionals and Oregon State 88–69 for the right to go to the final round of four in Louisville.

We lost to Cincinnati in the semifinals 72–70, but we just as easily could have won. I have never been more proud of a winning team than I was of this team, even in losing. As is often the case, they were equal in every way to the Cincinnati team that won. The line between champion and challenger is fine.

Many of our teams over the years have been good enough to win, but didn't. Just as with this one things didn't fall in place. That's why I feel so fortunate for the record we compiled in NCAA play during the last two decades.

There is no doubt that the talent was present in 1961–62. We had three seniors—Gary Cunningham and Pete Blackman at forward and Johnny Green at guard—plus two fine sophomores, Fred Slaughter at center and Walt Hazzard at guard. Though our season got off to a slow start these fine young men meshed together as the season progressed and came within an eyelash of being our first champions. After letting Cincinnati build up an early lead, our team made a courageous comeback

125

to tie the score at the half. The second half was close all the way with Tom Thacker of Cincinnati hitting from outside in the final second to win it. Ironically, it was his only basket of the game.

The talent was present. Maybe the coaching still lacked something. Who knows? I don't. I know that fine group of boys played their hearts out all season long. And they had fun, too, but within my bounds. They were all definite, different personalities who respected one another, jelled together as the season rolled on, and became a strong, strong team.

I've always liked fierce competitors who play with the desire and determination necessary to enhance some natural ability. One of that type whose play I have always admired, even when I might be yelling to the officials about it, was Ken Stanley of USC. Similar in some respects to Curtis Rowe, one of my championship players of whom I am very fond, Ken was not spectacular—just a strong, consistent, all-around fine player and tough competitor.

Rugged, tough, hard-nosed competitors like Stanley, Bill McClintock of California, and Tony Ckervinko of Arizona State have always appealed to me. They were living proof that players can be aggressive without being dirty. And you could always guarantee they would play the same, steady, almost flawless game against UCLA. Dick Banton, Jack Hirsch, and John Green should be singled out along with Curtis Rowe and some others as UCLA players of that breed. They seldom got the credit they truly deserved.

I had seen positive signs in 1961–62 that the change in the practice regime was showing. When replacements came in they showed their familiarity with the others. We had greater unity, greater rapport between players, and consequently a better team. Now to fit in with Slaughter and Hazzard, who were the only starters back in 1962–63, came two jaycee transfers, Keith Erickson and Jack Hirsch. They were to play dominant roles the next two seasons for UCLA, along with two fine guards, Freddie Goss and Gail Goodrich.

In a matter of days, I realized that those five plus Jim Milhorn, Kim Stewart, and Dave Waxman appeared to have the skills, speed, and desire to use a zone press as the basic defense. I had always had in the back of my head that with the right personnel it could be devastating at our level, as it had been for me at Indiana State and in high school. As a matter of fact, I had started out to use it several times and then decided not to. Early the year before, it hadn't worked too well, so I had junked it; in retrospect, I think far too soon. Now, I told myself, I had a young team that appeared to have the qualities necessary to make the zone press work, and I made up my mind to stay with it. I did not announce my intention to the squad, however.

Previously, I had used the zone press at UCLA only in certain situations—never as the primary defensive weapon. Not having really worked with the idea of using it full time since I left Indiana State, I decided this year it was basic. I was determined we would sink or swim with the press, rather than having to look back with regret for abandoning it. This time we would give it a fair test.

By the middle of the season, there was no question in my mind these boys could make it go. They began to destroy people with scoring blitzes that literally ended the games. Sooner or later it got to every opponent. The 2–2–1 basic zone press certainly built confidence in our overall game.

Once again we won the conference but got beat in the NCAA tournament by an amazingly red-hot Arizona State team at Provo 93–79. The fact that we lost the consolation to USF, 76–75, doesn't matter. Because I never liked consolation games, I played everyone, especially seniors and those who hadn't played too much before. In my opinion, the only time when a consolation game has any merit is in a preseason or holiday tournament when you can work on things that need it. I firmly believe you should never end the season with a consolation game.

As we flew home from Provo, dejected to a certain extent, I also had a great amount of confidence for the year to come. Everyone would be back, everyone who had made the press go and our fast-break offense work so well in going 20 and 9. We would be a year older, a year more mature, and I believed then that the 1963–64 season could be the ultimate success that I had predicted in my verse to Pete Blackman.

That first championship is always something special. This one pleased me greatly for two other reasons. Not only was it the first, but it truly established the zone press defense as an offensive weapon. And it was won by the smallest team, comparatively speaking, ever to attain that goal. Those boys, anchored by Keith Erickson in the number five spot, made it a slashing, dangerous, destructive force that probably earned more time and space in the sports news for UCLA basketball than anything before.

Though I have often been asked to name an all-time team of players I've coached, I never have and never will. It is less difficult, however, to answer a similar question about such a dominant force in our success as the 2–2–1 zone press defense. Many people have asked me who I think would make the best composite of my players for this sole assignment.

Two can be selected rather quickly. Erickson would be number five man. This position takes a special type of player. He must be quick, alert, courageous, and unselfish; able to read the man with the ball and very good at handling defense when outnumbered. But, most important, he must be able to make that instant decision to fly forward from his safety spot and attempt the steal of the long pass without fear of failure. Keith possessed every one of those attributes, mainly because he loved a challenge.

The number five man is the last man. Some call him the safety man, the safety valve, or the anchor man. He is the deepest man towards our basket and the last defender if our opponents break the press. I call him *the director*. Every man on the team must listen to him.

The number one man plays to the left of the basket the opponent is defending and harasses the inbound pass. One of the masters at this task was Gail Goodrich. Because of his boyish looks and because of his size (at 6′ 1″ he was the shortest and smallest of the starters on the 1964 and 1965 champions), he fooled many. But Gail played a lot bigger than his size and, like Erickson, was an intense competitor. He had exceedingly long arms, a factor that made him an ideal number one man because so many players trying to inbound the ball didn't realize how wide those arms could spread. Gail turned many a pass into a steal and, often, into an unassisted basket.

For the number two spot playing alongside Gail and to the

right of the basket our opponent defended would be Keith Wilkes. A highly intelligent player with a fine grasp of the game, he had extremely quick hands, instant reflexes, and stood tall at 6' 6". So fluid was he in his movements that he, too, caught a lot of people by surprise. Many loose balls were tipped off his hands and captured by the midcourt pair.

The number three man—and I want to emphasize that these selections are solely for the 2–2–1 press and nothing else—would be the late Walt Torrence. The three spot is behind Goodrich and a bit inside his right foot. Torrence, who played for UCLA in 1957–58–59 as a guard, stood 6' 3" and was as quick as any man I have coached. He had great anticipation and was especially adept at coming forward to tip a ball away on an inbound pass while still playing tight on any man working in his assigned zone. Walt was killed quite a few years back in an auto accident up in the San Joaquin Valley.

Number four has to be Sidney Wicks. Here was a man who measured 6' 8" plus, with the agility, quickness, and speed of a 6-footer. The number four spot is located to the right of the number three man as you face the end line, and just inside and back of the number two man. Wicks played the number five spot in his brilliant years, but he would be an ideal number four because of his range, quickness, and ability to handle both the quicker, smaller men who would be back trying to help the inbound man get the ball in play and the big men coming back to help out. Few big men are as quick as Wicks. Jack Hirsch at 6' 3" also played this spot exceptionally well.

That's almost an ideal 2–2–1 press unit. It's not my allstar team. It's not the best team offensively nor the best in total defense, but I believe it could more than hold its own with anyone playing the 2–2–1 press.

All of the team were well known to college basketball once we began our string of championships in 1964—except perhaps Torrence. I think it is obvious that Walt must have been a very talented young man to rate my choice for the number three spot.

It is a formidable unit, one I would like to be able to put on the floor in any game, in any year, just to play the press.

Each man could have been a master of his assigned duties. Each was well suited to meld in with the others, and Erickson was a master director. As the only man with a full view of the floor and what is taking place, the number five man is indispensable. Keith, who possessed that innate sense of when to charge and when to fall back on a long down-court pass, commanded the press with great effectiveness.

I always cautioned my safety man never to go for the interception unless he could get it. But though he must never guess, he can't just sit back and wait. He must have the courage to fly forward. He can't hesitate. If he does, it's too late. Erickson never lacked for courage and he seldom made an error in judgment.

20

Enjoy the present hour,
be mindful of the past;
And neither fear nor wish
the approaches of the last.

AFTER WE HUNG that first NCAA championship banner in 1964, there was considerable speculation whether we could join Oklahoma State, Kentucky, USF, and Cincinnati to win back-to-back NCAA titles. We had the number five and number one men back in Erickson and Goodrich, plus Freddie Goss, Doug McIntosh, and Kenny Washington, as well as two fine young sophomores in Edgar Lacey and Mike Lynn.

I believed we could. My prime concern was complacency. Many fine clubs had tried to win back-to-back titles but only four had succeeded since the NCAA began in 1939. I was convinced we had found the makings of a formula of success. The constant rotation of players into the floor unit in practice plus the arrival of the zone press seemed to be the answer, but one successful season doesn't make a career.

No one is more aware than the coach that every year marks a change in circumstances. With the graduation of young men who have established you as something of a success or a failure, depending on the season, new problems or opportunities present themselves in the form of new personnel and manpower grouping. My basic concepts, nevertheless, remained the same.

One of them, having to do with time-outs, was almost a fetish with me. I valued time-outs like gold, and I guarded them with the same zeal Uncle Sam does Ft. Knox. I tried to use them with great care and conserve them to the final minutes.

Never did I want to call the first time-out in a game. Once the game tempo had been established, or if we were making a

131

big run at an opponent, or even if we were behind, I preferred not to be the first to interrupt the game, under almost any circumstance. But sometimes I did.

Why not call the first time-out? First among several factors is condition. I always told my teams that we were going to be in better condition than the other team and we wanted our opponents to need time-outs for a rest. I didn't say that I *thought* we were going to be in better condition or that we were going to *try* to be. I said that we were *going to be* in better condition— a positive statement.

Being in better condition pays dividends if you can put the pressure on an opponent and keep it on, both offensively and defensively. This does not necessarily have to be done with a pressing defense. A tight pressure defense may serve the same purpose, providing, of course, that you are constantly and continuously applying offensive pressure also. I constantly repeated to my teams the admonition I had learned from Piggie Lambert at Purdue: "The team that makes the most mistakes will probably win." There is much truth in that statement if you analyze it properly. The doer makes mistakes, and I wanted doers on my team—players who made things happen.

Ninety percent of the time, the game is going to be decided in the final five minutes. When two teams are evenly matched, the better conditioned team will usually execute better when fatigue sets in, and will probably win. And if you have all your time-outs remaining, you can use them strategically to your advantage in the game situation.

Occasions when I called the first time-out were few indeed, averaging no more than once a season. But I did so in some pretty crucial games and at critical points where I felt a time-out was mandatory.

One of the most important came in the 1964 NCAA finals against Duke University in Kansas City. They had us down and were killing our press by getting through it to hit the jump shot. I was afraid our players might lose confidence, even though they hadn't all year long. Not wanting that to happen, I called time, reiterating that I wanted them to stay with the pressing defense; that Duke, although shooting exceedingly well, would ultimately start missing, and that the press would turn the game around.

In the next four minutes or so, we established our tempo and caught them at 27 all. Then *they* called time. After they got three points on three consecutive free throws, we broke the game apart and ran the score out to 41–30, when they called time again.

It was our pressure defense that broke Duke's stability. First taking its toll mentally, it finally did so physically as well. And that is what we always sought to do—to keep the pressure on, never letting up and always staying aware that pressure comes not only from the zone press defense but from every other thing we did. That's why I was so reluctant to call that initial time-out, or, for that matter, almost any time-out.

The next time I called time-out first was a full year later, in the 1965 NCAA championship against Michigan at the Portland Coliseum. It wasn't as critical this time, but our play was a little too loose and sloppy. After about five minutes Michigan was ahead by three points, and I wanted to tighten things up. My instructions: get a little more discipline, give Keith Erickson a little more help on Cazzie Russell, hit Edgar Lacey from the high post, set the double for Goodrich, tighten our press, and things would be all right. In a few minutes we turned things around, and captured the lead 26–24. Michigan called time with 8:56 to play. In the minutes remaining we outscored them 21 to 10 and left the floor ahead 47–34 at the half with the game in command.

There are many who disagree with me about my fetish of not taking the first time-out, but I consider my logic to be sound. Almost every time that I felt it was an absolute necessity to call that first time-out it was beneficial. I can't say every time because I can't recall every one, but it helped us win in 1964 and in 1965 in the NCAA finals, and it worked in 1970 against Jacksonville. It is true, however, that there may have been times when I should have called one and didn't. Perhaps I could have broken the tempo of Arizona State in the NCAA regionals in 1963 and prevented our defeat.

Against Jacksonville at Cole Fieldhouse on the University of

Maryland campus, we had played 6 minutes 52 seconds when I signaled for a time-out. Behind 14–6, we had hit only two for seven from the field while Jacksonville was seven for twelve, but I was concerned more with the defense than with Jacksonville's fantastic shooting percentage, a result of our giving up easy shots. I did not feel our players were giving them proper respect.

We had started with a defense I was convinced should work against Jacksonville, with Sidney Wicks against Artis Gilmore. I didn't care that Gilmore was over 7 feet and Wicks only 6' 8". There should have been no way that Jacksonville could lob the ball over Sidney. If Sidney could stand behind a 7 footer and get the ball or go up and block a shot on the turn, Sidney should have been able to keep Gilmore from getting the ball if he was alert and playing in front. Of course, we needed help from the weak side, but Curtis Rowe was very good at that.

But it was obvious from the bench that Sidney was concerned about the defense after Gilmore got one on him. I didn't want Sidney being concerned about anything but being Sidney and playing like only Sidney could play, so I called a time-out and changed things a bit. Little by little we whittled away at their lead, getting it down to 36–32 with 3:03 to play in the half. Once again condition told when we ran away from them with nine straight points to end the half 41–36.

Going back to back in 1964 and 1965—after losing three starters the second year—was a tribute to the players. Even so, we went into the 1964–65 season with what I thought might be nearly as good a team. Because we had two highly stable, highly talented starters back—Goodrich, the number one man in the zone press, and Erickson, the safety man at number five— we decided to alter our zone press from the 2–2–1 that had carried us to that perfect year. Instead we went with a 1–2–1– 1 almost all year long. We didn't have the really big man such as Oklahoma State had with Bob Kurland in 1945 and 1946 or USF had with Bill Russell in 1955 and 1956 to help us repeat. But we had fine range coupled with speed and quickness and I believed we had an excellent chance. Furthermore, I felt that the change to the 1–2–1–1 might cause confusion to our opponents who were expecting the 2–2–1.

That chance was almost obliterated in our first game. We went into Champaign-Urbana to meet Illinois in its new 17,000-seat Assembly Hall. We ran into a bunch of real sharpshooters. They had a tremendous game. Their fine ball handling, quick moves, and excellent outside jump shooting enabled them to work with great success against our press. They had a tremendous shooting percentage the first half. I know I didn't call the first time-out, even though Illinois couldn't miss. From the bench I kept assuring the boys to play their game, that Illinois had to cool off.

Only they didn't. They shot nearly 70 percent for the game. We were never close. And there wasn't much we could do about it. It was probably the worst lacing of my coaching career, a 27-point difference. We scored 83 points—which will win most ball games—but Illinois scored 110. It was no fluke. We just got slashed to bits. I told the team the next morning not to worry about it. It was true we could no longer match the undefeated performance of the year before but we were a very good ball club, and could settle down to do very well. With the pressure of a long winning streak gone, we could play our game.

The boys seemed to understand because the next night at Indiana State we scored a runaway win, 112–76. We rolled right along until the holiday when we went into Chicago Stadium to meet Iowa and Loyola of Chicago on consecutive nights. Then the Hawkeyes got to us, 87–82.

The raking by Illinois and the loss to Iowa were the only ones that year. Every player we had made a unique contribution to our second winning season. Seniors Erickson and Goodrich were superplayers, and sophomores Lacey and Lynn fit in very well with such veterans as center Doug McIntosh, guard Freddie Goss, and sixth man Ken Washington. Lacey, a very intent, sometimes moody young man, was highly skilled on the backboards despite his lack of weight. Lynn, on the other hand, was a rugged, boyish appearing youngster who had a deceptively quick pair of hands. Freddie Goss gave us fine outside shooting and endless hustle, McIntosh gave us good solid play at center, and Kenny Washington again was a tremendous sixth man. Quite naturally, however, it was Erickson and Goodrich who were constant sparks. What a pair they were!

Kenny Washington, who has to rank with the great sixth men in college basketball, seemed to thrive on supertough competition. The two greatest games of his career came in the NCAA championships in 1964 and 1965. A man truly shows his mettle in games like those. To go in under that kind of pressure and deliver, as Kenny did both years—that's a great sixth man.

Against Duke in the 1964 finals, Kenny went in early in the first half at forward and remained to score 26 points—his all-time high at UCLA—and get 12 rebounds. We were ahead 17–15, but fighting to stay even, when he made his first free throw, ending up with 9 points in the first half. But what he did to Duke in that second half was something else. When he wasn't hitting his jump shot, he was driving by his man for a lay-in or charging the boards for a tip-in, or making a mid-court steal to set up the fast break.

The next year against Michigan, Kenny was superb again. We were behind, 20–13, when in seconds he hit two jumpers to close the gap and then tied the game at 24 all with another one from the top of the key. Once again, cast as that vital sixth man, Washington was everywhere, blending in his fine shooting touch with his speed and skill. Working in harmony with his teammates, he sparked us to really destroy a great Michigan team led by Cazzie Russell. Washington scored 17 points in relief of the injured Erickson but the life he gave us was as instrumental in our victory as his points.

Although it was truly a team victory, the brilliant play of Gail Goodrich in that 1965 championship will never be forgotten either. Few players will ever play as well under such championship pressure. He and Keith Erickson, the only two returning starters from the 1964 champions, were both inspirational floor leaders. Gail responded to the added burden placed on him by Erickson's injury with a performance that easily made him the most valuable player of the tournament in my eyes. The record books show that his 42 points were his all-time high—this in his last collegiate game and for the national championship against a powerful team. What can never be measured statistically—his take-charge confidence and spirited floor leadership—was equally important.

We might not have had our NCAA string broken in 1966,

when we failed to win the conference, if we hadn't lost Lacey and Goss for the season. We looked like a very solid club going in with Lacey and Lynn at forwards; McIntosh, now a senior, at center; and Goss teaming with Mike Warren, a brilliant young sophomore from my old high school, South Bend Central, at guard; plus that number six man—Washington. Edgar sustained a knee injury, we never knew how, but he was never again the Edgar Lacey that we had known. Eventually he had to have surgery, was forced to lay off a year, and never came back to the brilliance we all expected of him. Goss was ill off and on all year, and though Warren was an excellent young sophomore, he needed the stabilizing influence of Goss. We ended up second in the conference (10 and 4), 18 and 8 overall for the year, and as spectators for the NCAA.

21

Dare to be a Daniel!
Dare to stand alone!
Dare to have a purpose firm!
Dare to make it known. *

ON TUESDAY, May 4, 1965, at Power Memorial High School in New York City, Lewis Alcindor announced that he would attend UCLA. With that announcement, the basketball world automatically declared that UCLA would be the first in history to win three NCAA titles in a row.

Up to that point in time, I had never seen Lewis play. He had visited UCLA the first week in April. As he returned to International Airport he indicated that he would enroll in the fall. About a week later he asked if I would come to New York to meet his parents. Jerry Norman, then my assistant, and I flew East where we met with Lewis and his parents for about an hour—at one o'clock in the morning because Lewis's father worked the four to midnight shift.

They, like Lewis, wanted their son to go to a university with high academic standing as well as a good basketball program. We felt UCLA met those requirements and we certainly wanted a young man of such talent and of such high intelligence. We were also realists. We knew that every university in America was after him. He had scholarship offers from every major college, and we felt the great distance to Los Angeles would pretty well rule out his coming to us.

After he announced his choice of UCLA, we began to hear all kinds of stories about how we had used the late Jackie Robinson, one of UCLA's greatest athletes ever; the late Dr. Ralph

---

* P.P. Bliss, "Dare to Be a Daniel!"

Bunche, a former Bruin basketball player, who was with the United Nations in New York; and Willie Naulls of the New York Knickerbockers, an All-American for us in 1956, to recruit Lewis.

If Jackie Robinson ever talked to Lewis about UCLA, he did it on his own. Jackie never talked to me about it. Dr. Bunche did contact Lewis. He wrote Lewis a letter, with a copy to me, about Lewis's coming to UCLA, in which he said that at UCLA Lewis would have an equal opportunity, the basketball would be good, and the academics good. I would never presume to have a man of Dr. Bunche's stature call on a basketball prospect. That he did so on his own is something for which I have been forever grateful.

Willie Naulls was definitely working to get Lewis to UCLA. The Knicks, in those days, practiced in the Power Memorial Gym once in a while. But I never really believed we had much of a chance at getting this great young man who ranked, as a prospect, with the likes of Wilt Chamberlain, Jerry Lucas, and Oscar Robertson.

Today Lewis Alcindor is Kareem Abdul-Jabbar. The Chamberlains, Lucases, and Robertsons—all of basketball recognize him by the name he has legally taken. While I accept this change in keeping with his faith and try to honor his request that I call him Kareem, I continually find myself using the name by which I knew him so well. And I am sure that his parents have the same problem, perhaps to an even greater degree. Try as I may, this fine young man will always be Lewis Alcindor to me. I hope he will understand my using the name by which we all knew him at that time in describing the years he spent with us.

Lewis was one of a kind. I hadn't really expected to get him, and, even after he made the announcement, I wondered if he would really show up in September for classes.

Actually, Lewis was no stranger to UCLA as a player or a person. When Lewis was a junior in high school, I spoke at the Valley Forge Basketball Clinic in Philadelphia. His coach, Jack Donohue, wrote that he was going to attend the clinic and would like to talk to me some time during it about "his big fellow." We did talk. I did express a great interest and I did tell him that if it were at all possible, UCLA would like to be the last school Lewis would visit during his senior year. I believe that is how it ultimately worked out.

After Lewis's sophomore season in high school, Edgar Lacey, who had been such a great player for Jefferson High in Los Angeles, was picked on the *Parade* magazine prep All-American, as was Lewis. Edgar and Lewis met for the first time when the team appeared on the Ed Sullivan show in New York. That summer, Edgar went to the Catskill Mountains in New York to work and play summer basketball, and so did Lewis.

There was no doubt in my mind of Lewis's potential. If there was doubt of any kind, it was in my ability to live up to the forecasts that were immediately made: three straight NCAAs, no defeats—things like that. I didn't know exactly how I could use a big man to the best advantage. I had never had the chance to experiment. All I had were ideas, but with no valid way to determine whether they were sound or not. All the concepts that I believed would work with a big man needed one in order for me to find out.

What Lewis could do and how he could dominate a game were instantly obvious at his first practice as a freshman. And after the first game, there was no doubt that my theories would work with the big man, especially such a fantastic big man.

As his first varsity season approached, UCLA was hit with two major losses in experienced personnel. Edgar Lacey, with whom Lewis roomed when he first came to UCLA, never got over his knee injury of the year before. When finally surgery was necessary, Edgar was lost for the year. And Mike Lynn, who had teamed with Edgar so well at forward or center, was lost through disciplinary action of the university.

We went into the season with four starting sophomores and one junior. Probably as young a team as any major college had ever put on the floor was burdened with living up to the press's forecast that they would be the national champions. Lewis, of course, was the center. Lynn Shackelford, a 6′ 5″ sophomore from Burbank, was one forward, and Kenny Heitz, a 6′ 3″ product of Righetti High in Santa Maria who was recruited as a guard or possibly a sixth man, was at the other wing.

Our only varsity experience rested with Mike Warren, a small but gifted player from South Bend Central. He was as smart and valuable a guard as I had ever had. Mike was a junior. Going with him was Lucius Allen, a 6' 2" All-State guard from Wyandotte High in Kansas City, Kansas. Allen had almost the same kind of potential at guard as did Alcindor at center.

Still, there was concern and skepticism in my mind whether what I wanted to do with these youngsters was right, whether it would take full advantage of Lewis's potential greatness.

In this, my first chance to build around an outstanding big man, I scrapped my whole offense and went to a totally different one than I had ever used. A complete low post offense placed the center deep, near the basket and well inside the free throw line. I had used a double post, a double low post, a double high post in a limited way, but never a single low post. To take full advantage of his height, I wanted Lewis Alcindor no farther from the offensive basket than he could reach. I almost wanted him to be able to stick his arm out and dunk the ball— no more than eight feet away.

I had spent literally hundreds of hours from the time Lewis entered UCLA as a freshman and the beginning of his sophomore year in 1967 talking to coaches whom I respected about the low post offense, diagramming plays and analyzing the consequences and trying to determine just how this seven foot plus youngster would fit in with the others.

The fit was instantly obvious. We opened the season against USC with an easy win and then decisively defeated a strong Duke team on consecutive nights, 88–54 and 107–87.

Immediately, the press again predicted the perfect season, the NCAA title, everything. Sometimes I wondered if they even expected our opposition to score a basket. It was well recognized that Shackelford's forte was shooting. He was not an outstanding all-around basketball player, but as a pure shooter he was something else, especially from the corner. If his defensive man floated in on Lewis, it meant that Shack would get not only more shots but more of them open shots. On the other hand, if the defense came out on Shackelford, then Lewis would have more freedom underneath.

Kenny Heitz, our other forward, was a quick, driving player

with good speed. The fact that he had to wear glasses on the floor did not keep him from being tough on defense and an adequate shooter. Neither forward was a superstar, but they were solid, dependable youngsters who played it my way. When you coupled them with the super super in Alcindor and one of the greatest guard combines—Warren and Allen—that I have ever coached, it was a formidable squad.

There was little question after that first weekend against archrival USC that we were going to be some kind of an offensive force. There was still a large question about our defense. Once again I was confronted with the same question: how do you play it with that big man with such fine reactions, great anticipation, and great desire?

I had long had a cardinal defensive rule that a forward should never give up the baseline at the end of the court and allow a man to slip through the back door to the basket. Where always before we had tried to drive people away from the basket, away from the baseline, now it was a different story. We wanted them to drive on Lewis. We wanted our forwards to free-lance more on defense, gamble more, take more chances. With Lewis underneath, we could do it with a certain degree of safety.

I also decided after a game or two that we would not be the greatest fast-break team I had ever had, nor would we use the zone press as much. It was obvious we were not going to be as adept at that as I thought, although Lewis had great speed and was a lot quicker and niftier than many believed. But we were so strong with both our set offense and set defense that I decided not to make the press a basis of our defense and to fast-break only when Lewis could outlet the ball for a definite and obvious advantage.

It was a great year. We won the Pac Eight. We won the NCAA, beating Dayton in Louisville, 79–64. But the most impressive thing was that we were undefeated in thirty games with four sophomores and an average team age of 19.1 years—the youngest ever to win the NCAA and the youngest ever to go undefeated.

The season was not without problems, nonetheless. Lewis Alcindor was always being challenged, and not only on the court by our opponents. His mere presence created problems among society in general and even among his teammates, for neither of which could Lewis be held responsible. Some of our players objected to the tremendous amount of space he received in newspapers and magazines and on radio and television. I recognized this and tried to avoid it as much as possible. Mostly, however, I tried to get the point across that Lewis's mere presence at UCLA was going to get all of our players far more publicity than they could possibly get otherwise. It made good sense for them not to be envious and jealous of the attention being paid to Lewis, especially since he was personally unselfish and deserving of all credit he would receive.

All our boys were fine players who worked exceptionally well together and made an ideal team. At the same time, it was obvious that Kenny Heitz at 6′ 3″ wouldn't be starting at forward on such a strong team unless there were an Alcindor in there. Shackelford was not a driver so he needed an Alcindor to open up his jump shot from the corner. Their abilities, fortunately, fit in well with what we had. Warren and Allen, by contrast, were an exceptional pair of guards who ranked with the Hazzard-Goodrich and Vallely-Bibby pairs. They would fit in with any team, but not our forwards as a pair.

While the problems with the squad were minimal and were more often than not resolved within our team, it was entirely human that there should be difficult moments. A few times they spilled out when some players complained to the press. Once a couple of them charged that I gave Lewis special privileges, which is true, to a degree. They also knew that I never treated them all alike in every respect and never professed that I would. However, they needed to accept my concept of trying to give each individual the treatment that he earned and deserved.

Another gripe was that Lewis got two glasses of orange juice for breakfast and they only got one. True. But they didn't mention that Lewis didn't eat anything else. They said he often got to room alone. True. He often did. But they didn't mention that you couldn't get two king-size beds in a room, and that was why he roomed alone. Once in a while Lewis would have a migraine headache. Having had them myself, I know how they affect your ability to function. I would tell him to go into the training room, take a pillow, turn off the lights and lie down. If he felt like coming back to practice, fine. If he felt he would be better at home, go home. He'd lie down. He'd never leave. Often he'd come back to practice. I would do the same for any other boy with migraines, but some players considered this preferential treatment.

Lewis took the most unfair raps, however, from the public. The signing of autographs was a major problem not only for Lewis but for the team. I remember one time when he must have signed thirty or forty autographs before I came out from the dressing room. "Lewis," I said, "that's enough. We're keeping the rest of the team waiting." Little kids were running after him trying to get his signature.

One of the adults commented, "Look at that big——, too good to sign an autograph."

They didn't know he had already signed thirty or forty and that I had told him to board the bus.

On another occasion, when we were walking more or less together, some lady remarked, "Look at that big black freak."

I heard it. I was two or three feet from Lewis and I know he heard it. I tried to explain to him that she didn't mean to be rude, that his size did startle people, and that it had nothing to do with his race.

"Do you think, coach," he asked, "if Mel Counts [a 7' plus center at Oregon State and in the NBA] walked in she would have said 'Look at that big white freak'?"

"No, Lewis, she wouldn't, but that is part of the basic society."

We discussed the incident at length and I could see his point. "I understand your situation, Lewis," I said, "I think."

"Coach," he replied, "I think you would be as understanding as any white man that I have ever known, but there is no way you can really understand. You are white, I am black. You are 5 feet 10 inches tall and I am 7 feet."

That was another of the problems. How tall was Alcindor? I was asked that once a day for four years. I gave everyone the same answer, 7' 1⅝", but no one ever believed me. I don't think they would believe me if they stood beside the yardstick while he was measured.

I can say without equivocation that in the four years Lewis Alcindor played for me at UCLA his mere presence created problems that shouldn't have existed, but the young man himself personified cooperation as exemplified by his greatness on the basketball floor. He was the least demanding of any superstar I have ever known. In fact, he should never have been held responsible for the problems that seemed to surround him. Such tremendous ability often brings out petty jealousy and envy from both teammates and opponents.

22

A gentleman is one who considers the rights of others before his own feelings, And the feelings of others before his own rights.

LEWIS FERDINAND ALCINDOR, JR., was, in my opinion, the finest truly big man ever to play basketball up to his time. He could do anything you asked of him, and do it almost to perfection. His tremendous physical ability, however, could not have been nearly so effective had it not been for his intelligence and exceptional emotional control. Seldom would he strike back in anger despite the fact he took more of a physical beating in his three years of basketball at UCLA than anyone I have ever seen.

The ability to keep his emotions under control was as much responsible for our winning three successive NCAA championships in the so-called Alcindor era as anything else. He had total control of a ten to fifteen foot circle around his position on the floor. He completely intimidated opposing players merely by the threat of moving out to meet them when they were driving toward the basket.

Lewis probably could get higher in the air than any man of his size. I don't think his timing was quite so good as Bill Russell's, but it was excellent nonetheless. It's almost impossible to make an objective comparison of men who played their collegiate ball more than ten years apart.

Russell was the first of the great intimidators at the defensive end of the floor, while Lewis was the first of the great intimidators at both ends. They were completely alike in one most important attribute: everything they did was subordinated to the team.

Russell was tremendous on defense. People have forgotten that at USF he was also excellent on offense and scored more

146

points than they can remember. But there was a wide difference between Russell and Alcindor at the offensive end. Lewis possessed a fine touch and was such a beautiful jumper that he could shoot either straight in or off the glass. His hook was also excellent and, although our style didn't really permit him to use it going to the base line, he became very proficient at using it in deep across the lane. Most people weren't aware of his hook at UCLA, but it was pretty good.

Lewis was really more like Wilt Chamberlain than Russell in all-around ability. He was more maneuverable than Wilt but not nearly so powerful. Had Wilt been surrounded by the playing cast that Russell was with the Boston Celtics, and had he had a Red Auerbach as coach, his team might well have won all those championships. Suffice it to say that Bill, Wilt, and Lewis all belong among the all-time greats.

One of Lewis's impressive statistics is that of the 88 games he played for us, in 87 he shot at least 50 percent from the floor. The only game in which he fell below that was in our loss to Houston at the Astrodome—when he had vertical double vision in the eye that had been scratched at Cal two weeks before. His three-year shooting percentages were 64.9, 61.6 and 63.5.

For only the second time in my coaching career, in 1967–68 all five starters were back from the year before. In addition, we had two other outstanding starters from our 1964–65 champions, Edgar Lacey and Mike Lynn, competing for starting positions. Both expected to be starters automatically. There was no way, however, that I would move men back who had started all season the year before for two men who had been forced to sit out the year.

Lacey and Lynn were going to have to work their way into that first unit. Physically they were good enough, probably better than either Heitz or Shackelford. But Edgar, gifted as he was two years before when he was hurt, was never able to regain his form—physically, mentally, or emotionally. Lynn was capable, but when the two joined as a combine, a harmonious relationship and desirable team play became impossible.

I moved Heitz back to guard, a more normal position for

him, and alternated Shackelford, Lynn, and Lacey at forwards for a while. I was trying to find the strongest line-up, not appease Lynn and Lacey. If I had not had Alcindor both of them would have been in the line-up, but Lewis and Shackelford complemented each other so well that I felt Shack deserved to be there.

The line-up was almost a juggling act for the first thirteen games. Then came the big scene in the Astrodome, with the largest crowd ever to see a college basketball game and an even larger crowd watching on coast-to-coast television. "The Big A," as someone wrote, "versus The Big E." But it really wasn't. Alcindor was just half of himself because of his injured eye. He had been in a dark room and had not practiced in over a week. Lewis at far below par, however, was still a potent psychological force. His mere physical presence forced opponents to alter their game—both offensively and defensively.

It had not been an easy year, as most would have supposed. The internal problems of having too many standouts had confirmed my long-time conviction that if you have more than seven or eight players who could be considered starters you may be breeding discontent. All this in spite of the fact we were going along undefeated, were physically very strong, and had the best bench ever.

But the Astrodome ended our streak of wins and, much to my concern, the playing career at UCLA of Edgar Lacey.

I started Edgar and gave him probably the toughest assignment possible—playing Elvin Hayes. Going in, I was concerned about Hayes. Maybe there was no way Edgar or anyone else could have contained him. I didn't think anyone could but I wanted Hayes played a certain way and Edgar wasn't doing that. I had asked him to play Hayes high on the side to prevent his receiving the ball. If he reversed for a pass, he would be running into Alcindor, and I did not think he would like that. If Edgar had played Elvin that way and Elvin had scored at will, I would have allowed him to try his way. But Edgar didn't try what I had told him to do, so I pulled him and put in Jim Nielsen, a 6' 7" reserve who had size and determination but nowhere near the skills of Edgar.

Early in the second half, I told Jerry Norman to get Edgar ready. "Look at him, coach," said Jerry. I surveyed the bench and saw Edgar at the far end, head down, not watching the game, really hanging, so I didn't put him back in. We lost, 71–69. Afterwards, I was asked by reporters why I had not played Edgar in the second half. "Edgar didn't give me the impression," I told the press, "that he wanted to play. He told me he could not handle Hayes and that was the reason."

That was in the papers, and Edgar was upset. But he had taken it wrong, somehow, because every man who has ever played for me knows that I demand attention to the game from those on the bench. They must be ready when they are called. Edgar felt my remark to the press was uncalled for and that it was a tremendous criticism of him as a player. I didn't think so then, and don't now. Convinced otherwise, Edgar told me he was going to leave the team. I told him I could understand his unhappiness, but that in my opinion he would be making a great mistake to quit. Nevertheless, he did.

I left the door open for him to return, but never pursued him, and he dropped out for good. Much to my surprise, we became a better ball club almost immediately. Some say it was the loss to Houston that made us a better ball club, and some say it was the loss of Lacey. I think it was a combination of things.

From that time on, with Lynn and Shackelford at forward and Alcindor at center, we became probably as strong a basketball team—a college team, that is—as the game has ever seen. Though not as good an outside shooter as Shackelford, Lynn was excellent as a number one on the 1–2–1–1 zone press because he was so deceptive. He was not fast, but, oh, how quick were those hands, so alert to tip the ball loose on the inbound pass.

Warren and Allen, together for the second season as guards, were a superb combination. Having Mike Warren on the floor was almost like having a coach there. He totally understood my philosophy and ran the game the way I wanted it.

With Mike in command of things, that second year of the Alcindor era—as the press called it—we improved steadily all season, from our Houston defeat in the Astrodome to our triumph over Houston in the semifinals of the NCAA Championships at the Los Angeles Sports Arena. That was the night Lynn Shackelford rose to the occasion. Assigned to Hayes as the chaser in the diamond and one, Shack did an excellent job. His sole assignment was Hayes. He was to chase him, no matter where he went. If he got the ball, Shack was to get right on top of him, try his best to keep him from shooting. Let him drive by you, I counseled him; then Lewis will take over. Our primary charge to Shack was to try to keep Hayes from ever getting the ball, to play him so tight they wouldn't pass to him. It was a tremendous individual defensive effort by a player who was not normally a good defender.

But our young men went out that night supercharged. In fact, I worried about their being too high. All remembered the Astrodome, and all remembered the comments by the Big E of what Houston was going to do to UCLA. It wasn't too good a ball game for ten minutes or so, but then the press and the diamond and one began to tell. Hayes got his first field goal at the 10:57 mark of the first half. That cut our lead to 20–19, but that was really the end. In the next five minutes—with probably the greatest blitz any of my teams has ever put together—we outscored Houston, 21–5. They were down, 41–24, with six minutes still left in the half. They got two scattered field goals in that run but, most important, they kicked the ball away eleven times in the first half, most of them during this streak.

Every one of our players was dedicated to that game. The fact that we beat North Carolina the next night for our fourth NCAA title, the second time we had two in succession, was anticlimactic, at least for the spectators. They came for the Houston affair and that's what it was. Quite an affair, and an impressive victory. One writer, I believe from the East, expressed to me later his amazement that our players didn't seem too jubilant about winning from North Carolina, 78–55.

I told him what I told my players on the bench as the clock ran down. "I don't want any out-of-control celebration. I want you to feel good, cut down the nets—but I don't want any jumping around, no dancing on the floor or acting like fools.

No excessive jubilation, no spectacle." What I was really saying to them was, don't climb a mountain. And when we lost, as we did earlier that year at the Astrodome, my words of caution, "Don't hang your heads, don't bellyache, walk out with your heads high," were to remind them not to descend into the lowest valley, but to climb a steadily rising plane as they strove to reach their ultimate potential.

Just give me a group of gentlemen who play the game hard but clean, and always on an upward path. Then the championships will take care of themselves if the overall ability of the team warrants them.

23

Ability may get you to the top, but it takes character to keep you there.

By the time of Lewis Alcindor's senior season in 1968–69, it was obvious that all the glowing forecasts about him were true. My only problem was to see that the infection of success didn't set in to spoil the team's final year.

We had already been beset with a major problem that cost us a great guard in Lucius Allen. He had become entangled with the police on a charge of possession of marijuana. It was dismissed, but within a year to the day of that charge he was hit with another. It was not generally known, however, that he had actually quit school before that happened.

It was a tremendous loss for Lucius and UCLA. I felt more concern for Lucius than for our problem because I felt his future was unlimited. It is a tribute to him that he came back from this adversity to become an established star in the NBA. He has tremendous ability, is one of the most likable young men I have ever known.

We were going into the year again built around the low post offense tailored for Lewis. Shackelford was back, but now both Allen and Warren were gone from the back line. That's one place where I always planned for experience, but man's best plans often go astray, and this was an example.

We had plenty of power up front. Two highly talented sophomores were on hand—Curtis Rowe and Sidney Wicks—and a top back-up center, Steve Patterson, who had been held out a year. But who would run our offense was a real question mark.

152

Kenny Heitz was back at guard, but I didn't think he was strong enough to be the lead guard and direct the attack. Our hope seemed to rest in reserve Bill Sweek and another senior who had sat out a year, Don Saffer, but there simply was no established back court general.

Coming in from Orange Coast was a new man I had seen play once as a forward. John Vallely, at 6' 2½", had been a high school center and later a jaycee forward. There was something about him, however—his quickness, his shooting ability, and his competitive desire—that seemed to me to spell guard. It was difficult to say why.

A year before, I had talked to Jerry Tarkanian, now coach at Cal State Long Beach but then at Pasadena City College, about Vallely. Jerry thought he could play the back court. Ironically, when we really decided we wanted Vallely, Jerry was at Long Beach and was the toughest competition we had for the boy. We were the only two schools, I believe, who were seriously interested.

Whether John could be a starter for us or even do much I didn't know, but I sure wanted to give him a try. We had to have someone. And it helped that Vallely came to Los Angeles that summer and played in a lot of pickup games at guard with Mike Warren and some of our other kids. It was a good way to get a little familiar with what we were doing.

By the time we opened the season against Purdue, I had pretty well established that Vallely would be a starting guard and run the offense. That was a tremendous decision for me to make and accept. Normally, I didn't think it best to bring a new man in and give him such a task unless he was out of this world, like an Alcindor or someone of that caliber. I preferred to have a man earn his way into the top unit, but when no one had established himself, my hand was forced.

Vallely adapted rapidly. Unfortunately, just when it was time to open in the Midwest for games with Ohio State and Notre Dame, he came down with the flu and couldn't play. That set him back so far that it appeared he might not be able to come up to the challenge of starting. By the opening of the conference, however, Vallely had convinced me. He had a fine series in the Holiday Festival in Madison Square Garden, getting 31 points against St. John's in the championship game.

Now we had the floor leader we needed to complete the five for Lewis's senior season. Lewis had reached a point where it was difficult to find even a small flaw in his game. As a sophomore and junior his timing had been a little uncertain on occasion, but now it was precise. Experience with our style and general maturity had developed this finesse and all the other necessary ones to near perfection. For a player as gifted as Lewis, it would have been simple to become blasé, to take things too easily. Not Lewis. He was a competitor, always pushing himself, always pressing to become greater.

Today, Lewis has long been an established superstar in professional basketball. In my view, he is the most valuable player one can have. His record in the NBA seems to support that. He has been on five championship teams. Six times he has been named most valuable player. Ten times he has been selected by his peers to the all-defensive team. Nineteen times he has been an All-Star. In the 1983-84 season, Kareem passed Wilt Chamberlain as the League's all-time scoring leader.

While he has passed 41 years and has talked about retirement, who is to say this gifted man can't go on for more than a year or two?

One of Lewis's greatest attributes was his ability to adapt to any situation. After the so-called Alcindor rule was passed—the outlawing of the dunk shot—some skeptics said he wouldn't be as great. They ignored his tremendous desire and determination. He worked twice as hard on banking shots off the glass, his little hook across the lane, and his turnaround jumper.

We were 29 and 1 again his senior year—88 wins and 2 defeats in three years—and while we had some fine talent to team with him, I do not believe we would have established that kind of a record without Alcindor.

That lone loss his senior year was our first ever in Pauley Pavilion. It came at the hands of USC. That year we closed the Pacific Eight season with back-to-back games—Friday and Saturday—against the Trojans at the Sports Arena and Pauley.

It was probably as great a two-game series as those two rivals ever played—or any two teams, for that matter.

We won Friday night in a double overtime, 61–55, and were lucky to do it. USC seemed to have the game won in the first overtime, 47–45, with just four seconds to play. I am sure USC expected the ball to go to Lewis but two quick passes found it in Shackelford's hands. Deep in the left corner, twenty-five or thirty feet away, Shack jumped and popped. As the buzzer went off, the shot dropped through for another tie. It was Lynn's first shot of the game, but probably one of the most dramatic he ever took. We came back in the second overtime to put the Trojans away. Once more, I felt that superior condition and confidence turned things around.

Bob Boyd's deliberate, slow-paced attack against us had been very effective. On the next night at Pauley he used the same tactics, and again it was a classic intracity battle. Lewis tied things up at 44 all with 1:15 to play. USC, as it had all night, worked deliberately, moving carefully as they tried to find an opening. With 19 seconds remaining, Bob Boyd called time for his Trojans. As the clock began to tick, USC worked cautiously, until finally Don Crenshaw set a screen and Ernie Powell jumped up to pop one in. We had seconds to go as we came down court for one shot, but this time Shackelford was not free. Then when Sidney Wicks's 20-footer with a second to play hit the iron and bounced away, USC won, 46–44.

Much as I hated to lose, especially to USC, this defeat was beneficial. We went into the NCAA regionals in Pauley and had little trouble in beating New Mexico, 53–38, in another slowdown game, and Santa Clara, 90–52, in a racehorse game.

Next stop was Louisville. If we could put it all together we would have an unprecedented third straight NCAA championship in the Alcindor years. We drew Drake in the first round. They were a fine club but I really didn't foresee the trouble we were to have. We might have lost if it hadn't been for John Vallely's timely baskets. As it was, John fouled out and so did Kenny Heitz.

That's the night I had a little trouble with Bill Sweek, who had played the sixth man role quite ably all year. Toward the end of the game, with Vallely out and Heitz in foul trouble, I had switched Lynn Shackelford back to guard. Bill thought he should be in the game instead. Finally, when I called him to go in, he sauntered up at a rather lackadaisical pace that irritated me. I told him if he didn't care to play any more than that to go back and sit down. Well, he went back all right, but instead of to the bench to sit down, he went to the dressing room.

Now I was irate. But we still had a game that wasn't won. Shack was not a guard and with Sidney Wicks inbounding the ball, we managed to blow a six or eight point lead. We finally hit two free throws to win, 85–82, but I was so upset over Sweek's leaving the floor that it was difficult to maintain my composure.

We had a real set-to in the dressing room. I almost went in the shower after Bill. I was very disappointed at his attitude for not wanting to go in when he was needed. We went round and round, but while I may flare up—as I did that night—I try never to hold a grudge. Bill was in there when we won against Purdue, 92–72, in the championship the next night, hitting three for three from the floor and providing that extra spark so vital in the sixth man role.

I know how a boy feels in such a situation. I know how I felt when I was in grammar school in Centerton and Earl Warriner didn't play me. It's a tough situation for a competitor, and Bill Sweek was a competitor.

Shortly after that, Bill asked me to write a letter of recommendation for him to get into the Peace Corps or the ministry, and I was glad to comply. He chose the Peace Corps.

It's when you have boys like Sweek, who'll fight you as hard as the opponent, and boys like Alcindor, whose talent is so great it's hard to appreciate, that you reflect back over your career and thank the Lord for allowing you to be the coach of such fine young men.

24

I will get ready and then, perhaps, my chance will come.

WITH THE GRADUATION of Lewis Alcindor, Kenny Heitz, Lynn Shackelford, and Company, a tremendous era in UCLA basketball ended. Many people believed that I would regret the departure of such a dominant force. I did, just as every year I regretted losing any of my boys to graduation regardless of whether they might be number one or number fifteen.

Coaches become extremely attached to their players and to their managers. Because they work with these students under conditions of severe emotional and mental stress, as well as physical, it is understandable that they establish closer relationships with them than are usual in the normal classroom situation.

While three brilliant seasons were now history, for the first time in 1095 days—three years—I could look forward to one thing. "It'll be nice to know," I told the news media, "that I'll again be doing my best to win rather than to keep from losing."

Throughout the Alcindor era, from day one, there was not, in the eyes of the public, a question of winning, but of not losing. Now I could revert to a more normal program. In 1969–70, since we had a fine, but not unusually tall, post man in Steve Patterson, that meant going back to my regular high post offense. While Steve was not a superstar of the Alcindor style, he was nonetheless a talent any coach would be pleased to have. He was a good blocker and screener, and in his way, a rather impressive feeder to men cutting through to the basket. His ability to shoot from the key made our high post offense more effective.

157

With Patterson on the post we could present probably the most powerful front line, from a purely physical point of view, that I had ever had. Steve was 6' 9" and weighed 221. Curtis Rowe, who started virtually all the way as a sophomore, was on one side. He was 6' 6½" and 216. A certain coming star, Sidney Wicks, at 6' 8" and 220, would be at the other forward. Although as a sophomore he had some trouble fitting into my style of play, I was confident that he was to become a superplayer. He was the quickest and fastest big man I had ever coached. That gave us real power, and tremendous board strength at either end of the floor. The quickness present in those three men would surprise a lot of people.

Our back court situation looked good. John Vallely, who had made such tremendous strides in the transition from a junior college forward to a UCLA guard, was back for his final year. As the floor leader, he ran the show, but now he had a real hand running with him in Henry Bibby, a 6' 1" sophomore from Franklinton, North Carolina. Henry had been an impressive shooter on our freshman team and I looked forward to three years of such shooting with the varsity.

Regardless of what was expected of a new season, there were always certain rituals to liven up the early weeks. One of my annual little stands came in mid-October. Although it varied a bit each time I wrote it, my fall letter told my prospective players almost the same thing every year. "You must report for practice with no beards, no goatees, no mustaches. Sideburns can be no longer than the beginning of the lobes of the ear and the hair must be a reasonable length. I will be the sole judge of what is reasonable." This policy was again made clear at the meeting I had about two weeks before practice started.

No matter what my letter said, occasionally some player or players would test me. Under the rules, organized practice cannot be held until October 15, but press and picture day may be scheduled one day earlier. One year, and I won't say what year, one of our stars came with extra long sideburns, one with a goatee, and another with mutton chops to draw their game equipment. Always on hand for this, I just stopped them, looked at my watch, and said: "You have twenty minutes to decide whether you're going to play basketball at UCLA this year or not. There are clippers and razors in the training room."

"You'll be crucified," one of them said.

"That may well be, but you won't be around to see it."

They decided in a hurry. Well within the allotted time they were back and passed inspection. Later they kidded me about it occasionally, and all of them at one time or another tried to find out what they'd been afraid to test me on earlier. "You really wouldn't have stuck to it, would you, coach?"

"You'll never really know, will you?" My reply still didn't commit me. "I'm the only one who really knows that."

Once during the summer when his hair was quite long, another very prominent player asked me, "What would you do if I refused to have my hair cut?"

"I won't do anything."

"I thought you wouldn't let us wear our hair real long."

"I won't. It's quite all right; you can wear your hair any way you want. I can't determine how long you wear your hair. All I can determine is whether or not you play."

"I thought there was a catch," he said, as my words sank in.

"That's right."

During my coaching career I managed to stand firm on the haircut issue. In other areas involving appearance I gradually relented some. One needs only to talk to any player of fifteen, sixteen, or twenty years ago to find that out. I was flexible to a point and that point I established from year to year.

It's just like our style of play. Basically, I never changed from the fast-break, pressure defense I had used my first day at Dayton High. But anyone who can objectively evaluate my teams over all those years can see the changes made necessary by the talent, the rules revisions, and the tremendous increase in the physique and the physical skills of the athletes.

The 1969–70 team was a striking example of that last factor. How many times in history has one team had a front line with such power as we did? You don't often put together three physical specimens like Wicks, Rowe, and Patterson. Furthermore, John Ecker, the first front-line replacement and a fine young man, was also of their size. They looked more like tight end candidates for the Los Angeles Rams than front-line men for a college basketball team. Even the two guards, Bibby and Vallely, were big for guards on my team. Surprisingly often, I would have one outstanding guard on a team who would be 6 feet or under, such as Eddie Sheldrake, Ron Livingston, Mike Warren, and others.

Bibby is an example of how much a team means to the individual man. As a sophomore with John Vallely, Bibby was third in scoring with 468 points and a 15.6 average while shooting 50.1 percent from the floor. That year it was Vallely's responsibility to bring the ball down court, direct the offense, and handle the ball in most of the pressure situations. Seldom had a sophomore guard shot so well from outside as did Bibby. He probably had more leeway from me as to how far out he could shoot from than any first year man I ever coached. His success was excellent.

The next two years, with Vallely gone, the whole burden of bringing down the ball, directing the attack, and handling the pressure situations was Henry's. He never shot as well again. He began to force his shots and failed to concentrate as much on the act of shooting.

Perhaps I was remiss in giving Henry so much freedom, but I kept thinking that he would come back to his form of that sophomore season, and I never wanted to hurt his confidence. In all other respects, Henry Bibby became one of the great guards in the country, tough on defense, sure of himself, confident in our concept, and ultimately one of the many outstanding guards I have had in my coaching career.

My goal every year was to make basketball a pleasure, not a poison. This year, 1969–70, was one of the really fun years I have enjoyed in coaching. We had a unique bunch of players. Most of the team had basked in the fame of Lewis's senior season. Some of them, like Rowe and Vallely, had achieved a certain amount of personal acclaim as well, but basically, UCLA was an unknown quantity.

One of the big ifs was that awesome looking young man, Sidney Wicks. As a sophomore, Sidney had disappointed me almost as often as he had made me happy. Feeling that he didn't have his game under control, I didn't start him many times that year. He was still too much of an individual to work into my concept of team play. Sidney, of course, did not like the fact that he wasn't starting all of the time when he knew he was physically better than others.

That year, Rowe played 912 minutes, Shackelford 469, and Sidney 473. Rowe, who was also a sophomore on the final Alcindor team, played almost twice as much as Sidney who had more physical equipment and greater individual talent. But Curtis was also talented and was, perhaps, the most consistent three-year starting forward that I have ever coached. He didn't have bad games; some were just better than others.

When I wrote my annual letter to the team on July 7, 1970, it was pointed probably more to Sidney Wicks than I realized at the time. I must emphasize, however, that Sidney was never selfish. Quite the contrary, he was always a fine team player, but his individual style did not fit in at first, and tended to make his play and our team play somewhat inconsistent.

"In group activity," I wrote, "there must be supervision and leadership and a disciplined effort by all, or much of our united strength will be dissipated pulling against ourselves.

"If you discipline yourself toward team effort under the supervision of the one in charge, even though you might not always agree with the decisions, much can and will be accomplished.

"Your lot is certain failure without discipline.

"I am very interested in each of you as an individual but I must act in what I consider to be in the best interest of the team for either the moment or the future.

"Your race or your religion will have no bearing on my judgment, but your ability and how it works to my philosophy of team play very definitely will. Furthermore, your personal conduct and adherence to standards that I make will undoubtedly be taken into consideration either consciously or unconsciously.

"There may seem to be double standards at times as I most certainly will not treat you all alike in every respect. However, I will attempt to give each individual the treatment he earns and deserves according to my judgment, in keeping with what

I consider in the best interest of the team. You must accept this in the proper manner for you to be a positive and contributing member. . . ."

It had been difficult for Sidney as a sophomore to fit into the wing style of play that was necessary with Lewis on the deep post. Sidney wanted to drive the basket, but with Lewis deep underneath and the defense always sagging in on him, there was no place for Sidney to drive. He reached on defense, he tried to steal too often, he slashed in on the board to grab the spectacular rebound; but being out of control he would often come down and foul an opponent or miss out on a rebound he should have had.

It was difficult, too, for him to see Lynn Shackelford pop them in from deep in the corner—twenty, twenty-five, and, rarely, thirty feet out. Sidney felt he should be allowed to shoot from farther than the eighteen-foot halter I had put on him. One day during his senior year, after I had jumped him pretty hard in a game for taking low percentage shots, for him—out beyond eighteen feet—he asked:

"If I can hit ten in a row from here," he said, pointing to an imaginary line about twenty-five feet out and at a little more of an angle than I preferred, "will you let me shoot from here in a game?"

"I sure will." This was well out on the side in an area that I consider to be the most difficult, lowest percentage shot in basketball, because you can't use the board and the angle is bad.

Sidney, I guess, didn't believe what he had heard.

"If I get ten in a row, can I?"

"Sure, Sidney, if you get ten in a row, I'll let you shoot from there."

Do you know, that determined competitor got out there and hit nine in succession, nine low percentage shots, before he missed?

"That ought to be good enough, huh, coach?" Sidney asked.

"Not for me. You won't do that when somebody is snapping his hand in your face." Sidney just laughed and went on to the next phase of warm-up. He knew deep down I was right, that he had had a run of good fortune and that the odds were too much against him to take another try, but he was very pleased at what he had showed me. What he did not know was that I was equally pleased.

The 1969–70 team won the conference, although we lost two games, one to Oregon, 78–65, and the other to USC, 87–86, the latter only our second loss at Pauley. We ended up with a 28 and 2 season and a fourth successive NCAA title, two more than anyone else had ever been able to win.

And that power line of Sidney, Curtis, and Steve was something else. When I automatically put Sidney in opposite Curtis, he arrived. Not immediately, but dramatically, as the season progressed. Now our style was cut out for a power driver like him. With Patterson working off a high post, both Wicks and Rowe could effectively cut and drive.

Those three had quite a year. Wicks led us in scoring with an 18.6 average, Rowe had 15.3 and Patterson 12.5. That was an average of 15.4 for the front line.

But I feel the team really came together in defeat. Once more this appeared to be the catalyst. USC had whipped us by a point in another wild battle at Pauley and again we were to close out the season on Saturday night with the Trojans in the Sports Arena. I never wanted to lose to the Trojans and never back-to-back games, but especially not the week before the NCAA playoffs. This would get to the players subconsciously, I felt, hurting their morale and bothering their tempo.

This night was not Sidney Wicks's night. From the start, he was miserable. Everything he did was wrong and every time he made an error, USC seemed to capitalize on it. When I took him out, we had a nose-to-nose confrontation right there on the Arena floor. I finally told him to go down to the end of the bench and stay there until he felt he was ready to play.

After about five minutes he came stalking down to me, looking like he was going to eat me alive, and announced he was ready to play. I let him sit another couple of minutes. In the next four and a half minutes, plus about seventeen minutes or so in the second half, Sidney played the greatest basketball he ever played. He had 16 rebounds and was 9 for 11 from the field and 13 for 18 from the free throw line for a total of 31 points.

This moment, coupled with his tremendous display in the NCAA championship game against Artis Gilmore of Jacksonville where he literally destroyed this great 7 footer, turned Sidney Wicks around from an erratic, great player into a superplayer.

Sidney was a skilled talent. But once again my belief was substantiated that a youngster must practice self-discipline and get his game under team control if he is to reach individual stardom and team success. Sidney certainly did that rather dramatically in his junior year, and no one was more pleased or happier for him than his coach. Sidney still feels that he should have started as a sophomore, and I do, too. I also believe that I was right in not starting him then and that Sidney was the one that prevented it, not his coach.

25

*The main ingredient of stardom
is the rest of the team.*

ONCE AGAIN IN 1970–71, we were picked to win the NCAA. We had now won six in the past seven years—four in a row— and if one was to believe the experts in the news media, all we had to do to add another was to show up for thirty consecutive games.

We were going to be tough, there was no doubt about that. We had four starters back from the sixth NCAA champions— Wicks, Rowe, Patterson, and Bibby—but we were faced with the problem of trying to come up with a floor leader. We needed a replacement for the graduated John Vallely, who had been dubbed "Money Man" by his teammates because of his clutch shooting.

Before the season began, I warned the returning starters of the pitfalls and problems we would encounter. An impressive lot of seniors, they might tend to become intolerable, and I was going to be sure that didn't take place.

We didn't have that able ball-handling guard that I could foresee, which meant we had to go with our strength, our power line. Our immediate problem at the outset of practice was to determine who would be the starting guard alongside Henry Bibby. There was no real standout. But in the weeks between the opening of practice in mid-October and our first game with Baylor, I had narrowed it down to one of two men, Kenny Booker and Terry Schofield. Both were seniors, and in spelling Bibby and Vallely both had logged considerable playing time the year before. The final selection was difficult and required careful analysis.

Schofield, the better shooter of the two, had come to UCLA from Santa Monica City College. Beaten out of an expected starting role when Vallely came in from junior college to earn it with no prior exposure to our style and system, Terry had been an unhappy youngster the past two years.

Now I decided that Terry still wouldn't be a starter—that I would go with Booker, who was just an inch taller at 6' 4", but who played just a little better defense and worked in more smoothly with the others. Our new starting five of Wicks, Rowe, Patterson, Bibby, and Booker averaged just a shade under 6' 5½"—the tallest and heaviest starting team I had ever coached.

Before announcing the decision between Booker and Schofield, I talked to Terry about it, pointing out that he was the sixth man, that he was probably going to play as much as, perhaps even more than, Booker, and that he was vital to our hopes. The team needed not only his outside shooting but his ability to come off the bench and inject that propulsive spark and drive that would get us untracked. Terry accepted that analysis and had a fine year for himself and the team.

I had feared that an irreparable gap might come between us over that decision. But it didn't. Terry Schofield played the role of the sixth man to the hilt, doing a tremendous job for us. Later he told me that he "grew up that year." Seeing him arrive as a basketball player and as a young man is the sort of gratification that makes a coach happy. All the effort is suddenly worth it because Terry Schofield, like so many others who have crossed my path in all these years, eventually found his place in the sun.

It is difficult sometimes to reach a team that is so weighted with experience. Most of them had been on two national championship teams and had already been labeled by sportswriters and sportscasters for a third. These were big, strong, experienced players who knew they were big, strong, and experienced players. It was difficult to keep them from becoming complacent. My hardest job all year was to fight the "I-can-get-the-job-done-when-I-turn-it-on" attitude and to keep them striving to improve.

It was difficult, too, to keep their minds on the problem at hand when the world, especially the pro basketball world, came knocking at their door. I never saw any more mail under the names of the various pro clubs than arrived for Wicks, Rowe, and Patterson. When we were flying to Houston for the NCAA finals in the Astrodome, Sidney was sitting directly in front of me and Mrs. Wooden. He had a cassette player with him, and I'll never forget the song he was listening to. "If I Were a Rich Man"—something like that. I reached over and tapped him on the shoulder.

"Sidney," I said, "I wish I had your opportunities to be a millionaire."

There was no player aboard who had gone to Houston with us in the Alcindor years when we lost that mid-season affair in the Astrodome. All of them, though, had either seen the game on television or had read and heard about it. They were quietly determined to change our record in that "Eighth Wonder of the World" arena—which definitely is not the best place in the world for the basketball fan.

We had had a good year in 1970–71, losing only once, to Notre Dame in South Bend, 89–82. Although it was not one of our better games, Notre Dame had a fine ball club. Led by the great Austin Carr, they purely and simply outplayed us and richly deserved their victory.

We had several other struggles that year. One was a 64–60 win at USC in which we had to come from behind, but we beat them quite easily in Pauley Pavilion later on. Instead of playing these games on consecutive nights as we had been doing recently, one took place about mid-season and the other was the final conference affair.

We had two extremely tight games in Oregon. On a Friday we barely beat Oregon at Eugene, 69–68. A late steal by Henry Bibby was the key play. The next night, we went down to the wire with Oregon State before we could win, 67–65, and this time it was Sidney Wicks who won it. After getting well behind in the early going, we had to labor through that whole game.

Eventually we tied it up, and in the closing minutes, with the ball in our possession, we were playing out the time for Sidney to drive by the big man guarding him. He was playing Sidney a little loose, giving him the outside in order to protect the drive where Sidney might either get the basket, the foul, or both. Finally Sidney got just a bit of an edge, faked the drive to freeze his man, then put up a jump shot from just outside the circle. It dropped through the loop just about as time ran out.

One thing that I learned over the years in which we were so fortunate in NCAA championship play was not to work the team too hard once we had the conference won and were certain of going into the playoffs. We kept them in top shape but without too much contact. We did a lot of group work—two on two, three on three, etc.—to keep up the momentum and the unity. I also built confidence. I pointed out to them that they had gotten this far with what they had been doing and that now was no time to change. We played our game and tried not to permit an opponent to force us into theirs.

One of basketball's prime tenets is discipline. You must maintain it. Most of my players who have gone into professional basketball come back to tell me how valuable the discipline they learned at UCLA has been in the pro leagues.

There is no replacement for sound fundamentals and strict discipline. They will reinforce you in the toughest circumstance. The importance of little things cannot be overemphasized—like double-tying the shoestrings; seeing that uniforms and shoes are properly fitted; and forming the habit, based on the assumption that every shot will be missed, of getting your hands above your shoulders when a shot is taken so you can come down with the rebound.

I've heard coaches say that you can't do much with a player's shooting ability, his speed, his quickness, or the height he can jump. I agree to a certain extent, but I also believe you can improve those skills.

At the 1964 Olympic basketball team trials a study was made by Joe Brown, a trainer with the physical education department at the University of Kentucky. Six members of our first NCAA champions were trying out for the Olympic team—Kenny Washington, Keith Erickson, Fred Slaughter, Gail Goodrich, Jack Hirsch and Doug McIntosh. (Hazzard did not participate in the test.) All candidates were given what is called the sergeant jump and reaction test. This is a vertical jump test where each player stands sideways to a wall with his feet together and the arm next to the wall extended upward as high as he can reach without rising on his toes. An observer indicates that spot with a chalk mark. Next the player squats and jumps as high as he can. The observer again marks the extent of the player's reach. The jump is repeated three times and the score based on the difference in inches between the first mark and the highest mark corrected to the lowest number.

Washington and Erickson tied for first with a 36 score. Slaughter was third at 30; Goodrich—probably the smallest man— was fourth at 29. Jack Hirsch tied Dave Stallworth at 28 and McIntosh was at 27 with the likes of Rick Barry, Jeff Mullins, Bill Bradley, "Cotton" Nash, "Bad News" Barnes, Jerry Sloan, and "Butch" Komives.

"UCLA's success in overpowering these [taller teams from Duke and Michigan] for the national championship," Brown pointed out in his report, "can be attributed to many factors; but, in this author's opinion, a very important contributing factor may have been the great jumping ability of the UCLA players."

He also concluded that "UCLA's work index is 8 percent greater than the NCAA Olympians, 10 percent greater than the NCAA alternates and 12 percent greater than the NCAA Olympic trials participants."

He concluded that "a basketball team with players who can jump with power and efficiency, regardless of physical height and weight, will generally have a much better chance to win the important games on its schedule."

We continually drilled on jumping, rebounding, and timing. Thus, when we got a big club like the 1970–71 team with that power line of Wicks, Rowe, and Patterson, we were tough on the boards for balls that went up in a scramble. Once again, every drill had its purpose. Not only were they devised to improve general condition, but also to improve some basic fundamental of the game.

The proper execution of fundamentals can become instinctive if taught properly, just like breathing or walking. The crucial factor in basketball is that most of them must be done at full speed, running. When they become instinctive under these circumstances, you're tough. That's what became second nature to most of the NCAA champions.

Such instinctive control was very visible in the power line during our final two games in the Astrodome. We beat Kansas in the NCAA semifinals, 68–60, and then had a real set-to with Villanova in the finals. When it was all over, we had a six-point edge, 68–62. (I'm still not too proud to settle for one more than our opponents.) Sidney Wicks, incidentally, played with a very sore foot in the championship game and, although not up to par, made some very key plays.

One of the most gratifying moments in my entire coaching career came afterwards in the Astrodome as I walked in our dressing room door. I heard some writer ask Curtis Rowe, "What kind of racial problems did you have on the UCLA team?"

Curtis, without hesitation, looked at him in that firm, strong way of his, and said, "Coach Wooden doesn't see color."

Then he turned and went into the shower.

26

Young people need models, not critics.

"IT HAS BEEN A LONG TIME since I have looked forward so eagerly to a coming basketball season and I hope that you share this enthusiasm."

That was the opening sentence in my annual letter to the squad on July 28, 1971. It was a most sincere and forthright declaration. Even though that power line of Wicks, Rowe, and Patterson was gone and only one starter, Henry Bibby, was back, I was eager to get going. I felt that the squad epitomized the saying "Youth must be served."

I wrote: "The 1971–72 Bruins will be short on experience in comparison with most of our recent teams, but it will not be short on talent, and I would much rather have talent without experience than experience without talent."

There was talent. It was led by another big man who some claimed was of the Alcindor caliber but from a different mold. Bill Walton, an angular redhead from San Diego who stood 6' 11", had potential defensive skills that could have been compared to those of the fabled Bill Russell. There were two excellent sophomore guards in Greg Lee, whose father played at UCLA prior to my arrival in 1948, and Tommy Curtis, a quick, but smaller sophomore from Tallahassee, Florida. A strong contender at forward was Keith Wilkes, a 6' 6" sophomore from Santa Barbara, who was only a few months past his eighteenth birthday when practice commenced October 15.

There were two junior forwards who had played well in relief to the power line the year before. One was Larry Hollyfield, a

6' 5" all-everything from Compton. He probably possessed as good a one-on-one talent as anyone out but had problems adapting to the system. Larry Farmer from Denver, Colorado, also 6' 5", was a steady cornerman with good rebounding talent.

There were others—Gary Franklin, a 6' 5" sophomore forward; 6' 5½" Vince Carson, who had been hurt his senior season at John Muir High in Pasadena; Swen Nater, a 6' 11" center, who had transferred from Cypress Junior College and had sat out a year. Swen was born in Holland and had played only two years of basketball.

To bind all this youthful skill together, we had Henry Bibby, now a senior and twice a key back-court man on NCAA champions. A tireless worker who fully understood our philosophy, he gave our team the assurance, security, and leadership so vitally essential to its eventual success.

This was the talent. On paper, and based on the freshman season, they had fine potential. I was convinced that if everything would fall in place, if the players would accept all our precepts of play, conduct, condition, discipline, team welfare, and avoid any individual personality clashes, it could be a "very rewarding year."

How did I forecast the season in my little envelope locked in the top drawer of my desk? I foresaw 24 wins, 2 defeats.

I feared we would probably lose to Oregon State in Corvallis early in January. They loomed as very strong, and it would be the first road game for our extremely young team. Fortunately, we would have time to build our confidence in a pre-conference schedule of eight games all to be played on our home court— Pauley Pavilion. Although I was worried about our conference opener, I anticipated we would have the Pacific Eight Conference won going into the final regularly scheduled game with USC at the Sports Arena. I figured we would lose that one because I expected to be concentrating that week on preparations for the NCAA regionals at Provo, Utah.

I told no one, of course, except my wife, of my prediction.

One of the attributes of the 1971–72 team—which our sportswriter friends tagged the Walton Gang or Bibby's Bunch—

was its intelligence. Not only basketball intelligence—the players as a whole probably had more academic brilliance than any team I have ever had. Walton, Wilkes, and Greg Lee were all fine students; and Farmer and Bibby, the other two starters, were good students—not brilliant but good.

It was an easy team with which to work. With the big man once more in Bill Walton, I went back to a set offense similar to the one I had used with Lewis. Our players' balance around the big man and the fact that they got along so well as a team was important in getting it all together.

Once more we had someone other than a guard to lead us on the floor. Just as Sidney Wicks in his senior year had taken command of both ends of the court, Bill Walton now came forward. Visibly happy playing basketball and all-seeing on the court, this gifted young man talked more during a game and called out more warnings and advice to his teammates than any player I have ever had.

Every expert saw something else of great import in Walton's talent. In my mind, next to tremendous ability and unselfish team play, his foremost offensive skill was on the outlet pass. Never have I coached a player who was more skilled at outletting the ball to initiate a fast break. He always had the ball ready to throw even before he came down with the rebound. In fact, there were times when the ball was nearly at mid-court before Bill's feet hit the floor. On defense his intimidating shot-blocking was his greatest asset.

With no great speed in the guards to compare with what we had had in the years with Walt Hazzard or Mike Warren or earlier with Eddie Sheldrake, we still capitalized on the break. Once that was stopped, however, we had a strong set offense with Walton underneath, Bibby on the left wing where he was a definite shooting threat, and Farmer on the right wing. In this offense, Larry, a strong rebounder, was vital on the side away from both the big post man and most effective outside shooter. Pencil-thin Keith Wilkes, a good passer and feeder, was excellent coming up from the low to the high post. Not nearly as strong as Curtis Rowe, Wilkes was equally adept at doing a job that few recognized, and he seemed to have been born just as consistent. Seldom did he have a bad game. If his shooting was off, his defense, rebounding, and general play contributed greatly.

Once again, I was confronted with a difficult problem in determining how to place the fifth and sixth men—sophomores Greg Lee and Tommy Curtis. Each had attributes the other didn't. Going down to the wire again, I finally selected Greg. He was taller and bigger, and a little headier on what to do. And since he got the ball into the high post a little better than Tommy, I felt he would complement Walton more.

On the other hand, Curtis was quicker and stronger on the pressing defense, but the thing that clinched my decision was Tommy's ability coming off the bench. I felt he would be far more valuable coming in as that sixth man than starting every time as the fifth. Yet the one game when Greg couldn't play because of an injury the night before, Curtis started, played a tremendous game, scored 14 points, and did everything one could possibly ask of a starter. Furthermore, it was against Ohio State, our most respected and capable opponent up to that date.

Tommy showed what a fine young man he was when in the very next game I started Greg again. I know that was a bitter pill for Tommy, but he never brooded about it. Convinced that Greg could never give us that dynamic thrust we needed from time to time out of the sixth man, I had to hold Tommy in readiness for those crucial moments. There was many a time in winning those 30 games in 1971–72 without a single defeat that his teammates turned to Curtis. "Come on, Tommy," I would hear them say during a time-out or a brief break, "liven us up. Get us going."

By the time we went on our first road trip to Oregon State in January, I was convinced that we had a superclub. Just how super a club so young could be over a full season was yet to be demonstrated. But it had really matured in those eight games at home without defeat. We had averaged 108 points, including our 79–53 win over Ohio State in the finals of the Bruin Classic, while our opponents averaged only 63 points. It was now obvious that not only were we a pretty strong offensive force despite our youth and inexperience, but exceptionally tough defensively.

Many pointed to the big man, Walton, as the reason for the defensive strength, and it was obvious that he was a major contributor. But everyone else was tough on defense, too. With Bill directing things vocally, they played it tight and we didn't get burned too often.

Youth must mature with experience, but this squad matured with more rapidity than I had any right to expect. It certainly must have been the youngest team in average age to go through a season undefeated and win the NCAA. It was a delightful team with which to work, with a minimum of problems and a maximum of success. The never-ceasing hustle of Henry Bibby, our only returning starter from the year before, in each and every practice was an inspiration to the younger players.

Not an overly emotional group, they let their play speak for them. Most of the boys would probably agree that our victory against Cal State Long Beach in the regionals at Provo, Utah, was the most satisfactory moment in a perfect season, but our toughest game was in the NCAA finals against Florida State at the Los Angeles Sports Arena.

We were never in danger of losing a ball game, as far as score was concerned late in a game. The NCAA record we set for average margin of victory over the season attests to that fact. In thirty victories we averaged 94.6 points against 64.3 points for our opponents, or a difference of 30.3 points per game. This was accomplished with no player averaging over thirty-one minutes of playing time per game. Bibby and Walton had the most, averaging just under thirty-one minutes per game.

It was a fine team. We got great play all year from the starting five—Wilkes, Farmer, Walton, Lee, and Bibby—plus some brilliant service from Curtis, Swen Nater, Larry Hollyfield, and the others.

Every game, I was asked the obvious. Who was the better big man, Alcindor or Walton? I never make comparisons, even of which is the best team I have coached or which is the best player.

For the record, here are some statistical comparisons of the UCLA years for Alcindor and Walton. The numbers in parentheses indicate standing in career UCLA records:

	Alcindor	Walton
Career scoring leaders	(1) 2325 points	(2) 1767 points
Career rebound leaders	(2) 1367	(1) 1370
Career FG percentage	(2) .639	(1) .651
Career FG scored	(1) 943	(2) 747
Career FG attempts	(1) 1476	(8) 1147
Career FT scored	(1) 699	Not in top 10
Career assists	Not in top ten	(3) 316
Season scoring leader	(1) 870	(9) 633
Season rebound leader	(3) 466	(1) 506
Season FG percentage leader	(1) .667	(2) .665
Season FG scored	(1) 346	(4) 277

One conclusion is obvious from these statistics. They both were very talented; both were excellent team men, both were very unselfish, and both were superb defensive men. But my comment when I was first asked to compare them after our first 1971–72 win was the same as after our NCAA championship, and it will always be the same:

"I was most happy and pleased with Lewis for three years and I was most happy and pleased with Bill for his three years."

27

When we are out of sympathy
with the young,
then our work in this world is over.

On August 1, 1972, I sat down to pen my annual letter to the squad. My profession is truly a pleasure, I reflected, as I thought about the continuing inspiration I had received from the many young men who had played for me. The group I was addressing myself to had gone 30–0 the year before, and the great majority were now only juniors.

"It is my sincere hope," I wrote to each, "that the 1972–73 UCLA varsity basketball team will be made up of players who love a challenge. Not only will there be a real battle for the top seven or eight playing spots, but the team pressure from the press and public will be far more severe than last year because now you will be expected to win.

"Many of you are partially responsible for this enviable, or unenviable, position as far as team pressure is concerned because of what you have accomplished in the past. I choose to consider it an enviable position that has been earned and that is a mark of respect. Furthermore, if you are the competitors that I think you are, you will justify the position.

"I must caution you that you cannot live in the past. The 1971–72 season is now history and we must look toward the future. The past cannot change what is to come. The work that you do each and every day is the only true way to improve and prepare yourself for what is to come. You cannot change the past and you can influence the future only by what you do today."

Shortly before we opened the season against Wisconsin, I

performed another annual ritual I had begun several years earlier. Weighing carefully all the factors that would affect our upcoming season, I wrote a little message to myself, placed it in an envelope, and locked it in my desk drawer.

I devoted considerable thought to what I had said to my team back in April 1972 after our perfect season. I had complimented them, of course, telling them what a fine group of young men they were and what a pleasure it had been to work with them. But I had also added a word of caution.

"You've won a championship. You've gone through an entire season undefeated. Next year most of you will be juniors. You'll not be nearly as easy to work with because, after accomplishing the feat you have, you're going to 'feel your oats.' You won't be listening quite so well or working quite so hard. You may want to give just as much, but, subconsciously, I don't think you'll do it."

I couldn't resist adding a parting remark:

"And by the time you're seniors," I prophesied, "you'll probably be intolerable."

My prediction for each year never went beyond our regular season. Any team that gets that far is capable of eliminating any other in the "sudden-death, one-loss-and-you're out" NCAA championship tournament.

Once again we were in a position of trying to prevent a defeat rather than win. Although we were lacking a little in outside shooting because of the loss of Henry Bibby, that would be offset by a year's experience and greater maturity overall. And the tremendous skills Bill Walton showed as a sophomore promised to be even greater.

There was one last question mark in my mind before I wrote down my forecast of our season's record. That was the final game with USC. I figured we'd have the conference won by then and there might be a letdown. Furthermore, I knew that if we did have it won, I'd be preparing for the playoffs and this could be all that such a prospectively fine team would need. Nevertheless, I picked us to win them all, 26–0.

There was always a certain amount of concern at the beginning of a new season. Little did I know how much would arise very shortly, December 11, to be exact. During the wee hours on that Monday, I awoke with a severe pain in my chest. Not wanting to admit what might be happening to me, I tried to tough it out. But finally I woke Nellie, and at 1:45 A.M. was admitted to St. John's Hospital in Santa Monica.

Now I wasn't worried about our pressing defense or our post play—only about how long a mild heart problem would keep me away from my team. For the first time in thirty-eight years, I missed a game. When we went against the University of California at Santa Barbara, my assistant, Gary Cunningham, directed the team's play while, from my hospital bed, I impatiently awaited news of the outcome. That was the only game I missed.

One special experience following my eight-day hospital stay served to remind me again what a wonderful profession I am in. Nellie had gone to the store, so I was at home alone when the doorbell rang. When I opened the door, there stood that big, lovable redhead, Bill Walton. He had come from the campus to the house on his bike just to see me in person. You know, that perked me up about as much as anything could have.

There is a lot of disparaging talk about the young these days—how callous they are, what little regard they have for their elders. But to know this young man had ridden his bike more than ten miles to visit an old gaffer who is on him all the time made me realize how false such generalities are.

Bill and his teammates were a fine group. They never failed to do what was necessary. The end was another perfect season, another NCAA title, and, more important, another season of fond memories.

How can I ever forget the magnificent performance of Walton in the championship final against Memphis State? The inspiration and effective play of Tommy Curtis in many games, especially in the NCAA tournament against USF and Indiana? The smooth, polished brilliance Keith Wilkes displayed game after game? The solid, all-around performance of Larry Farmer? The startling steals and vibrant play of Larry Hollyfield?

Or those beautiful lob passes of Greg Lee to Walton and Farmer, especially against Memphis State? The vast improvement and productive play of David Meyers and the good humor and the fine touch provided by Swen Nater? Then, of course, there was the unpublicized but tireless dedication of those who didn't play as much but helped prepare those who did—Vince Carson, Casey Corliss, Ralph Drollinger, Gary Franklin, Pete Trgovich, and Bobby Webb.

Each year I felt I was blessed with a remarkable group of young men. Gifted as these players were from the standpoint of basketball talent, we also wanted them to have the ability to get along with others, especially their teammates. This 1972–73 team had that to a remarkable degree. Their closeness, coupled with their high intelligence, stood them in good stead as we approached the University of San Francisco's all-time consecutive win record of sixty. Only the two crucial games—number 60 to tie and number 61 to break the tie—seemed to betray added strain. Once past that milestone, we could all relax. In my opinion, in fact, every game we played was in hand before we reached its last few minutes.

During the season someone asked me what would have happened if Walton had been hurt and forced to remain out. My instant answer was, "We'd win with Swen." I had great confidence in this group as team basketball players. Whether or not we could have won without Walton no one can know, of course. Naturally, our play would have been a little different with Nater, but I firmly believe we still could have won.

This was a responsive crew who always answered a challenge, no matter what it might be. I remember the Sunday before the finals against Memphis State on Monday night. I was concerned at how taut they all seemed—perhaps even nervous. In the semifinals against Indiana we had lost our composure a bit as Indiana staged a brilliant rally to cut our 22-point lead to two, and this had not happened in any previous game. I watched them as we dressed for a late Sunday afternoon workout. They just didn't look good. How could we loosen them up?

Although our practice was not planned to be formal, as we took the floor I even cast aside what schedule I had. Near the close, still not liking the way they were reacting, I made up my mind to do something I never thought I'd do: I decided we'd finish practice with a "dunk shot" drill. No team of mine had done that since they outlawed the shot after Alcindor's sophomore season. When I told them to dunk, the change was almost miraculous. That little bit of levity dissipated all the tension. They were alive. They moved more quickly, with better speed and greater determination.

That dunking drill seemed to do more to ready us for Memphis State, both mentally and emotionally, than any other immediate preparation. If you ask me why, I can't tell you. All I can say is that it gave us the lift we needed to relax.

Very probably the drill may have relaxed Bill more than anyone else, because he dearly loves to dunk the basketball. His performance in that game was one of the finest by an individual that I have ever seen, not only from my own particular team and players, but from any player I've seen in any championship series. Only in the 1965 finals when Gail Goodrich scored 42 points—the record Bill broke—can you find a comparable effort.

In view of Gail's height (only 6′ 1″) his play was truly amazing. But regardless of Bill's advantage in that respect (he is 6′ 11″), his play was equally amazing. He showed tremendous timing and body balance as he handled those lob passes and hit twenty-one out of twenty-two shots from the floor. And he could have had twenty-four out of twenty-five, because he had three taken away for offensive goal interference.

The basketball world lauded Walton for that effort, and rightly so. Bill , however, would quickly tell you that it was Lee's fourteen and Hollyfield's nine assists that enabled him to have such a stunning night.

It's ironic that Bill played that well. Some of the media during our four days in St. Louis had Bill jumping the team and about to sign with the pros. The rumor ballooned so out of proportion that the true story never did appear.

When we arrived in St. Louis there were no seven-foot beds at our hotel. After sleeping Friday night in a regular bed, Bill acknowledged that the semifinal win over Indiana had completely exhausted him. J. D. Morgan, our athletic director, who had a second room at another hotel, the Chase Park Plaza, informed us that it had a king-size bed, and, while we don't like to divide our players, we decided to transfer Bill to his room. But about 1:00 A.M. on Sunday, however, Bill was ejected from the room because the room clerk had mistakenly sold it. That left Bill in the lobby without any room in which to sleep. Finally, after determined efforts by Mr. Morgan, Gary Cunningham, and a sportswriter, we got Bill back in a room with a king-size bed. And, as we always do with our players to insure more privacy, we cut off calls to his room.

The next morning, writers tried to find Bill at the team's hotel and at the Chase Park Plaza, but of course they couldn't. So the story exploded that Bill had jumped the club, quit the team, and was in hiding waiting to sign a contract with a pro team. This was not the case at all. While Bill spent the rest of the nights at the Chase Park Plaza, he took all his meals with the team, as well as participating in all the practices and meetings.

Some writers tried to predict all kinds of dire things, and a lot of them got burned, so to speak, assuming something had happened without getting the facts. These were the things about the media that disturbed Bill. Naturally a very reticent, quiet young man who didn't want to be uncooperative, Bill was an entirely different person from what the press often implied. The claim that he disliked granting interviews probably arose from the fact that immediately after a game Bill wanted to get away quickly and relax. He probably expended as much individual energy as any player I ever coached. This, coupled with his aversion to large crowds, seemed to create difficulties for him with the media. But as Bill matured, he began giving them more time. For instance, after the NCAA in Atlanta, Georgia, where he received the Naismith trophy (basketball's equivalent to the Heisman trophy in football), he was a very fine, cooperative, and willing interviewee, and the media seemed pleased with his honesty and openness.

Who is to say how Bill felt physically after a game? I doubt if I ever had a player go through so much to play. He had to get to the arena a good hour before the rest of the team to use heat hydroculators on his knees, a treatment he kept up until we went on the floor. After the game, he spent another thirty to forty-five minutes sitting with his knees packed in ice so they wouldn't swell. Every day we practiced or played, Bill had to go through this same routine. That alone nearly doubled the time he devoted to basketball in comparison to most other players.

This season Bill was given permission to call a time-out whenever he felt he needed one. This was a rare privilege, but no one I've ever coached has had a knee problem like Walton's. During our thirty games, there were times Bill elected to call time-out when I would have preferred not to. But no one could see into those knees. Only Bill could judge when they were causing him such trouble that it was best to give them a rest.

Bill was also charged with having special privilege because he was allowed to judge whether or not he practiced the Monday following a game. Again, he was the first player I ever gave that option, but that was because of the nature of his physical problem. I am sure Bill would not want to skip practice.

Missing Mondays seemed to be beneficial to Bill. Indirectly his absence was quite beneficial to the team too, in that it allowed me to give more work and attention to Nater and Drollinger. They'd get a good go against each other, a welcome respite from having to work against Bill, who is so awesome on defense that I sometimes feared it might destroy their incentive. Each also had a good workout against a different style of play.

All players are individuals. Occasionally we all—coaches, media, spectators—expect too much from them. Sometimes we tend to see them as outstanding performers and forget how young they still are. We need only to analyze ourselves to realize that we adults do not always act like adults in everything we do.

These talented young men of the 1972–73 UCLA basketball team were part of a win streak of seventy-five straight games. They and those before them had won forty-three games without defeat in our conference, the Pacific Eight; they had won thirty-five games in a row on the road; but, what I believe is the most impressive statistic of all—our teams had won thirty-six games without defeat in NCAA tournament play.

Yes, this was a remarkable group who fulfilled all that was expected of them and more. The season was a trying one for me, primarily because of my little heart flare-up, but the end result was extremely gratifying and made this one of the most cherished of all our championships.

28

Talent is God-given; be humble.
Fame is man-given; be thankful.
Conceit is self-given; be careful.

No MATTER HOW you total success in the coaching profession, it all comes down to a single factor—talent. There may be a hundred great coaches of whom you never have heard in basketball, football, or any sport who will probably never receive the acclaim they deserve simply because they have not been blessed with the talent. Although not every coach can win consistently with talent, no coach can win without it.

Over the years, particularly in the last decade or so of my coaching career, I was fortunate. UCLA had some remarkably talented basketball players. There was sufficient talent right here in Los Angeles that I needed to go no farther to search for it. Often I would hear that our success was due to the out-of-state boys who came to Westwood. We had some great ones, to be sure—like Alcindor, Hazzard, Warren, Lucius Allen, Bibby, to name a few. But we also had some remarkable players from our own southern California area—players like Wicks, Rowe, Green, Cunningham, Patterson, Naulls, Erickson, Goodrich, Vallely, Lacey, Walton, Wilkes, and others.

Within ninety miles of our campus, there was—still is —a fountain of talent unequaled anywhere else in America except, perhaps, in other really large metropolitan areas. We didn't get it all, but we got our share and that's all we asked. Probably 90 percent, or possibly more, of our time was spent evaluating youngsters right in the Los Angeles area, with the remainder elsewhere in California, the Northwest, and in other states.

We did not initiate contact with players from out of state;

185

usually they contacted us by some means—coach, principal, or mutual friend. Then we might look at a film or talk to people whom we respected about them. If the prospect met our entrance requirements and fit in with our player needs, we might then extend a scholarship offer.

We had considerable competition for the talent in our immediate area. We had several strong basketball powers right at hand in USC, Pepperdine, and Cal State Long Beach. And of course everyone else in the Pac Eight, the state colleges, and the smaller colleges on the West Coast looked here also. And the rest of the nation discovered long ago that this was a large fountain of talent.

Although it was probably no different from other schools in our conference, we had a pretty good built-in scouting system of our own. We had a rather large, interested alumni group of former players and managers who had a good eye for basketball talent. Some had become coaches, other officials, but most were still buffs who loved to watch the game whether on a local playground, a neighborhood high school, or junior college. Hardly a day went by during basketball season that one of my former players didn't call to tell me about a prospect he'd seen. We even had a father or two—Marvin Lee, Greg's father, for instance—who had a son we could use.

There was one tremendous advantage to this. Each of those men (I have to pick that word carefully, because even though they may be fathers they are still youngsters to me) was well versed in the Wooden philosophy. They knew what I wanted in a young man, and what it took to play for me at UCLA. They automatically eliminated many, which was a fine screening system for us. Of course, I don't want to imply that my former players spent day and night seeking talent, but if they saw someone they believed was a bona fide prospect, they called.

Among the most active alumni supporters of our program were the ex-managers. They were largely responsible for organizing an annual dinner meeting for the alumni group. Held in January at the recreation center on the UCLA campus, it always had an amazing turnout, particularly among those alumni from my earlier years. Many of the ex-managers never missed a game. No more loyal friends could be found anywhere than such men as Steve Aranoff, Gary Walls, Ted Henry, Dennis Minishian, George Morgan, Harold Crawford, Bill Anderson, Herb Furth, and numerous others who served in that position. Quite a number of them worked with us for years—charting shots, turnovers, and other statistics that weren't normally provided in every game. Some of them never missed a home game, a few went on the road, and some saw all of our NCAA championship games. Furthermore, it was a labor of love, on their own time and at their own expense.

The managers, over all these years, remained steadfastly devoted to our team. Today, they are friends I value dearly, and men of whom I am equally as proud as I am of the boys who played in the games. No honor is more fulfilling than the accomplishments of the young men you have worked with so closely— players or managers, All-American or average.

Honors are fleeting, just as fame is; I cherish friendship more. I am very flattered, very honored, and very appreciative of the fact that in 1960 I was elected to the Basketball Hall of Fame as a player and in 1972 as a coach, the only man to date to be in the Hall in a dual capacity. While such an honor is great recognition for any man in his profession, I didn't get there alone. Every man who has been with me from my grammar school days on a dirt court in Centerton, or in Martinsville, Purdue, Dayton, South Bend, Indiana State, or UCLA holds a share of such honors. They have all been kind to me in helping me achieve what success has been mine. Their contribution reminds me of these few words from Lao-Tse:

> Kindness in words creates confidence,
> Kindness in thinking creates profoundness,
> Kindness in giving creates love.

I hope that in some way each of my boys, whether he may now be thirty or fifty, will understand somewhat why I do things the way I do. From my friends in the media, I used to keep getting one persistent question. "John," they asked, "when you retire, will you pick your all-time team?"

I always gave an immediate answer, always the same: "Never."

And my answer is the same today. Can I truthfully say whether Lewis Alcindor is better than Bill Walton? Who are the two best of all the guards—Eddie Sheldrake, Dick Banton, Walt Hazzard, John Green, Mike Warren, Ron Livingston, Don Johnson, Morris Taft, Walt Torrence, George Stanich, Lucius Allen, Gail Goodrich, Henry Bibby, and others? Who are the two best of all the forwards—Alan Sawyer, Willie Naulls, John Moore, Jerry Norman, Dick Ridgway, Don Bragg, Gary Cunningham, Keith Erickson, Pete Blackman, Jack Hirsch, Curtis Rowe, Keith Wilkes, Sidney Wicks, and others?

Who can say which ones should rank above the others? My only reply is that at the given time in the given year the man doing the job was doing his best. For that moment, he was the best that played for me. I have always contended that the great players of a past era, if transported into the present with the fine coaching, the fine equipment, and the fine facilities now available, would be every bit as great as those men being called superstars today.

Players who attained that pinnacle in my regime as a coach did so on individual merit, but in all honesty I feel that their accomplishment was at least partially indebted to having come within our system. Nevertheless, though the system gave many an opportunity, it couldn't make the man unless the latent talent were present.

An example that comes to mind immediately is Keith Erickson. He blossomed into greatness by hard, diligent work, but his ultimate success depended upon those who surrounded him and worked just as diligently as he to make the system an effective, dynamic force. Of course, he had to possess the inherent ability and competitive spirit.

Another striking example of ultimate individual success through melding into our system was Sidney Wicks. On and off the bench as a sophomore, Sidney acquired a partial understanding of the system as a junior, truly found it in the USC game and the NCAA championship against Jacksonville that year, and became totally accomplished within its limits as a senior.

In his final year of 1970–71, Sidney became the dominant force. It was one of the few times in my career that a forward had done so. He directed us at both ends of the floor and when the pressure became the greatest, the players went to him. Innately possessed of great individual talent, Sidney subordinated his personal desires to fill the need of the team. A genuinely great performer has such supreme confidence in his own ability that he is not afraid to take that risk.

Sidney genuinely personified what an individual could accomplish within the bounds and limitations of our system. He reached as close to the maximum potential as a young man can. Most of it came together when he was able to channel his emotional and physical abilities into our team effort.

Those who saw Sidney's last performance for UCLA in the Astrodome in Houston in the NCAA finals remember his brilliance. It's an example I continued to point out to equally talented youngsters as they came along. When Villanova was pressing us hard, Sidney was the man we had bring the ball down court, in spite of the fact that he was playing on a very sore foot. He was an excellent dribbler and ball handler, and I knew that no one would outmuscle such a courageous competitor in a pressure situation.

That was an inspiring night. What a contrast it was to the earlier game with Houston that year when Alcindor was hurt. This time, with the game all but over, there was no way we could lose our seventh NCAA. As the ball came down toward our end of the floor for Henry Bibby to shoot two free throws, there were just seconds to go.

The benches in the Astrodome are below floor level, and all of a sudden Sidney came over to the pit. Forgotten was the little difficulty that we had had only a day or two before. Sidney, exuberantly happy as he leaned over and grabbed my hand, literally radiated his feelings. A smile covered his whole face and his eyes were sparkling.

"Coach," he said, "it's been great. A great career, coach."

With that he bounded back onto the floor. As I waved my program and yelled my thanks for a fantastic effort, he suddenly stopped, turned back, and declared:

"Coach, you're really something."

Yes, as Glennice Harmon has put it so eloquently in her poem "They Ask Me Why I Teach," where else could I find such splendid company?

29

*Goals achieved with little effort
are seldom appreciated and
give no personal satisfaction.*

WHEN I SAT DOWN in late November of 1974 to make my little prediction of the coming season, I had no inclination that it would be the last time. As I had done for forty years, I jotted my prediction down on a piece of paper, sealed it in an envelope, and locked it in my desk drawer.

As I did so, I couldn't help thinking back over the disappointments of the previous season. The 1973–74 UCLA basketball team had confirmed my long-held belief that veterans who have unusual success as sophomores and juniors will find their senior season their most difficult. Our front line, consisting of Bill Walton, Keith Wilkes, and David Meyers, had played well, but we had had continual problems at guard. Both Tommy Curtis and Greg Lee had been inconsistent. And neither Pete Trogovich nor Andre McCarter had been quite ready; I had used them only sparingly.

After beating North Carolina State 84–66 in a pre-season game in St. Louis, we had seen our all-time win-streak record snapped at 88 by Notre Dame in South Bend. In that game, we'd had an 11-point lead, only to allow Notre Dame to run off 12 unanswered points and win 71–70.

Later, we had lost back-to-back games at Oregon and Oregon State and had barely pulled together to win the Pacific Eight Conference and enter the NCAA playoffs. Then we had had tremendous problems with Dayton in the first round of the regionals. We had gone into three overtimes to win 111–100,

191

and we could have just as easily lost in either of the first two periods.

We had come back to play respectably in the regional final, beating San Francisco 83–60. But then in the first round of the Final Four we had lost to North Carolina State in double overtime—our first NCAA championship loss since 1966. We had come back to beat Kansas 78–61, but that had been in one of those infamous third-place consolation games I had so detested all my coaching career.

All in all, 1973–74 had been a disappointing season. But now a new season was before us, full of promise and uncertainty. My annual letter to the squad that year was more detailed than in the past, because for all practical purposes I was dealing with a new team. Bill Walton, Keith Wilkes, Greg Lee, and Tommy Curtis had graduated. Those four had played key roles for us over the years, and they would be difficult to replace—especially two like Walton and Wilkes, who as history has now shown would go on to successful roles in professional basketball.

Many felt that Ralph Drollinger, taller than Walton by two inches, would be our center. Like Bill, Ralph was an excellent student and had great determination on the basketball floor. However, he lacked much of the skill and drive Walton had exhibited during his college years.

The absence of Keith Wilkes would be keenly felt. Keith had a knack for always being in the right spot at the right time. And even though his shooting style was not one of accepted technique, I never tampered with it. Without doubt, Keith was one of the most graceful men to play on any of my teams.

As practice got underway for the year, it soon became obvious to me that, although Drollinger had the experience and size, Richard Washington at 6'9½" was going to play more and more of a role at center. In my points to be considered for the 1974–75 season, I noted: "Prepare Richard Washington for both the high and low center post as well as forward." And then I added, "Use the weak-side post drill without shooting more frequently— possibly as a pre-game warm-up." The thought about Richard proved to be rather prophetic.

Although our guards lacked starting experience, Andre McCarter and Pete Trgovich worked together well and gave us considerable size. And much to the surprise of many, they developed into an outstanding defensive pair.

When I wrote my forecast, I figured we'd win the conference and have a reasonable opportunity to take our tenth NCAA title. My prediction for the season was a 23 and 3 year. We actually ended up 22 and 4.

Our 1974–75 team was made up of as fine a group of young men as I have ever had the privilege of working with. Not one gave me any trouble on or off the floor during the entire season. The prognosticators didn't expect us to win, either at the outset of the season or when the NCAA tournament began. But to a man our team played as if they were not aware of what the experts believed. They showed tremendous courage and determination.

Our leader and captain was David Meyers, who as a senior was truly an All-American at each end of the floor. Pete Trgovich, who had switched back and forth between forward and guard, settled in with McCarter in the back court. He had matured tremendously between his junior and senior seasons and was at his best when the pressure was the greatest. And as I mentioned earlier, he and McCarter developed into as fine a pair of defensive guards as I had ever coached.

Our two sophomores, Marques Johnson and Richard Washington, despite their youth and inexperience, joined up with David Meyers and Ralph Drollinger to give us a strong front line. It was not surprising that each went on to greatness following my retirement.

This team of fine young men captured the Pacific Eight title and qualified to meet Michigan in the first round of the NCAA tournament held in Pullman, Washington. Although we won 103–91, it wasn't that easy and the game went into overtime. However, much like our 1970 team, this group seemed to come together under pressure.

The victory over Michigan put us into the West Regionals in Portland against Montana University, who also gave us quite a battle. We eventually won, 67–64, but we had to fight every inch of the way. We just couldn't seem to get things together, particularly on offense, and Eric Hayes, their great forward, put the pressure on our defense by scoring 32 points.

We played Arizona State in the West Regional final and won substantially, 89–75. It was in this game that Marques Johnson really "arrived," even though he was only in his second season. This happened in spite of the fact that he had to be brought along carefully because he had contracted hepatitis just before the season. Throughout most of the season the doctor had cautioned me not to use him too much or let him get too tired. So his playing time was quite restricted, and although the situation was disappointing to him, he accepted it without grumbling.

Against Arizona State, however, the doctor told me Marques could go a little longer. As the game progressed, I felt he was all right. His statistics confirm that he had a tremendous game. He made 14 of 20 field goals, 7 of 8 free throws, 12 rebounds, and only one personal foul. His 35 points led all the scoring. He was simply outstanding—a beautiful player with his action and motions—and he played all but four minutes of the game.

In our semifinal game in the Final Four we faced Louisville, an outstanding team that was coached by one of my own, Denny Crum. Denny had played for me after two years at Pierce Junior College in the San Fernando Valley, just over the hills from UCLA. Then he had come back from Pierce where he had success as a coach to become my lead assistant. We had no secrets from each other when it came to basketball, and played almost identical styles. The outcome would be determined by poise and execution.

As the game progressed, both teams were playing superb ball. In fact, I believe it was one of the finest games of my entire coaching career. Considering the way both teams played, it seems rather logical that we were tied at the end of regulation play.

Both teams played well in the overtime, too, but when we got down to the last fifty seconds, Louisville was ahead 74–73. At this point, I sent Jimmy Spillane, a young and fast sophomore guard in to help pressure the ball.

A few plays later, with twenty seconds left on the clock, Spillane fouled Terry Howard, who went to the line for a one and one. Howard missed and Richard Washington came down with the ball. We got across midcourt and called time with five seconds left in the overtime. We set up a play for a side court shot for Richard. This was the situation play I had mentioned in my pre-season analysis, and it worked beautifully. From about ten feet out and at just the right angle, Richard arched it in.

Later, I was asked why we set up the play for Richard, since he was only a sophomore and there were more seasoned players on the court. My reasoning was that, since Washington was 6'9½", his shot would be hard to block, and I also knew that Richard wouldn't feel any pressure. Others might feel the strain, but I don't think Richard ever knew the meaning of a pressure shot. Of course, the fact that he was a fine shooter also helped in our decision.

Washington's basket gave us a lead of 75–74, and with two seconds left Denny signaled for a time-out. I was certain he wanted to set up Allen Murphy for that one last shot, and I was right. Murphy had already scored 33 points, but this time he lost control of the inbound pass for just a moment. This forced him to attempt a long desperation shot that fell short. The game was over.

The San Diego Arena was in bedlam and exuberant UCLA fans poured onto the court. Wherever I turned there were well-wishers. Some I recognized; others I had never seen before. I had a hard time getting to Denny, but I finally forced my way through and we embraced, although neither of us could hear what the other said. Then I moved slowly through the crowd, shaking the hand of one person, smiling to another, waving my program to someone else.

I was thinking to myself, "I'm really wrung out." I should have felt elated. These young men of mine had done what no one expected. They had played a superb game against a fine team. It was a shame someone had to lose.

"Gee," I said to myself as I walked slowly through the throng, "if I'm feeling like this after such a beautiful game, maybe it's time to get out."

At that moment, I decided 1974–75 was my last year. When

I finally arrived at the dressing room, I told my players I had decided to retire after the finals on Monday. I wanted them to be the first to know—even before my family.

It was, in a sense, a sudden decision, but in another way it wasn't. Previously, I had considered the possibility of retirement at the end of this season, but up until then it had just been a thought.

As I have since reflected, I have realized that something else may have also influenced my decision—possibly even unconsciously. A year or so before that, the NCAA Basketball Tournament Committee had passed a rule that at tournament time coaches would have to give the media access to the dressing rooms. I was opposed to that rule because I always felt it wasn't fair to the players, coaches, and other support people to allow the press into an area that was already overcrowded. Then, too, the press usually were interested in talking to only two or three of the players, and the others were left out. It just had never seemed to me that all the hubbub was in the best interest of the team as a whole—and a coach is responsible for the morale of everybody involved. So I had always spoken out in vigorous opposition against allowing the press in the dressing rooms before or immediately following the games.

When the chairman of the committee had announced the passing of the rule he had said, "That will take care of John Wooden." That attitude really hurt me, as I had always tried to be cooperative with both the committee and the press. However, I still feel that closed dressing rooms are in the best interest of the players.

I had determined years before that when I retired I wanted to leave UCLA with outstanding talent. I didn't believe it would be fair either to my successor or to the university to leave behind a "bare cupboard." I had seen that happen elsewhere, and I had wanted to be sure it didn't happen at UCLA. I knew that for the next two or three years UCLA was going to be in excellent shape because of the new players that would be coming in and the returning members of the squad. So I felt all right about leaving the team in someone else's hands.

I could have coached for three more years before mandatory retirement, but I've never faulted the decision I made that evening. It was right, and it was timely. The season was finished on an upbeat; we had won our tenth NCAA championship. And don't they say something perfect is a 10?

30

The journey is greater than the inn.

SINCE MY RETIREMENT from active coaching at UCLA in 1975, I have spent a great deal of time speaking at basketball clinics for coaches and teaching the sport to young people at my summer camps. Both are enriching experiences for me in many ways, because it gives me the opportunity to see my old friends still working as teacher/coaches and make new friends with the young people that come to my camps each summer.

But I've always enjoyed the luxury of doing some reflecting, such as my regular self-criticism after each of my seasons as a coach. Not that I live in the past—far from it. My thoughts are on the present and even the future as I approach my eighth decade. At the same time, though, what many of us are today, irrespective of age, is a combination of the events, the experiences, and the people who help make up our past. All of this shapes our thoughts, and our thoughts shape our future actions.

As I write this, in 1988, reflecting back to my first coaching assignment at Dayton, Kentucky in 1932 and my last experience at UCLA in 1975, I have no desire to take off on a nostalgia binge. This is no ode to the "good old days." Instead, I want to share my feelings about certain trends, events, and people as a means of help and encouragement to young men and women who are just getting started and who are reading this book for the first time.

Of course, there are some who have read the book many times. One of those is Gary Carter, a catcher with the New York Mets. He was born in Southern California and was an excellent all-around athlete at Sunnyhills High School in Fullerton, the city that produced the famed Walter (Big Train) Johnson. Car-

198

ter was the captain of his high school football, basketball, and baseball teams in both his junior and senior years. He signed a letter of intent to play football at UCLA in 1972 but decided to sign a professional baseball contract with Montreal. Gary graduated in the top 50 out of a class of 550 and had a 3.40 grade-point average.

We first met while I was flying east and Gary was seated beside me. He told me he had read *They Call Me Coach.* Later I learned that he traveled with a copy of it throughout the baseball season, reading certain segments before each game. The last time a friend saw him reading the book in the clubhouse, it was dog-eared from his constantly thumbing through it.

The fact that he had read the book pleased me. The fact that he read it almost daily flattered me. My objective in writing it was not so much to recite a history of my coaching career but to emphasize to readers the teaching role all coaches play in working with young people.

Before going any further, though, I want to make some additional comments about my retirement from active coaching at UCLA. Possibly if my duties could have been restricted to just coaching basketball behind the scenes, I wouldn't have retired when I did. The NCAA title we captured in San Diego in 1975 was our tenth championship in twelve years, and we had a powerful momentum going in our basketball program. The future looked bright.

However, I had begun to feel the presence of the limelight and the crowds of people. This is not to say that I don't like and need people; I do. I've always deeply appreciated the recognition from the fans that comes with success in my profession. As the years passed, though, the pressure of the crowds at our regular season games and especially at our championship tournaments began to disturb me greatly. I found myself getting very uncomfortable and anxious to get away from it all.

Perhaps my feelings crystallized after we defeated Kentucky in 1975, 92–85, in the Final Four. One of our most visible boosters suddenly appeared beside me on the floor as we awaited the awards ceremony. He grabbed my hand, shaking it warmly, and yelled in my ear over the roar of the crowd: "It was a great victory, John." Then he added, "After you let us down last year." Needless to say, I was shocked. Only minutes before we had won our tenth NCAA championship, and his memory was only of our 80–77 loss to North Carolina State in double overtime in the 1974 semi-finals.

Furthermore, I had been surprised to find out that the more championships you win, the more criticism you receive, the more suspicious people are of you, the more there is expected of you, the less appreciation there is of what has been accomplished, and the less personal satisfaction you have. In many ways my experience reflected the words of Cervantes: "The journey is greater than the inn."

These were certainly key factors in my 1975 decision, and I must say that I have not for one moment regretted retiring from my teaching position at UCLA. I use the word *teacher* purposely, because I've always considered a coach to be a teacher; the only difference is that he is teaching a particular sport rather than English or chemistry or philosophy. I do believe, however, that a teacher/coach has a better opportunity than the regular classroom teacher to build cooperative values and the acceptance of responsibility. Furthermore, I believe most coaches—not all—attempt to do that.

Happily, my activities since formal retirement have still been associated with basketball in one way or another. A big difference is that now it is by personal choice and not out of necessity or duty. I do these things that I enjoy, and I'm not burdened with that part of basketball that was becoming a chore. This is one of the small rewards of retirement.

I still speak at a number of coaching clinics across the nation under the auspices of the McGregor Sports Education Coaching Clinics. At times I wonder aloud to the folks at McGregor if I really should still do this kind of speaking. I always have the question in my own mind whether what I have to offer now might be passé. But they continue to reassure me that, according to their annual polls, I'm right at the top of the list of speakers requested for the next year. That is very gratifying.

Another thing I have truly enjoyed since retirement is speaking at business and sales conventions and seminars across the nation and in several foreign countries—Mexico, Canada, Australia, New Zealand, Spain, Belgium, France, Germany, and England among them.

One of the pleasures of such assignments was having Nellie along as we went from place to place, enjoying the luxury of visiting unusual and lovely places in our country and foreign spots. But after a lengthy illness, Nellie passed away on March 21, 1985. For me it was the ultimate tragedy. The girl I had known for most of my life was no longer beside me. We would have celebrated our fifty-third anniversary on August 8, 1985. Now I live with fond memories and do my best to carry on in life as she would want me to.

One thing that has helped me during the years without Nellie is the number of bright, interesting young people who come to my summer camps at California Lutheran College in Thousand Oaks. We share the facilities at times with the Dallas Cowboys. We accept campers who will be entering the third grade in September up through the eleventh grade, and place them in groups compatible with their age, size, and ability. I especially enjoy working with the beginners.

What an interesting activity; each group is different and has an appealing makeup. I feel the greatest value for young people coming to my camp is not how much basketball they learn but the association they have with all the others in the camp. Being away from home for the first time teaches many how to get along with others. We insist on all being courteous and polite to each other and on their taking advantage of the opportunity to make new friends.

We stress conduct, attitude, and attention in every session of the week-long camps. Our subject is not just basketball. We try to develop the full personality, just like I insisted on at every place I taught basketball. We believe the youngsters should be neat in their dress, keep their rooms in order, bus their dishes after each meal, and maintain proper decorum in their rooms, and we insist they listen attentively to instructors.

All these things, in my opinion, are more valuable to them as people than the basketball instruction they receive. In our concept of teaching basketball we begin with the simple rudiments of how to dress: how to put on their socks, how to tie their shoelaces, and how to prepare for our daylong sessions.

Basketball instruction is directed to the simple fundamentals of the game. It begins with the position of the feet and maintaining good body balance. We spend a lot of time on that to hopefully get the campers to understand the messages that come from the brain to their feet.

I have told all who apply that if their main objective is to play games or be entertained, they should not come to my camp. Our emphasis is on teaching the quick and proper execution of the fundamentals and on being considerate of others. I consider, the playing of games a small segment of my camps. I firmly believe it is the least important part of what we teach.

I believe—and always have—that a player must first have mental and emotional balance in order to have the proper body balance essential to the quick execution of the fundamentals. All three make the whole. Body balance is controlled by the extremities—hands, feet, and head, with all joints flexed and relaxed. We stress the many fundamentals necessary to make a good basketball player within the human limits each possesses. I really don't expect too many of them to make a great mark in the sport. I feel, however, that they can have a solid base that will enable them to understand the game in later years, when they might attain some stature or just be a spectator with a good feel for the nuances of basketball.

We emphasize half-court fundamental work rather than scrimmages, although some competitive games are played. In those games, however, I try very hard to keep the coaches working with me from getting carried away. It doesn't matter whether they outscore the other team or not. I want to see if the campers are practicing what they've learned about the principles of proper body balance in the execution of the fundamentals, and about team balance, both offensively and defensively. I want to see if they are floating off on defense and playing a team defense, and not just running around trying to steal the ball from someone. I want players to always be in a helping situation, whether on offense or defense. We try to do away with as much dribbling as possible. We do not permit a full-court press when we do have games, and we encourage field goals to come from the end of a pass rather than at the end of a dribble.

I have repeated time and again at each of my camps that never, under any situation, is it our goal to make a young man into a star. The Lord makes stars. What we can do is help someone make a squad at his high school or junior high that he might not have made. We can help someone become a starter on the team who might not be able to do it on his own.

But stars, no. Not that we would hurt a star. If they have the physical ability to begin with and then develop the interest and desire, we might be able to help them. Those lacking in God-given skills can never attain so-called star status from our camp, but we can help bring about improvement at every level if they are attentive and industrious.

Of the hundreds of youngsters who have attended our camps since they began as day affairs at Pacific Palisades High School in the summer of 1963, at least three *have* gone on to gain some recognition nationally. Paul Westphal, who attended our camps for several years, had a fine college career at USC followed by a long career in the NBA, including three years as a first team selection on the All-Star team.

I had hoped that Paul would come to UCLA. I was very disappointed when he enrolled at our crosstown rival, where he made several All-American teams, but I always held him in high esteem. He told a reporter that he selected USC to help end the dominance of UCLA. I am happy to say that such an aspiration did not materialize.

Greg Lee, whose father played basketball at UCLA before my time, came to several of my camps. Greg was an excellent student and played on our UCLA championship teams of 1972 and 1973, and on our 1974 team which lost to the champions, North Carolina State, in a double overtime semi-final game. Ralph Drollinger, another camper and a fine student, played in 1974, 1975, and 1976, and was on our title team in my final year. He played a great game in our NCAA championship game against Kentucky in 1975. This was especially gratifying because it was played in his hometown, San Diego.

I guess I am an exception to the rule, but I have never been in favor of the all-star camps that have swept the nation in recent years. I think summer camps should be teaching camps. I want campers to leave with a better understanding of the great game of basketball. I never said no to a star-to-be like Westphal, Lee, or Drollinger, but stars were never stressed at any of my camps even when we had such campers. Those the Lord has given great natural ability can become stars or even superstars, but I don't think camps should be directed to their development.

Many parents have sent their children back to camp year after year even though they did not have the potential to become players, let alone stars, in high school or college. I can honestly say that the greatest satisfaction and pleasure I have gotten from my camps is feedback from parents. They tell me that their children were more considerate at home after a camp, that they kept their rooms cleaner and in better order while doing chores like making up their beds. I definitely feel that is one of the goals we set at our camps.

I feel one reason for such reactions is the discipline we establish from hour one. We have a coach and counselor for every fifteen campers. In my initial talk to each group, I stress that we are guests at Cal Lutheran: we tolerate no littering anywhere on campus; I tell our campers to stay on the sidewalks and not create any new pathways across the grass, although it is difficult for youngsters to understand this when they see older people doing those things; we expect politeness and decorum in the cafeteria; and there is to be no teasing or harassing fellow campers. I want them to make new friends—not just buddy around with the ones they came to camp with. I tell them not to throw their old friends aside, but since they are going to be together when they get home, take advantage of the opportunity to make new ones.

We have had a few altercations over the years, but never anything of a serious nature. I can't recall anything you would actually term a fight. We are very strict about that, as well as about the language they use.

The campers should leave with pleasant memories of their experience. They get an individual color photo taken with me and a photo of their group. When they arrive they also get a fundamentals book that they can take home, as well as a camp T-shirt and a pair of basketball shoes.

Twice during the week we bring in guest speakers, usually after lunch on Tuesday and Thursday. I also take one session where I speak to them about the Pyramid of Success. Then we also bring a coach to lecture, like Jim Harrick, now at UCLA; Walt Hazzard former UCLA head coach; Steve Patterson from Arizona State, or Gary Cunningham when he coached the Bruins (he now is the athletic director at Fresno State).

We also bring in some of my former players who have gone on to the NBA to talk with the campers. Among them are Jamal Wilkes, Bill Walton, Greg Lee, David Meyers, Sven Nader, and Sidney Wickes.

Essential to the success of the camps are the counselors and workers who work for us. Some have been on the scene for all the years I have done camps for Max Shapiro and Sports World. One, Tom Desotell from Sheboygan, Wisconsin, has had a state championship team. Another regular through the years is Mike Kunstadt from Irving, Texas, who has brought campers who later became counselors and, even later, coaches. Don Showalter from Iowa is another regular. As they always bring their families, I have watched their children grow over the years.

For the past five years we have held a Fantasy Camp for adults. One of these was held on the UCLA campus and the others have been held at Pepperdine University's beautiful Malibu campus, overlooking the Pacific. The Fantasy Camp is for adult men from almost every profession. It stretches over a long weekend, from Friday morning to Sunday afternoon.

All participants have one thing in common: a highly dedicated interest in basketball. Some were frustrated players. Some were decent players who want to know all the nuances of my coaching concepts. I think they have spread the age bracket from 29 to 70. A lot of them played high school basketball. A few played in college. None that I can recall are of great renown, but all have a love of the sport with a desire to learn more about it.

One consideration is made for this group. Because of their average age and the short period of the camp we do not work them as hard as we would, say, the top level of high school juniors. Very few of them are aware of the basic drills, although those who are repeaters have a better understanding of the fundamentals. We have a lot of sessions where they just ask questions. Many want to know about the style of play some of the famous coaches used against the Bruins in title years. Others want to know about various players for UCLA or one of our big rivals. They want to know what my ball control is or my deep penetration game, how we run the various presses, how we counter teams that hold the ball on us, how I work with various personalities, how I maintain discipline, and so on.

We limit the number of participants to fifty, and one man has been at all of the adult camps. One year Max Shapiro registered fifty-four, and instead of having last minute dropouts, they all showed up. Another year we held the number to fifty, and ten or eleven dropped out. Each day begins with an early breakfast and runs into evening time.

One day we bring in members from our 1964 NCAA championship team. We have had the likes of Walt Hazzard, Gail Goodrich, Jack Hirsch, Fred Slaughter, Keith Erickson, and Kenny Washington. Kenny has been out every year, and he looks just like he did in 1964.

We bring the 1964 group in for dinner on Saturday night and spread the players around among the group so they will get to talk to them one-on-one. Then we adjourn to the gym and I set up the '64 team to show how they ran the press. After that we put a camp team on defense and the campers try to break the press when they gain possession after a score. We run the adult teams in and out so they all have the experience.

It's quite a test for my old players. The adults love to break the press and, no doubt, go home and tell their friends how they broke the press against the 1964 NCAA championship team. The players are having a little tougher time each year keeping up with multi-groups, but 1964 will always be special to them.

Essentially, the campers are getting a mini-version of what the 1964 team did on a daily basis. I give them a version of the introductory remarks I have given to every team over the years. I cover the more important points, but time doesn't allow me to present what each of my Bruin teams received on the first day every fall.

Each adult, like the youngsters, comes away with mementos of his experience. Each receives a UCLA game sweat suit, jersey, and shorts, a pair of pro-styled shoes, and a copy of *They Call Me Coach,* which I personalize with a message and autograph. They also receive a videotape of various drills and games where they see themselves in action, and excerpts from various philosophy talks and question and answer sessions. These items plus an autographed copy of my Pyramid of Success seem to be greatly enjoyed, but, if I may judge from the comments on the questionnaires we have them fill out, it is the pleasant memories and new associations that are most treasured.

Surprisingly, I didn't want to do an adult camp. Max had to talk me into doing it. I have found that I enjoy it very much and have been surprised at adults' interest level and their desire to learn the intricate aspects of a college basketball program.

How long will the camps continue? I am not sure. I have told Max to put in his 1988 brochures that this will probably be my last year of summer camps. However, if I am up to it physically, I will continue. It is all a question of whether my arthritic knees will allow me to do all the standing that is required. I don't want to be a figurehead. I want to be as active as I have been over the years, and that will depend on my health and the good Lord.

31

The harvest of old age is the recollection and abundance of blessings previously secured.

My life has been exceedingly full since I walked off the San Diego Arena court for the last time on March 29, 1975. I've truly enjoyed what I've been doing and have not looked back with any regret. I've probably most enjoyed keeping an eye on what's been going on in the game of basketball. I follow the sport with as much intensity as I ever did as an active coach. My interest level has never waned.

Frequently, in conversations both with my peers in the coaching profession and with basketball fans, I am asked if there are any developments and trends in today's game that concern me. I always try to approach such questions from a positive point of view. To be honest, however, I do have certain concerns that I want to share briefly.

First, while I firmly believe the players get better and better with each passing year, I am not sure we are seeing a constant improvement in team play. Tremendous individual ability has produced more one-on-one basketball, but somehow that seems to take some of the beauty away from team play. It tends to produce grandstand players who are obsessed with showmanship.

Perhaps this showmanship is epitomized by the various dunkshots. Some are marvels of aerial gymnastics. But how often do they miss those dunks—the ball ricocheting off the rim or the board and setting up a fast-break basket the other way?

I feel that if I were actively coaching today, I would discourage the use of dunkshots in most situations. I am sure there would be great consternation among the players, but the goal is to minimize mistakes and play to our potential. When you blow an easy two points with an errant dunk, and your opponent turns the break into a basket, there has been a four-point swing. I don't like such swings.

I've always been opposed to showboating. I rarely permitted the use of the behind-the-back passing and dribbling that the late Pete Maravich was so good at. If I were coaching today, there would be minimal use of either on my teams. I feel this aspect of the game has been so amplified by the professional game and television, that it has even trickled down to the high school and college ranks.

Although I would be the first to agree that television has contributed greatly to the increased popularity of the sport and has enriched all aspects of it financially, I also feel that the presence of the cameras encourages individual showmanship on the court at the expense of the true beauty of the sport.

After all, the opportunity to be seen by millions on regional or national television is pretty heady stuff. The temptation to concentrate on one's own performance, instead of giving attention to the quick and proper execution of the fundamentals within a team framework, can be very strong.

You constantly hear references to television. When some young man from the West Coast opts to enroll at a Big East, Southeast, or Atlantic Coast Conference institution that "gets more national TV exposure," it suggests that the exposure enhances the player's opportunities at the professional level. It appears today that a college education is a distant second or even third to a pro career. Yet less than one percent of college basketball players ever have a successful pro career.

Nevertheless, each one believes he can be another Kareem Abdul-Jabbar, Larry Bird, Magic Johnson, or Michael Jordan. All forget that the good Lord gave those men superb talent that, when combined with their intense dedication to the game, has made them into almost one-of-a-kind models. I believe young people, basketball players included, should have role models— but they should be realistic. Every once in a while I will overhear some young college player talking about beating Magic Johnson in a summer pickup game in Pauley Pavilion. I almost have to bite my tongue to avoid pointing out that the *real* Magic Johnson was not out on that floor. The real one stands up in the NBA against a Larry Bird or a Michael Jordan. There is a great difference. Young college men find it difficult to realize this, and consequently more often than not live to see their dreams shattered.

In my judgment, one of the reasons for the success of the Los Angeles Lakers is that, while they have great individual players like Magic and Kareem, Coach Pat Riley has been able to instill a team concept as the governing demand. Yet, within the environment of the Lakers' superb team concept, these great players are able to display their unique skills. Few professional coaches have achieved this blend and balance as Riley has.

Showmanship has become almost an essential part of the game—too important in my opinion. I think the emphasis on showmanship is subconscious on the coach's part, and perhaps subconscious on the part of the players. But there is definitely too much emphasis. You seldom see a star player in the NBA called for carrying the ball, even when carrying is done consistently. You seldom see traveling called—as it should be—when they come in to make a fancy dunk. Most players travel if they are dunking at the end of a dribble.

You see the traveling time after time, especially when they rerun the slam dunk in slow motion. It is instantly obvious. I don't think it is good for the game. It makes for bad habits in high school and college ranks. We'd have a better game without it.

Another thing that concerns me about the way television has affected basketball is that it seems to have brought on a change in coaching style. Like some of the players, many coaches are becoming performers. Their dress and antics are styled for the cameras. I believe this is a diversion that takes something away from the game. The fans come to watch players, not coaches. Hopefully, this is a fad that will pass in the interest of the game, but as the years pass on I haven't seen any halt of coaches' sideline antics. Nor have I seen strict enforcement of the coaches' box. Once coaches step out of those boundaries they should be warned. The next time it should be a technical foul. I doubt if many would test a second excursion and face banishment.

I am equally disturbed by the way television seems to regulate the scheduling of games. We now find that collegiate basketball is played at almost any hour of the day and night on every day of the week. I have always been opposed to playing intercollegiate and interscholastic games on Sunday—even though I did play some—and I doubt if I will ever change in that regard. It is not that I am a religious fanatic; the student athlete just needs that day off.

I'm waiting for a game in Los Angeles to be switched to a 7 A.M. Sunday start so East Coast cities will have a 10 A.M. game to watch during breakfast. Or maybe a midnight start for prime time in the Pacific Islands. It's all ridiculous.

I also object strenuously to the way games are spread out over the week. Our Pac 10 teams, UCLA and USC, may leave here to play a Thursday game in Northern California or the Northwest. Maybe one will play a second game Saturday afternoon and the other on Sunday. Oregon came down here one year to play USC on a Thursday then had to wait over until Sunday afternoon to play UCLA. That means they didn't get back to Eugene until Sunday night, five days away from the academic environment. They could just as well have played on Saturday, except for the consideration of a TV game on Sunday afternoon.

In all the years I coached we played mainly on Friday and Saturday in our conference. I saw nothing wrong with that schedule then. I see nothing wrong with it now. Only television dictates schedules that require a five-day absence from classes. Have the university and college presidents lost all perspective on what these students are here for? Isn't that objective still an education? Aren't all sports a distant second?

Along with that, the game philosophy has been altered by the mandatory TV time-outs. They're prefaced in many arenas with the announcement, "There is time-out on the floor." That's for TV. I have wondered a time or two if we might not have one for the *Los Angeles Times* or maybe the Associated Press, so a writer can catch up on the action.

These time-outs can easily break game continuity and team momentum. And they do. Time and again you see crucial sequences where one or the other team is on a run and the TV clock takes command and halts play. So important have these commercial breaks become, that the rules committee has even changed the number of time-outs in a game to coincide with the needs of television. This definitely alters the flow of the game and is much more detrimental to college basketball than college football.

I am fully aware of what television means to every institution in terms of dollars available to support all athletic programs. Without TV income, many of the non-income programs for both men and women would have to be cut. Only two sports, as a rule, produce income—football and basketball—and the income producers are responsible for funding the rest.

Before I leave the matter of television's impact on collegiate basketball, I want to react to the present sums of money being paid out in the NCAA championship tournament that we all refer to as the Final Four. I am concerned about what the event is becoming.

The four teams in the Final Four in 1987 each received $1,056,027 out of a total distribution to all 64 participants of $26,189,456. Television money has made it so profitable to get to the Final Four, it can cause not just coaches but also presidents and athletic directors to look the other way and let some things go by that they normally wouldn't tolerate.

We all know that too much money in almost any area can be a problem, just as too little can. I don't think that intercollegiate athletics is an exception.

I would like to suggest a resolution to the problem: that the tournament leading up to the NCAA title game be patterned after the Indiana State High School Championship. Every school in the state that is not under disciplinary sanction participates.

It is possible for every team playing NCAA Division I basketball to participate in the championship tournament. Today 64 are invited. They could get to the same 64 teams with one additional weekend.

The perfect pairing would begin with 256 teams. Last year there were 253 teams that shared in the funds. If less than 256 teams participate, some kind of a by-system would have to be worked out. If more, an elimination round might be necessary. Starting out with 256 entries, the first round would trim the field to 128. The next round would reduce the teams to the 64 that we now have.

Unlike the NCAA's present distribution, all 256 teams in Division I would get a share with additional shares being added on for every victory. Take the 1987 distribution of $26,189,456 and let's round it off to $26 million.

After the first round, there are going to be 128 survivors. Each of the losers in the first round will get one share of $51,792 or a total of $6,629,482 divided among them.

Now the 128 play in the second round and after that you have 64 losers and 64 winners. Those 64 who were eliminated would get two shares each for a total of 128 shares. Those 64 losers will get $103,585 each for a total of $6,629,482.

We're now down to 32 and after this round, the 16 losers will each get three shares or a total of 96 shares worth $155,378 each and a grand total for that round of $4,972,111.

Now the field is down to 16 and the eight losers will get four shares each worth $207,171 for a total of 64 shares for a grand total of $3,314,741.

There are now eight survivors and the four losers will each get five shares worth $258,964 per team or a total of 40 shares totaling $2,071,713.

The semi-finals involving four teams will have two survivors. The losers will each get six shares worth $310,756 or a grand total of $1,243,027.

The loser in the NCAA championship game will get seven shares worth $362,549 which is the total out of the $26,000,000 pot and the champion will get seven shares plus one share for winning or a total of eight shares worth $414,342.

The figures for the final four is considerably less than the $1,056 million each they received in the 1987 classic. However, every single participant in the 256 team bracket got at least $51,792 up to the champion's share of $414,342.

As it was, the 64 participants in the tournament did very well financially. Losers in the first round, according to the *NCAA News;* received $211,205. The second-round losers received

$422,410. Regional semifinalist losers received $633,615. Regional finalist losers received $844,821 and the Final Four each received the $1,056,027.

I admit you can't make comparisons with decades between events. However, when UCLA won its final NCAA title in 1975 in San Diego, each Final Four team received $133,381. I don't think inflation has increased that much. I don't think the hike in dollars is good. And I don't think that the teams which usually make the Final Four really need it. There may be a rare exception, but most programs do very well with their regular season incomes from basketball.

You can be sure that there would be many, many members in Division I who could support their entire basketball program with a first-round loser's share of $51,792.

The dollar figures for the 1987 tournament boggle my mind. The gross receipts, according to the NCAA, came to $49,092,205. Of that, 74.6 percent came from television revenue; 21.6 percent from ticket sales; 2.0 percent from radio rights; and 1.8 percent from other rights. The total attendance in all 1987 tournament games was 654,744, an increase over the 1986 attendance of over 150,000. The average per session was 19,257 attendees, exceeding the 1986 average by 6,433.

Out of the $49,092,205, the NCAA retained $17,459,645 to finance its operations. I can remember talking with our late athletic director, J. D. Morgan, after our historic televised game in the Houston Astrodome with the University of Houston. He was very enthused about the future television income for the Final Four. All of his dreams have been far surpassed with the income of 1987.

I think that having every Division I team participate would eliminate another major objection I have to the selection process as it exists today. I think it has totally taken away from the various conference races across the nation. Some teams get in the tournament with more losses than victories. Many get in with nearly double-digit losses. UCLA in 1980 finished fourth in the conference and had eight losses, yet it made the Final Four. If teams with records like that—and UCLA's record was better than some since—then all Division I teams not on probation should be included in the tournament.

Can you imagine the interest that would sweep the nation when 256 of the Division I institutions began to take their shot at the national championship? I think the attendance would mushroom. TV income would be increased since there would have to be regional games. And just think—3,840 men in years to come could tell their grandchildren that they played for the national basketball championship.

The distribution of the funds might possibly help to sustain a well-rounded athletic program for men and women on every campus. I personally feel there should be no distinction between sports, as sometimes happens at schools that give different letters for major sports vs. minor sports. Every sport is major to the participants. I, for one, used to enjoy many of the non-income-producing sports on campus at UCLA. I found them all enjoyable to watch, and I felt it took great athletic skill to play them.

I remember when Keith Erickson, off our first NCAA championship team and one of the finest athletes I ever coached, elected not to try out for the 1964 Olympic basketball team. Keith had grown up on the beach at El Segundo and was a brilliant volleyball player. He tried out for the U.S. volleyball team and played in Tokyo. Do you think Keith considered volleyball a minor sport? No, sir! It was a tough game as shown then, and it has developed to phenomenal standards today.

Since my retirement, there have been two major rule changes that have had a great impact on basketball. One is the adoption of the 45-second clock and the other is the three-point shot. I believe that the clock has definitely been good for the game. It has eliminated that occasional farcical game where two teams with outstanding talent have been known to play a 7–5, or once a 3–2, game. They were playing within the rules, but I think it was a mistake for the rules committee not to take care of that situation.

The adoption of the 45-second clock has eliminated those types of games. At the same time, however, it has not forced the coach whose philosophy is ball control basketball to change his style of game. I am quite certain that one of the great coaches of the game, Hank Iba, would have had no problem with the 45-second clock.

As a matter of fact, while I was a member of the rules committee in the 1960s, a survey checked Iba's teams and they seldom,
if ever, violated a 30-second clock—and then only when it was
late in the game and they were protecting a lead.

I would not have favored a time clock if it forced teams to play
a certain type of basketball or prohibited them from playing their
coaches' preferred style. That's also why I think it would be
wrong to bar the zone defense. I don't think zone defenses have
had any particular impact now that we have the clock.

Now the three-point shot, which I wasn't totally in favor of,
has added a very exciting dimension to our game. I feel that
19′9″ is entirely too close for college basketball. I would have
liked to have them try a 20′ line for high schools, 22′ 6″ for colleges, and 25′ for the pros. Then a three-point shot would be
more meaningful. I believe it is far more difficult and notewor-
thy for a team using their set offense to work the ball inside to
get a close shot than it is for someone to cast off from 19′9″ and
hit. It seems to me that if you worked the ball in to where you
got a lay-up, maybe that would be worth three points.

Since the rule has only been in one season, I wouldn't want
to take a stand either for or against it although I feel 19′9″ is
just too close.

The last thing I want in making these observations is to sound
negative. I'm a positive thinker from the very core of my being.
But to make television and money such an important part of basketball goes against so much of what I stand for in intercollegiate
sports. I feel our first objective is to educate and build responsible
young men and women. Therefore, it is important that we
model for them the highest educational, social, and moral
values.

A further concern that I have about basketball today is the tendency of officials to permit the game to become excessively
physical. Basketball was meant to be a game of finesse and ma-
neuverability, not a game of brute strength. I am not suggesting
that it be a noncontact game, but merely that excessive contact
should be controlled. As it was originally conceived, basketball
is a beautiful game—almost majestic. It is a game of skill. It can
be argued that a more physical game produces higher scoring.

That may be, and I enjoy that part of it. But the fact remains that championships are usually won by defense.

Frequently, I'm asked about my reaction to changes in the game since the time of my retirement. Actually, I believe, the basic concept of basketball hasn't changed at all. For example, Piggy Lambert, my old coach at Purdue, had a very simple but enormously effective approach to the game. He was decades ahead of his time. Lambert was one of the great teachers of basketball because he felt it was important to work closely with each player. He understood the young men who played for him and knew how to get the best out of them.

Coach Lambert was one of the first men I knew who stressed how important the right mental attitude is to the success of a player and a team. This emphasis was part of his three fundamentals: (1) conditioning—getting a team in the best possible physical and mental shape to play; (2) quick and skilled execution of the fundamentals in an uncomplicated series of offensive and defensive plays; and (3) the development of strong team spirit that included consideration at all times for one's fellow players.

Coach Lambert's emphasis on keeping the game simple is one that greatly influenced my own coaching style. I think that something is lost when the style of coaching and playing fails to be simple. The sheer beauty and grace of the game fades behind complex maneuvering and showmanship.

A present-day example of a coach who insists on an uncomplicated approach to basketball is Bobby Knight of Indiana. It is true that many people criticize him for the way he goes about the business of coaching, but the fact is that Bobby is one of the premier teachers in the game today. He holds to a simple game plan. You always know the style of offense and defense that will be used by his teams—his plays are simple to read. But they will be executed beautifully, and although you may know *what,* you won't know *when.* Bobby Knight keeps the game simple, and yet he is an outstanding success. This could be clearly seen in the performance of the 1984 United States' Olympic team, which he coached. He took a group of superstars and had them playing with the true team concept.

Basketball is not a complicated game, but we coaches complicate it. This, I believe, is a growing problem—a change I hate to see occurring. For example, we coaches try to get involved too much during a game. It seems that players spend too much of their time watching the bench for hand, towel, or card signals that call for a change in offense or defense.

I think the coach's job is to prepare players to play and then let them do it. Failure to prepare is preparing to fail. And the preparation process has to take place before the game, with any needed adjustments made during time-outs and at half time.

Another development that seems to have emerged in very recent years is the emphasis now being placed on substitutions. Over and over again I hear coaches say, "I want to keep them fresh," or "We did not have enough depth."

It seems to me this is just a coaching gimmick. After all, a college basketball game is only forty minutes long, and even that isn't forty minutes of continuous action. Time is spent bringing the ball up court for the set offense, resetting the offense, shooting free throws, stopping for time-outs. These provide frequent breaks in the hard running and battling for the ball off the board. And there is also a fifteen-minute break at the half. I just feel there's something wrong if a young man of nineteen, twenty, or twenty-one who is working out every day can't play at maximum peak through forty minutes of game time.

I remember so well a comment made during our NCAA Final in 1975 against Kentucky by Billy Packer, the television analyst. He said that Kentucky would "wear UCLA down" because I was not substituting and resting my players. But I knew they were in top condition, and at the end of the game I believe most observers would have said that my players were running faster, jumping higher, and executing better than our opposition.

It was my experience that if my players were physically and emotionally fit and were prepared for the game, they could play good basketball for the entire game. So I never went in for the razzle-dazzle of running players on and off the court during the game. Furthermore, I feel that too much substituting disrupts team play.

I have frequently been asked what changes I would make in my style if I were to return to active coaching. While I have no intentions of returning, I have reflected on the question. Frankly, I don't see anything about my coaching philosophy that I would change—or if there *were* changes, they would be minor. I'm sure I would stick to a man-to-man defense with zone principles helping out on the weak side. And I would want my style of offense to fit my personnel and to be a threat from both sides and through the middle, so as to provide balance.

Balance is one of the most important things in basketball—and in life, as well. Some might think that work or concentration or enthusiasm or persistence are more important than balance, but I don't agree. *Balance* is the most important single word for an athlete or coach to keep in mind—even as it is vital for a productive and satisfying life.

Physical balance is controlled by the extremities of the body—the head, feet, and hands. A player must be constantly alert to keeping his feet just wider than his shoulders. His head must be directly above the midpoint between the two feet, and his chin should be up so floor vision will not be impaired. Hands are to be held close to the body on both offense and defense. And all joints should be flexed and relaxed.

But balance for a basketball player involves more than just the physical. It means keeping everything in proper perspective: maintaining self-control . . . never getting emotionally too high or too low because of unexpected good luck or misfortune . . . not permitting things over which you have no control to affect attitudes and actions . . . remaining calm in stressful situations. It also includes the proper handling of academic and social responsibilities.

I also happen to believe it is important for a coach to maintain mental and emotional balance at all times if he or she is to teach well and make productive decisions that will be accepted by everyone. An excitable and uptight coach can throw players out of balance and cause them to lose their winning rhythm.

Recruiting is one aspect of coaching I can honestly say I haven't missed since I retired. It is an activity that some thoroughly enjoy and others heartily detest—I was one of the ones who didn't care for it. But recruiting is necessary for all coaches who hope to compete on a comparatively equal basis at the highest level.

When it came to recruiting I had six basic rules that I strongly believed in and almost always followed:

(1) I never wanted to talk a prospective player into coming to UCLA. It was important to me that they be truly interested in us without having any pressure put on them. I wanted them to want UCLA.

(2) I would not initiate contact with any prospect from outside the Southern California area. And I would not show any active interest in a player without first having a letter from him indicating his desire to come to UCLA.

(3) Whenever possible, I avoided visiting the home of a prospect. As I recall, I broke this rule only twelve times during my twenty-seven years at UCLA. Most of my competitors visited regularly in the homes of their prospects.

(4) I always refused to promise any prospective player that he would become a starter during his first year of eligibility. I felt that the offer of a scholarship was ample proof of my interest in him.

(5) It was against my policy to attend high-school All-Star games or to visit high-school super-star camps.

(6) I always reminded every prospect that during his first and second years there would probably be times when he might think he should have chosen another school. But I also told him that he would probably feel the same way if he *had* gone somewhere else. I tried to impress upon my recruits that their academic progress should always come first, even over basketball, but that basketball should take precedence over good times and social functions.

I always placed a high priority on academic skills when I was recruiting. Throughout my coaching career I would sometimes have to make a choice for a scholarship between two players of almost equal talent. In such cases, the deciding factor to me was grade averages. Academic achievement was always very important to me in my evaluation of a prospect. And if I were recruiting today, I would take an even tougher position than I used to take when it comes to academics. I believe more firmly now than ever before that a college coach should not only search for talent in a given sport—he should also give high priority to high academic ambitions.

My approach to recruiting was somewhat different from that of most coaches, and it sometimes brought me criticism from alumni and disagreement from my assistants. But I believe my recruiting record speaks for itself. Such outstanding players as Lewis Alcindor, Lucius Allen, Henry Bibby, Larry Farmer, Walter Hazzard, Andre McCarter, John Moore, Fred Slaughter, Mike Warren, and Kenny Washington all expressed interest in UCLA without being approached by me first. We never saw any of them play and never visited their homes prior to their decision to enter UCLA. (I did visit Lew Alcindor's home *after* he had made his decision.) I have described how most of these young men were recruited and told something of their success earlier in this book.

Two or three additional recruiting stories really stand out in my memory:

KEITH WILKES: Here is an example of how easy it might be to miss out on a potentially outstanding player. Wilkes expressed an interest in UCLA. After getting his transcript and finding he was an outstanding student, my assistants arranged to see him play.

They returned with a lukewarm opinion. He was rather a frail-looking 6'6" center who played close to the basket. He never showed an outside shot, which he would need as a forward for UCLA, although he had a crazy back over-the-head shot from the free-throw line. On the whole, he hadn't played very well that night.

But after a lengthy discussion, we decided that since Keith was such a fine young man and an outstanding student we would all arrange to watch him play again. And on the next occasion he played very well; we all agreed he was a brilliant prospect. Keith's story proves that seeing a prospect only once may be worse than not seeing him at all!

PLAYER A: This player will be unidentified. He was an outstanding young man with whom I had quite a close relationship, and his grades were very good. On the Saturday before a letter of commitment was to be signed, I had dinner with him and his family. He assured me then without any question that he would be coming to UCLA.

But much to my disappointment, on the following Monday this player signed a letter of intent with a rival in our conference. This was the greatest disappointment I ever had in my recruitment activities. A little later, when newspaper reporters asked him why he had changed his mind, he said that he would rather go to another school and beat UCLA than just help us do what we were doing. And I should add with some bit of satisfaction that this young man never had the pleasure of playing in a winning game against us.

PLAYER B. This is another young man I won't identify. He was an excellent prospect and a good student. His was one of the few homes I visited over the years of my career. While I was chatting with his parents, his mother asked me a question. Before I could answer, the young man interrupted and said, "Mom, how can you be so ignorant? Anyone so stupid should just keep still." I was appalled, although neither parent seemed to take offense at his rudeness.

Very shortly I said that we must be going, and as we left I withdrew our offer of a scholarship. This was just not the kind of young man that I wanted on our team. Admittedly, he went on to a successful career at one of the rival universities in our conference. But I never regretted my decision.

Yes, there are always ups and downs for a head coach in the recruiting process. It is impossible to always guess right 100 percent, but I'm extremely grateful for the high caliber of young men that came to UCLA during my career there, most of whom (over 90 percent of my lettermen) received their college degrees either on time or eventually.

Since my retirement, the Los Angeles Athletic Club has created the John Wooden Award for the college basketball player of the year. I had wanted the trophy to depict six players—five of whom would represent the major skills of the complete basketball player: passing, defense, dribbling, shooting, and rebounding. The sixth figure would exemplify academics—a person in cap and gown holding a degree. I was overruled on that sixth-figure idea, but I'm pleased that to this point all of the winners have completed their college education. They were Marques Johnson, 1977 (UCLA), Phil Ford, 1978 (North Carolina), Larry Bird, 1979 (Indiana State), Darrell Griffith, 1980 (Louisville), Danny Ainge, 1981 (BYU), Ralph Sampson, 1982 and 1983 (Virginia). The 1984 winner, Michael Jordan of North Carolina, decided to turn professional after completing his junior year but has since graduated, as has Chris Mullen, 1985 (St. Johns), Walter Barry, 1986 (St. Johns), Ensign David Robinson, 1987 (Navy), and Danny Manning, 1988 (Kansas).

Without question, there is absolutely nothing more important to a basketball coach than the acquiring of talent. And, happily, there is more raw talent available today than ever before. But the coach must be able to analyze the talent and recruit for his needs. It must be the right kind of talent, and it must be fitted to the coach's particular style and blend with the talent of the other players on the team.

There are coaches who can't win with talent, even as there are those who can win with just certain types of talent. And there are those coaches who have the knack of doing well with the talent available to them. But no coach can win consistently without talent. Now, when I use that term "win consistently," I'm not necessarily talking about winning national championships. I'm referring to coaches who have the gift of developing teams that play close to their potential.

There are many fine coaches for whom I have great respect who never won an NCAA championship or even came close. Tony Hinkle, a dear friend who coached basketball at Butler University in Indianapolis for many years, never won a national championship. But I know of no coach who ever came closer to getting full potential out of the talent available to him. He played a tough schedule year after year and probably won about 60 percent of his games, but I believe there are very few coaches who would have done as well with the talent that was available to Tony.

There is an art to putting a basketball squad together. It is what separates the winners from the losers. But again I have to say that whoever the coach might be, if he doesn't have the right talent, no amount of skill in the world will produce the desired results.

Every coach gets tremendous satisfaction out of every team with which he works, no matter what level of competition is involved. But sometimes the satisfaction comes in ways no one would expect. In looking back over my UCLA teams and naming the ones that gave the greatest personal satisfaction, I often surprise people by my choices.

The first I want to mention was my 1948 team. I had come to UCLA from Indiana State on a three-year contract. My Indiana team had done well, even playing in the National Association of Intercollegiate Athletics championship game. And I wanted to get off to a good start at UCLA. But when practice began in October I began to have second thoughts about the move. At the time, basketball was second class in Los Angeles. Interest was very low, and there was no field house or arena. As I analyzed the UCLA teams on game films, I could see that the team I had left behind at Indiana would have taken them apart without any trouble.

Our team that year was picked unanimously to finish last in the Southern Division of the Pacific Coast Conference—the same spot they had been in the year before. But as practice went on, I began to see some improvement. We changed the style of play, and that seemed to change the attitude of the players for the better. There was some talent in the squad, and they began to work together. We went on to win twenty-two games and the Southern Division title. Winning as we did after being picked to finish last gave me a great deal of personal satisfaction.

The 1962 team stands out next in my memory. At the start this wasn't a particularly good team, but by the end of the year we had made remarkable improvement and were among the very best. That year Walt Hazzard was a sophomore guard, and was probably more responsible that anyone else for our making it to the Final Four for the first time. The improvement in this team over the course of the season was very gratifying to me, especially as they gave me my first trip to the all-important Final Four and had an excellent chance to win it all.

Next, we jump to my first championship team in 1964. This was my first undefeated season. What we lacked in size, we made up in quickness. This was the finest pressing team I ever had. As a matter of fact, I believe it was the best pressing team I have ever seen!

The same five players started every game. Jack Hirsch at 6'3" was one forward—an outstanding competitor. Keith Erickson at 6'5" was the other forward. Keith was probably one of the most competitive athletes I have ever seen, and the finest when it came to natural athletic ability. He was a natural in most any sport and made the 1964 Olympic team in volleyball.

Our center was Fred Slaughter, and our guards were Hazzard and Goodrich. Gail Goodrich was another spirited competitor and a fine shooter. The other two whom I brought in off the bench were Doug McIntosh and Kenny Washington, two first-year men with an abundance of enthusiasm. McIntosh backed up Slaughter at center. He came in against Duke after about eight minutes of play and played most of the rest of that championship game. Washington, who I used at either forward or guard, also had a tremendous game against Duke. He finished with 26 points, one less than Goodrich. Slaughter went unappreciated by many, but he played his role well and his talents blended well with those of his teammates.

I'll jump ahead now to 1970, to the squad I dubbed "the team without." Without what? Without Lewis Alcindor. During Lewis's college career we expected to win as long as he stayed healthy and didn't foul out. But this first team after his graduation had to prove they could do it without him. And they did.

Many of the games that season were very close. I often said that if they could somehow stay close for thirty-five minutes, somehow they'd find a way to win in the last five minutes. This happened many times.

There were some fine players on the 1970 team: Sidney Wicks, Curtis Rowe, Steve Patterson, John Vallely, and Henry Bibby. These men had a big part in offsetting the comment made by several coaches: "When Alcindor is gone, UCLA will get their comeuppance." Happily for us, it didn't work that way. And as I think about that team now and about the way they overcame the odds against them (including the fact that nobody expected them to win when they went into the tournament), I get a very warm feeling.

The fifth team I am including here was my last one as an active coach. Pre-season polls indicated they had little chance for the championship, and several teams were rated much more highly. But as the season progressed, this fine group of men proved themselves in an amazing fashion.

This was also a "team without"—without Bill Walton. Actually, only David Meyers was back from the previous year's starting five. But every man on the team was anxious to prove to himself and to the world that they could be winners on their own. In addition to David Meyers, the starting team was composed of Marques Johnson, Richard Washington, Pete Trgovich, and Andre McCarter. All of them were fine, young Christian men, and to see them capture a championship was a wonderful experience. But I would have felt the same way about them even if they hadn't been winners on the court. Winning just adds a little extra to my glow.

As the years pass, people continue to ask me to select an allstar team from among those I've coached. And my answer today is the same as it has always been—no. There is no way I can pick such a team and do justice to all the fine players who played under me over the years. I was very fortunate. We had a number of great, great players. That's illustrated by the All-Americans—seventeen individuals who won honors twenty-four times. Eleven men I coached at UCLA were first-round selections in the National Basketball Association draft, and quite a few more went on to play professionally. And there were many others who blended in with those superior players to make a number of great teams.

While I will never select an all-time team or even an all-time squad, I will say that Lewis Alcindor (Kareem Abdul-Jabbar) is the most valuable player I ever coached. I believe he caused his opponents more difficulties both on offense and defense than any other player in the history of the game. And I would choose Bill Walton as the second most valuable player I ever had. Bill probably could do more things than Kareem, although he was not the dominant force that Lewis was.

Mike Warren from South Bend Central was probably as smart a player as I ever coached. Mike was our floor leader for three years. He proved that there is a place in basketball for the little man. (A theater arts major, Mike went on to star in the hit television series, "Hill Street Blues.") Lewis Alcindor was on the team for two of Mike's three years as floor leader, and they formed a blend of talent that worked beautifully. But, again, balance is important, for neither five Alcindors nor five Mike Warrens would make a great team by themselves.

Walt Hazzard, former UCLA head coach, was certainly one of the finest floor leaders I ever coached, and I never had a more spirited and aggressive guard than Gail Goodrich. Keith Erickson, who probably wouldn't be selected by others as one of our all-time great forwards, made a tremendous contribution to our first two national championship teams. Like many, Keith had a true value that could not be measured statistically.

I can't think of a nicer young man than Keith Wilkes—a delightful person and a good student who never seemed to have a problem on or off the floor. And then there was David Meyers, a spirited player who played basketball every second as if his whole life depended on it. And I also think of other players, such as Conrad Burke, who wasn't an All-American but who came about as close to realizing his full potential as any player I ever coached. Doug McIntosh was another like Burke. Doug wouldn't make any all-time team, but he gave himself to the game and was a valuable contributor.

Sidney Wicks was an outstanding competitor, one you would like to have to take the last shot in a crucial situation. Curtis Rowe was one of the most consistent players I ever coached; he never had an off game. Eddie Sheldrake was a great hustler on the court and an inspiration to every player on and off the court. And another great competitor was George Stanich—a bonus pitcher, a medal winner in the 1948 Olympic Games, an All-American guard. I get great joy remembering him.

But when I start mentioning names like this, where do I stop? It is so easy to forget and overlook great young men such as Dick Banton and Don Johnson and Don Bragg. And then there were Walt Torrance and Jack Hirsch and John Green and Gary Cunningham and on and on. . . .

There are so many. In my book, every man who played for me fits somewhere on my all-time team. Every one played an important role.

So . . . I will rest with my memories of all the men who played basketball for me—men whom I appreciate more with each passing day.

32

Serenity is ever with those who are considerate of and courteous to others.

JUDGING FROM THE questions asked of me most often since my retirement from active coaching, there is little difference between the average fan, writer, and broadcaster. Sooner or later they all get around to subjects that I will comment on.

Who was the best player you ever coached?

Of course, I refuse to answer that with a single name because too many factors are involved for me to give a valid answer. However, I do say, and have said, that Kareem Abdul-Jabbar, then Lew Alcindor, was the most valuable player I ever had under my supervision. Bill Walton might be considered the best, if all areas of the game were added up on the basis of one to ten for each. But Kareem posed a greater problem for an opponent at each end of the court than did Bill.

They were both very intelligent, unselfish team players—hard working, exceptionally quick and maneuverable for their height, and far more interested in the team results than in individual statistics. Less gifted players, such as Doug McIntosh, usually come closer to realizing their full potential than the unusually gifted, but I am not sure that would be true of Kareem and Bill.

Furthermore, less talented players may be more valuable on certain teams because of the characteristics and abilities of their teammates. For example, Keith Erickson, one of the most spirited and finest athletes that I have ever had, and Jack Hirsch, a long-armed and competitive "big play" player, teamed up exceptionally well with Hazzard, Goodrich, and Slaughter for our undefeated NCAA champions in 1964. However, Sidney

Wicks, who was very talented—being tall, quick, and strong—
fit in better with Curtis Rowe and Steve Patterson than would
either Erickson or Hirsch.

Keith Wilkes was one of the very finest all-around players and
persons that a coach could have, both on and off the court. He
would fit in well at any time with any group, as would Willie
Naulls, who had a fine pro career and was probably my finest
and most recognizable player in the 1950s. No forward was ever
more responsible for leading UCLA to a National Championship than was David Meyers of my 1975 and last team. He truly
led by example. I am certain this rubbed off to some degree on
our two young and promising forwards, Marques Johnson and
Richard Washington.

Yet, it would not be right to overlook the guards when considering my best or most valuable players. Consider the following:

—WALT HAZZARD was the best ball-handling and passing guard
I ever had, as well as being very competitive.

—GAIL GOODRICH, another fiery competitor, may have been my
best at working without the ball, as well as being a great shooter.

—MIKE WARREN was as smart a player as I ever saw play and ex-
celled in all the fundamentals of the sport.

—LUCIUS ALLEN possessed all the physical qualifications one
could expect in a guard from both an offensive and a defensive
point of view.

—HENRY BIBBY, along with Dick Banton, was perhaps the best
defensive guard I ever had and would have been a sensation if
the three-point rule had been in effect in his time.

It is quite possible that under different circumstances or in
another era, such guards as George Stanich, Don Johnson,
Eddie Sheldrake, John Green, Don Bragg, Morris Taft, and
others would be considered among the best.

What was your best team?

How could I honestly say which was truly the best team when

I had ten National Championship teams, four of which, 1964, 1967, 1972, and 1973 were undefeated, and three of which, 1968, 1969, and 1971 lost only one game? I am proud of the fact that my 1964 team, with no starter over 6'5", went undefeated and will probably always be the shortest ever to win the NCAA. I am proud of my 1967 team, the most inexperienced team ever to win the championship—with only one year of varsity experience among the starting five. My 1975 team also would have to be considered, as it won the championship after losing two superstars—Walton and Wilkes—and both starting guards from 1974.

Many coaches have expressed the opinion that my 1969 team was the best, even though we lost to Houston in the much publicized game in the Astrodome. We did destroy Houston in the semifinal of the NCAA tournament later in the year, leading by as much as 44 points early in the second half.

The following factors did tend to make my 1969 team an extremely difficult team to play:

Center: Alcindor/Abdul-Jabbar, the most dominant collegiate player of all time in my opinion. An intelligent, graceful, quick, and maneuverable 7'2", unselfish, and a superstar in every sense of the word. The only center to lead his team to three consecutive NCAA championships.

Forward: Lynn Shackelford, at 6'5" an excellent shooter from the corner, who complemented Abdul-Jabbar in the low post very well.

Forward: Mike Lynn, a 6'7" outstanding shooter, with the quickest and finest hands in and around the basket that I ever had.

Guard: Mike Warren, as smooth, smart, and intelligent a player as I have ever coached. Well-versed in all fundamentals, who could drive, shoot from the outside, or merely direct the play.

Guard: Lucius Allen, as physically gifted a guard as one could want. Very quick, good ball handler, and a dangerous scorer both inside and outside, who could also play fine defense.

Yes, this team posed extraordinary problems for every opponent, but I would not want to say that they were the best. A team, like a player, that comes the closest to realizing its own particular level of competency, is the best regardless of its record. But of course there is no way to objectively measure that.

What could be done to improve intercollegiate athletics, basketball in particular?

Here are some things I feel could be beneficial. Keep in mind that these are only opinions, and certainly my opinion does not make them true.

(1) There should be no freshman competition at all. Freshmen could practice every day and perhaps have some intrasquad scrimmages before the varsity game. But there would be no traveling, no missing classes, no pressure of competition in any way. This way freshmen would get a good, fundamental foundation for future competition and have a year to become academically and socially adjusted to the change from high school to college.

It is my firm belief that all high-school graduates need one year to get acclimated to college life. There is a great social adjustment as well as an academic one. They are now on their own with less supervision, and they are under more difficult competitive pressures, especially academically. We must always keep in mind that they are student athletes and not athlete students. Although many are ready athletically and many are ready academically, very few are ready from the combined academic, athletic, and social point of view.

(2) I would place small emphasis on the little technical infractions of the NCAA rules, but I would severely punish all involved with the buying of an athlete. Coaches personally involved, if proven guilty, should be barred from all NCAA sports, and players involved should be barred from NCAA competition at any school. The prospects may not know about all the technical violations, but they all know when they are being bought. When the rule is clear, the penalty should be severe.

(3) I would prohibit all in-home visits to prospects by all

coaches or representatives of athletic departments, and also all paid visits of recruits to a campus.

(4) In basketball, I would permit no games before the third weekend in November, schedule all games on weekends or when school is not in session, and permit no travel that would require missing more than one day of school in any week.

What do you think of the 64-team format for the NCAA Basketball Tournament?

Now that they no longer require a team to win its conference to qualify, and invite four or five teams from certain conferences every year, I am for using the method used in the Indiana High School Tournament. Every Division I school not on probation should qualify, and in one weekend they will have the number down to the sixty-four. All of the income—ticket sales, television, radio, parking, programs, concessions, etc.—minus tournament expenses and a percentage to the NCAA should be divided into the number of shares it would take to give each school one share for each game they play, plus one extra share for the champion. In this manner every school would receive at least one share. I am certain that many of those who would receive only one share need it more than the Final Four needed the $1,056 million they received in 1987. The teams that last the longest in the tournament usually are the greatest money-makers during the season because of things like television contracts and seating capacity.

This change would reduce the temptation to break the rules in order to receive the million or more. History has proven that even strong and good people are susceptible to temptation when big money is at stake. Athletic directors and even college presidents could be tempted, and their head coaches might be under greater temptation because of the present method.

Furthermore, no team should be permitted to play in an NCAA tournament game on its home court. There are so many fine facilities available today that it no longer necessary. It would be no problem to arrange alternate game sites.

Proper seeding would be a problem as it is in the present sixty-four-team format, but it could be done.

Who do you consider to be the top coaches in the game?

This can really open a can of worms, because there are many great coaches who have never won an NCAA championship or do not have an outstanding winning percentage.

Although no coach can have an outstanding winning percentage without outstanding players, not every coach will have it even with outstanding players. It would be as ridiculous to say that all coaches are equal in ability as it is to say that all players, lawyers, writers, or artists are equal in ability.

It is also true that some coaches can do better with certain types of players than with others, while a different coach might be exactly the opposite. I know a coach who is considered to be outstanding, but who finished last in his conference one year with what almost every knowledgeable basketball person in the area considered to be the very best material. However, he later won the NCAA with players that were not considered to be nearly as good. He was much more difficult to beat when he had good players than when he had star players.

It is rather odd that the coach I would go to for help with technical aspects of almost any part of the game was not a good coach in my opinion. He never had a really good record in spite of the fact that he usually had good talent. He always seemed to have internal problems on his team and was not a good teacher. His lack of success convinced me that a good teacher who communicates well with his players will always do better than one with much better knowledge who is not a good teacher.

My observation on some of the following coaches may surprise you but they are sincere:

MORGAN WOOTTEN, DeMatha Catholic High School in Hyattsville, MD, may be the finest coach of all. This is not because of his unbelievable winning percentage or because his players are so solid fundamentally, as many college coaches will attest, but because of the fact that all of his players, stars and substitutes, always receive academic scholarships. Morgan is a great teacher. I have no doubt that his history students are as fortunate to have him as their teacher as his basketball players are to have him as their coach.

PAUL (TONY) HINKLE, Butler University, is now retired. Although his winning percentage may not be the equal of some others, his teams probably came as close to their own particular ability level as any national championship team. This is also true of the football and baseball teams he coached. He is a truly great teacher and person.

JERRY TARKANIAN, University of Nevada, Las Vegas—this much-maligned man can coach. He has had outstanding success at every level, and he is the only coach I know who completely changed his philosophy of both offense and defense after many successful years and continued his winning way. He went from a 1–2–2 zone defense and ball control offense to a pressure defense and fast break offense. Not long after he began his college coaching career, I said that if he completed twenty years of coaching he would retire with the highest winning percentage of any college coach—but that he would never win the NCAA. I hope my reasons for this will not be taken in a critical manner. They are based on the fact that for many years he would have several transfer students on his team. It was, and is, my opinion that you cannot have the consistency necessary to win several sudden-death games in succession against quality competition with players who could not work out the problems that brought about their transfer.

However, I thought his 1987 team might accomplish that feat when I heard he had no transfer players and that he had five seniors, all of whom were going to receive their degrees. I was glad to see that. Yes, this man can coach. Furthermore, he cares for his players.

As long as the coach gets his players in the best possible physical, mental, and emotional condition; teaches them to not only properly but quickly execute the fundamentals; and has them playing together as a team, they will play to near their potential, regardless of the system of offense and defense.

In order to accomplish this, however, the coach must be a good teacher and must maintain discipline while still being able to communicate with the players.

Amos Alonzo Stagg, who coached in some capacity when he was over 100 years of age, displayed the philosophy that I most admire when he said, "I never had a player I did not love, although I had some I did not like and could not respect." When at the end of the season he was asked if he considered it a successful season, he replied, "I won't know for the next fifteen or twenty years."

In trying to rate coaches I am reminded of a verse from Thomas Gray's "Elegy Written in a Country Churchyard,"

> Full many a gem of purest ray serene,
>   The dark unfathomed caves of ocean bear:
> Full many a flower is born to blush unseen,
>   And waste its sweetness on the desert air.

Can one honestly feel that a Dean Smith, a Bob Knight, a Denny Crum, a Lou Carneseca, a Ralph Miller, an Adolph Rupp, a Hank Iba, or a Pete Newell is a better coach than one of the many Browns, Joneses, or Thompsons—or than the many who never won a national championship because of extenuating circumstances, but whose teams always play close to their own level of competency?

Suffice it to say there are many good coaches, known and unknown, whose records would be just as good or better than many of the highly publicized if their positions were reversed.

APPENDIX 1

DEPARTMENT OF INTERCOLLEGIATE ATHLETICS
University of California, Los Angeles
405 Hilgard Avenue • Los Angeles, California 90024
(213) 825-3236 or 825-3326

August 1, 1972

Dear

It is my sincere hope that the 1972-73 UCLA varsity basketball team will be made up of players who love a challenge. Not only will there be a real battle for the top seven or eight playing spots, but the team pressure from the press and public will be far more severe than last year because now you will be expected to win.

Many of you are partially responsible for this enviable or unenviable position as far as team pressure is concerned because of what you have accomplished in the past. I choose to consider it an enviable position that has been earned and that it is a mark of respect. Furthermore, if you are the competitors that I think you are, you will justify the position.

However, I must caution you that you cannot live in the past. The 1971–72 season is now history and we must look toward the future. The past cannot change what is to come. The work that you do each and every day is the only true way to improve and prepare yourself for what is to come. You cannot change the past and you can influence the future only by what you do today.

For maximum team accomplishment each individual must prepare himself to the best of his ability and then put his talents to work for the team. This must be done unselfishly without thought of personal glory. When no one worries about who will receive the credit, far more can be accomplished in any group activity.

You must discipline yourself to do what is expected of you for the welfare of the team. The coach has many decisions to make and you will not agree with all of them, but you must respect and accept them. Without supervision and leadership and a disciplined effort by all, much of our united strength will be dissipated pulling against ourselves. Let us not be victimized by a breakdown from within.

You may feel, at times, that I have double standards as I certainly will not treat you all the same. However, I will attempt to give each player the treatment that he earns and deserves according to my judgment and in keeping with what I consider to be in the best interest of the team. I know I will not be right in all of my decisions, but I will attempt to be both right and fair.

My maturity and years of experience surely enable me to be far more accurate in the selection of the playing personnel, the style of play most suitable to the abilities of the players available, and to what is in the best interest of the 1972–73 UCLA team, than the judgment of any player or other interested party.

There will be a meeting for all potential squad members about two weeks before practice starts where a number of things will be discussed. For press and picture day on Monday, October 16, you should:

1. Have your feet tough and in shape to run without causing blisters.

2. Wear no mustache, beard, or goatee; have sideburns no longer than the top of the lobes of the ears; have your hair of reasonable length with the coaches being the judge as to what is reasonable length.

3. Remember that you represent others who are responsible for you as well as yourself and your personal appearance and conduct should not reflect discredit in any way upon yourself or upon those whom you represent. Cleanliness, neatness, politeness, and good manners are qualities that should be characteristic of those who are of great influence on young people and you certainly qualify for that category. Be a good example.

4. Be determined to do what is expected of you by those who are responsible for you and the team.

I hope that you are having a pleasant summer and that your 1972–73 school year at UCLA will be most rewarding—both academically and athletically.

Best wishes and regards to you and your family.

Sincerely,

John Wooden
Head Basketball
Coach

JW:jd

Encl.

APPENDIX 2

1974-75 UCLA Varsity Basketball Practice

Mon. 10/14 - Press & Picture Day in game uniforms. Get all team and individual photos out of the way.

Tues. 10/15 - 3:00-3:30 - Indiv. attention + free throws. Reemphasize being dressed and on floor by 3:15. Wooden - work with guards; Cunningham - work with front line.

(5 lines of 3) 3:30 - 3:35 - Loosening up - stretching, twisting, bending, squatting, running in place; Imaginary jump shots (3 ways), Imaginary offensive + defensive rebounding; Tipping.

(5 lines of 3) 3:35 - 3:40 - Change of pace + direction, quick starts + stops, defensive sliding, defense with quick turn + catch up, one on one (with & without ball)

(5 lines of 3) 3:40 - 3:50 - Dribbling - in place (rt., left, + alternate hands); quick starts + stops; change of pace + direction; cross-over; stops + turns with pass back.

3:50 - 3:55 - Ante-over, rebound and pass out.

3:55 - 4:05 - 3 man lane - parallel, through middle, front + side

(3 groups of 5-2 balls fa end) 4:05 - 4:15 - Shooting - base line, board, perimeter jumper, perimeter jumper after a quick drive.

4:15 - 4:25 - 3 on 2 continuity + 3 on 2 for board shot.

4:25 - 4:40 - 1-3-1 offensive patterns

4:45 - 5:30 - Full court scrimmage with officials (Keep full statistics. Those not scrimmaging must be shooting free throws - shoot 5 + move. 15 min. ea. - 1 v 2, 1 v 3, 2 v 3)

5:30 - To showers on a happy note.

<u>Consider for 1974-75 Season - UCLA</u>
(<u>Compiled at the close of the 1973-74 season</u>)

1. Build confidence in Drollinger + Trgovich.
2. Get McCarter under control with the basketball.
3. Be patient in determining the proper pressing defense
4. Use 3 on 2 continuity drill at least three times a week.
5. Defense the passing game a little more.
6. Work on our offense against zone defenses a little more.
7. Use weak side post drill without shooting more frequently and possibly in our pre-game warm-up.
8. Organize our time-outs better
9. Try out the "4 corner" as a lead protector.
10. Make Dave Meyers "captain".
11. Be very cautious with Marques Johnson - Hepatitis.
12. Forget the past and concentrate on each day of practice - analyze, prepare, evaluate, etc.
13. Prepare Richard Washington for both high and low post as well as forward.
14. Be patient with players on floor, but firm in discipline both on and off the floor.
15. Do not take anything for granted just because we have done so well in the past.

<u>Sunday. 3/30/75 - San Diego Arena</u>
<u>UCLA</u>

Practice the day before the NCAA championship game vs Kentucky and the day after a great over-time victory against Denny Crum's fine Louisville team in a semi-final game. When you consider the play of each team, I felt this was the finest NCAA tournament game in which I had ever had a team involved.

This practice is primarily to prepare our team mentally and emotionally for Kentucky while merely tuning up from a physical point of view. We want to prevent a "let down" after our great, but emotional, victory over Louisville.

Emphasize that we must keep constant pressure, both offensively and defensively, on Kentucky so our superior physical condition and quickness can take effect. We must not get into a half court game with them as their superior size and physical strength will be to their advantage.

One hour practice - no contact.
5 min. - Stretching, loosening up & imaginary jump shooting and rebounding.

Sun. 3/30/75 (Cont.)

5 min. - Change of direction & pace, defensive sliding, def. sliding & catch up, 1 on 1 (with & without ball)

10 min. - 4 man break-end with jump shot.

10 min. - Shooting - base line, flanker off board, perimeter - after pass and after dribble (6 players at each end with 2 balls with each group).

5 min. - Team fast break (1 man on defense at each end).

10 min. - Set offense with no defense - break to pressing position after each score.

5 min. - Team fast break from set defense - coach will shoot the ball.

10 min. Pair up for shooting quick sets and jumpers. 3 pair at each end. Compete to see which pair can make 10 first, then each pair leaves ball and moves to other end to start another game at a different basket with a different ball.

John Wooden's Most Memorable Games As a College Coach

The following are the most memorable games in John Wooden's college coaching career. All but the first involved games played by UCLA during his 27 years as Bruin coach. Legend: N—played on neutral court . . . T—played on opponent's home court . . . *—UCLA defeat.

Year	Site	Opponent	Score	Wooden's Comment
1974–75	N	Kentucky	92–85	"My last game; 10th NCAA championship"
1974–75	N	Louisville	75–74 OT	"Semifinals; exceptionally well played by both teams"
*1973–74	N	N.C. State	77–80 2 OT	"Lost 7-point lead in OT; NCAA semifinals"
1972–73	N	Memphis State	87–66	"4th perfect season; 9th NCAA; 7th in row"
1972–73	T	Notre Dame	82–63	"Set NCAA consecutive game win record at 61"
1972–73	T	Loyola	87–73	"Tied USF's consecutive game record of 60"
1971–72	N	Florida State	81–76	"3rd perfect season; 8th NCAA title; 6th in row"
1969–70	N	Jacksonville	80–69	"6th NCAA title; 4th in row; minus Alcindor"
1968–69	N	Purdue	92–72	"5th NCAA title; 1st coach to win over 2 in succession"
1967–68	N	Houston	101–69	"Atonement game; NCAA semifinals"

*1967–68	N	Houston	69–71	"In Astrodome before over 55,000 people"
1966–67	N	Dayton	79–64	"3rd NCAA title; 1st coach to have more than 1 perfect season"
1964–65	N	Michigan	91–80	"2nd NCAA title; tied record 2 times in succession"
1963–64	N	Duke	98–83	"1st NCAA title; 1st perfect season; small, exciting team"
*1962–63	N	Arizona State	79–93	"Lost NCAA regional to finest outside shooting I had seen"
*1961–62	N	Cincinnati	70–72	"Lost NCAA semifinal on last shot of game—so close to title"
*1949–50	N	Bradley	59–73	"Lost 7-point lead in NCAA tournament with less than 3 minutes to play"
*1948–49	T	Oregon State	35–41	"Lost game in my first PCC playoff; cost us NCAA playoff berth"
1948–49	T	USC	51–50	"Won at USC on consecutive nights to win PCC championship and qualify for playoff; Won with crippled team that had been unanimously picked to finish last in our division; 1st year at UCLA"
	T	USC	68–65	
*1947–48	N	Louisville	70–82	"Lost the NAIA national championship game my second year at Indiana State. Took the first black player ever permitted to be in the tournament.

APPENDIX 4
The Wooden Years at UCLA

TEAM MEMBERS

The men listed on the following pages were candidates for the UCLA basketball teams during John Wooden's coaching career that began with the 1948–49 season and ended with the 1974–75 year. Of this list of 334 squad members, 166 earned letters; the asterisks (*) indicate the number of letters won by each player (playing under Wooden only). Included in the list are team managers.

Ackerman, Dick
Adams, Carroll**
Adler, Frank*
Alba, Ray**
Alcindor, Lewis***
Alio, Mike
Allen, Lucius**
Alper, Art***
Amstutz, Harlan
Anderson, Stan
Anderson, Tom
Aranoff, Steve**
Archer, Robert***
Armstrong, Douglas
Arnold, Jack*
Babcock, Henry
Bailey, Allen
Baker, Gary
Baker, Jim
Ballard, Bob*
Ballinger, John
Bane, Ron****
Banton, Dick**
Barnes, Duane
Barnett, Greg
Bauer, Ralph
Bell, Robert*
Bennett, Eldon*

Benoit, Robert
Berberich, John**
Berry, Robert**
Betchley, Rick**
Bibby, Henry***
Blackman, Pete***
Bond, Ernie
Bond, Howard
Booker, Kenny**
Boone, Bill
Borio, Courtney**
Boulding, Wayne*
Bragg, Don****
Brandon, Cliff***
Brewer, Jim
Brewer, Lathon
Bridges, Lloyd
Brogan, Alan
Brucker, Steve
Bryant, Bill
Buccola, Guy*
Burke, Conrad***
Camarillo, Al
Carmock, John
Carson, Vince**
Caviezel, Jim
Chambers, Brice**
Chapman, Jon***

Chasen, Barry*
Chrisman, Joe**
Cline, Neal
Clustka, Charles*
Coleman, Don
Conkey, Jim
Conwell, Alan
Cook, Bruce
Cook, Ray
Corliss, Casey*
Costello, Mark****
Cox, Bill
Crabtree, Fred*
Crawford, Harold**
Crawford, Russell
Crowe, Sam
Crum, Denny**
Cumberland, Dave
Cunningham, Gary***
Curtis, Tommy***
Daggott, Andy
Darrow, Chuck
Davidson, Jack*
Dexter, Dennis
Dishong, Roger
Dodwell, Dave*
Donagho, Chuck
Drollinger, Ralph**

Eberhard, Gil
Eblen, Bill**
Ecker, John***
Elerding, Steve
Ellis, Bill**
Elzer, Richard
Erby, Al
Erickson, Keith***
Evans, Jerry**
Farmer, George
Farmer, Larry***
Fields, Richard
Fisher, Robert
Franklin, Gary***
Frear, Robert*
Freeman, Wayne
French, Billy**
Friedman, Jerry
Friedman, Lenny*
Friedman, Les**
Frost, James
Galbraith, John
Gelber, Art
Glucksman, Richard
Glucksman, William
Goldman, Marvin*
Golnick, Clair
Goodman, Larry
Goodman, Marvin
Goodrich, Gail***
Goss, Fred***
Gower, Larry
Graham, Kent
Grandi, Don
Grandi, Tim
Grates, Tom
Gray, Fred
Green, John***
Griffith, Neil
Gruber, Edwin
Gugat, Rich
Hall, Dave*
Halsten, Jim***
Hansen, Dick
Harrison, Jim

Hazzard, Walt***
Heitz, Ken***
Helman, Jay
Henry, Ted***
Herring, Alan**
Hibler, Mike***
Hicks, Bill***
Hill, Andy***
Hirsch, Jack**
Hobbs, Doug
Hockins, Lee
Hoffman, Vaughn**
Hollyfield, Larry***
Holzer, Fred
Huggins, Mike**
Humphrey, Keith
Hurry, Jim
Hutchins, Art**
Irmas, Dick*
Jacobs, Ron
Jennings, James
Joeckel, Ralph**
Johnson, Don**
Johnson, Ernie*
Johnson, Marques**
Johnson, Nolan
Johnson, Rafer**
Johnston, Wm.*
Jones, Scott
Jones, Warnell**
Judd, Randy*
Katilius, Vytas
Katz, Dave
Kell, Lindy*
Kennedy, Kenfield
Killgore, Dick
Kilmer, Billy
Klein, Phil
Kligman, Eward
Knapp, Don
Kniff, Brian***
Kordick, Jack
Kraushaar, Carl**
Kropf, Ken
Krupnick, Sid

Kurtovich, Bob
Lacey, Edgar**
Land, Don
Lawson, Ron*
Lee, Chris
Lee, Greg***
Leeds, Art
Leigh, Barry
Levin, Rich*
Lewinter, Jeff
Lincoln, Jim
Livingston, Ron***
Lock, Steve
Logan, Gene***
Long, Bob
Luchsinger, Grover***
Lundy, Al
Lynn, Mike***
Lynn, Richard
Lyons, John
Marcuccin, Bob*
Matlin, Jack*
Matney, Ken
Matulich, John**
McCarter, Andre**
McCollister, Larry
McFarland, Jim
McFerson, Henry
McFerson, Jim
McIntosh, Doug***
Meerson, Steve
Meyers, David***
Mielke, David
Milhorn, Jim***
Miller, Denny**
Miller, Kent**
Miller, René*
Miller, Robert
Mills, William
Minishian, Dennis*
Mokree, George
Montgomery, James
Moore, Jerry
Moore, John****
Moore, Robert

UCLA ALL-AMERICANS (FIRST TEAM ONLY)

1950—George Stanich, g
1952—Don Johnson, g
1955—John Moore, f
     Don Bragg, g
1956—Willie Naulls, c
1959—Walt Torrence, g
1962—John Green, g
1963—Walt Hazzard, g

1964—Walt Hazzard, g
1965—Gail Goodrich, g
1967—Lew Alcindor, c
1968—Lew Alcindor, c
     Lucius Allen, g
     Mike Warren, g
1969—Lew Alcindor, c
1970—Sidney Wicks, f

1971—Sidney Wicks, f
1972—Henry Bibby, g
     Bill Walton, c
1973—Bill Walton, c
     Keith Wilkes, f
1974—Bill Walton, c
     Keith Wilkes, f
1975—Dave Meyers, f

ALL-CONFERENCE BRUINS (FIRST TEAM ONLY)

*1949—Alan Sawyer, f
     George Stanich, g
*1950—George Stanich, g
     Carl Kraushaar, c
 1951—Dick Ridgeway, f
     Eddie Sheldrake, g
*1952—Jerry Norman, f
*1954—Don Bragg, g
     Ron Livingston, g
*1955—John Moore, f
     Willie Naulls, c
     Don Bragg, g

**1956—Willie Naulls, c
     Morris Taft, g
***1959—Walt Torrence, g
***1961—Gary Cunningham, f
***1962—John Green, g
***1963—Walt Hazzard, g
***1964—Walt Hazzard, g
     Gail Goodrich, g
***1965—Gail Goodrich, g
     Keith Erickson, f
***1966—Mike Lynn, f
***1967—Lew Alcindor, c
     Lucius Allen, g

***1968—Lew Alcindor, c
     Mike Warren, g
***1968—Lew Alcindor, c
     Curtis Rowe, f
***1970—Sydney Wicks, f
***1971—Sidney Wicks, f
     Curtis Rowe, f
***1972—Bill Walton, c
***1973—Bill Walton, c
     Keith Wilkes, f
***1974—Bill Walton, c
     Keith Wilkes, f
***1975—Dave Meyers, f

  *All Pacific Coast Conference Southern Division
 **All Pacific Coast Conference
***All Pacific Eight Conference

OFFICIAL BOX SCORES FOR NCAA CHAMPIONSHIP TOURNAMENTS

On the following pages are official box scores and other pertinent information for UCLA's ten NCAA championship tournaments. Legend: **fg-fga**—field goals made-field goals attempted . . . **ft-fta**—free throws made-free throws attempted . . . **rb**—rebounds made . . . **pf**—personal fouls . . . **tp**—total points scored. Note other information below each box score: half-time score, officials, and attendance.

249

1964

SECOND ROUND
At Corvallis, Oregon
March 13, 1964

UCLA	fg-fga	ft-fta	rb	pf	tp
Erickson	3-13	1- 4	13	5	7
Hirsch	8-12	5- 5	13	5	21
Slaughter	6-10	1- 3	13	5	13
Goodrich	6-22	7-11	6	4	19
Hazzard	9-14	8-11	7	3	26
McIntosh	1- 1	0- 1	1	1	2
Stewart	0- 1	0- 0	0	2	0
Washington	3- 4	1- 4	3	4	7
Huggins	0- 0	0- 0	0	0	0
Hoffman	0- 0	0- 0	0	0	0
Darrow	0- 0	0- 0	0	0	0
Team			6		
Totals	36-77	23-39	62	29	95

Seattle	fg-fga	ft-fta	rb	pf	tp
Tresvant	5-15	10-16	20	3	20
Vermillion	6- 9	3- 3	5	5	15
Wheeler	7-16	6-11	8	4	20
Williams	5-20	2- 4	13	5	12
Heyward	3- 8	3- 5	4	4	9
Phillips	2- 8	2- 2	4	4	6
Turney	2- 6	4- 4	2	5	8
Tebbs	0- 0	0- 0	0	1	0
Team			6		
Totals	30-82	30-45	62	31	90

Half time: UCLA 49-39. Officials: George and Magnusson. Attendance: 9,661.

REGIONAL CHAMPIONSHIP
At Corvallis, Oregon
March 14, 1964

UCLA	fg-fga	ft-fta	rb	pf	tp
Erickson	3-10	1- 6	10	4	7
Hirsch	5-11	4- 5	7	3	14
Slaughter	4- 9	1- 4	8	4	9
Goodrich	6-18	3- 5	4	1	15
Hazzard	9-19	5- 5	3	3	23
McIntosh	0- 1	3- 5	4	1	3
Washington	2- 4	1- 4	3	1	5
Team			9		
Totals	29-72	18-34	48	17	76

San Francisco	fg-fga	ft-fta	rb	pf	tp
Lee	2- 5	2- 2	4	4	6
Mueller	6-12	3- 5	7	4	15
Johnson	6- 9	10-11	13	2	22
Brovelli	5- 8	1- 1	2	4	11
Ellis	5-14	1- 2	10	3	11
Thomas	0- 0	0- 0	2	2	0
Brainard	2- 8	1- 2	4	5	5
Gumina	1- 1	0- 0	1	1	2
Team			3		
Totals	27-57	18-23	46	25	72

Half time: San Francisco 36-28. Officials: Glennon and Watson. Attendance: 9,416.

1964

SEMIFINALS
At Kansas City, Missouri
March 20, 1964

UCLA	fg-fga	ft-fta	rb	pf	tp
Goodrich	7-18	0- 0	6	3	14
Slaughter	2- 6	0- 0	5	4	4
Hazzard	7-10	5- 7	7	2	19
Hirsch	2-11	0- 0	1	4	4
Erickson	10-21	8- 9	10	2	28
McIntosh	3- 5	2- 3	10	3	8
Washington ...	5-11	3- 4	6	1	13
Totals	36-82	18-23	45	19	90

Kansas State	fg-fga	ft-fta	rb	pf	tp
Moss	3- 9	1- 1	5	3	7
Robinson	2- 7	0- 1	5	4	4
Simons	10-17	4- 6	7	3	24
Suttner	3- 9	0- 5	10	2	6
Murrell	13-22	3- 5	13	3	29
Paradis	5- 9	0- 0	1	0	10
Williams	1- 1	2- 3	1	2	4
Nelson	0- 1	0- 0	0	1	0
Gottfrid	0- 0	0- 0	0	1	0
Barnard	0- 1	0- 0	0	0	0
Totals	37-76	10-21	42	19	84

Half time: UCLA 43-41. Officials: Mahalik and Honzo. Attendance: 10,731.

CHAMPIONSHIP
At Kansas City, Missouri
March 21, 1964

UCLA	fg-fga	ft-fta	rb	pf	tp
Goodrich	9-18	9- 9	3	1	27
Slaughter	0- 1	0- 0	1	0	0
Hazzard	4-10	3- 5	3	5	11
Hirsch	5- 9	3- 5	6	3	13
Erickson	2- 7	4- 4	5	5	8
McIntosh	4- 9	0- 0	11	2	8
Washington ...	11-16	4- 4	12	4	26
Darrow	0- 1	3- 4	1	2	3
Stewart	0- 1	0- 0	0	1	0
Huggins	0- 1	0- 1	1	2	0
Hoffman	1- 2	0- 0	0	0	2
Levin	0- 1	0- 0	0	0	0
Totals	36-76	26-32	43	25	98

Duke	fg-fga	ft-fta	rb	pf	tp
Ferguson	2- 6	0- 1	1	3	4
Buckley	5- 8	8-12	9	4	18
Tison	3- 8	1- 1	1	2	7
Harrison	1- 1	0- 0	1	2	2
Mullins	9-21	4- 4	4	5	22
Marin	8-16	0- 1	10	3	16
Vacendak	2- 7	3- 3	6	4	7
Herbster	1- 4	0- 2	0	0	2
Kitching	1- 1	0- 0	1	0	2
Mann	0- 0	3- 4	2	1	3
Harscher	0- 0	0- 0	0	0	0
Cox	0- 0	0- 0	0	0	0
Totals	32-72	19-28	35	24	83

Half time: UCLA 50-38. Officials: Mihalik and Glennon. Attendance: 10,864.

1965

SECOND ROUND
At Provo, Utah
March 12, 1965

UCLA	fg-fga	ft-fta	rb	pf	tp
Lacey	7-11	1- 3	13	3	15
Erickson	14-22	0- 1	9	4	28
McIntosh	1- 6	0- 2	9	3	2
Goodrich	16-27	8- 9	5	2	40
Goss	2-10	0- 0	2	5	4
Washington	0- 5	1- 1	4	5	1
Lynn	3- 9	2- 2	10	3	8
Hoffman	0- 1	0- 1	2	0	0
Chambers	0- 1	0- 0	1	0	0
Lyons	1- 2	0- 0	0	0	2
Levin	0- 0	0- 0	0	1	0
Team			11		
Totals	44-94	12-19	66	26	100

Brigham Young	fg-fga	ft-fta	rb	pf	tp
Kramer	5- 7	0- 1	4	2	10
Roberts	2-11	3- 4	6	0	7
Fairchild	8-17	7- 8	13	2	23
Gardner	5-10	4- 4	4	4	14
Nemelka	2-11	1- 5	1	2	5
Hill	2- 5	0- 3	7	4	4
Quinney	1- 5	2- 2	4	0	4
Congdon	2- 5	0- 1	1	1	4
Stanley	2- 3	0- 1	4	0	4
Raymond	0- 2	1- 2	4	1	1
Jimas	0- 1	0- 0	0	0	0
James	0- 3	0- 1	1	0	0
Team			7		
Totals	29-80	18-32	56	16	76

Half time: UCLA 51-40. Attendance: 10,766.

REGIONAL CHAMPIONSHIP
At Provo, Utah
March 13, 1965

UCLA	fg-fga	ft-fta	rb	pf	tp
Lakey	7-13	1- 2	7	4	15
Erickson	13-26	3- 6	11	4	29
McIntosh	2- 3	1- 1	6	1	5
Goss	6-15	1- 1	0	1	13
Goodrich	10-18	10-11	3	3	30
Lynn	2- 3	3- 4	1	4	7
Washington	1- 4	0- 1	1	2	2
Team			9		
Totals	41-82	19-26	38	19	101

San Francisco	fg-fga	ft-fta	rb	pf	tp
Gumina	6-12	4- 5	4	2	16
Mueller	4- 6	4- 5	4	5	12
Johnson	15-20	7-10	21	4	37
Ellis	7-13	2- 4	11	3	16
Thomas	3- 4	2- 2	0	1	8
James	1- 5	0- 0	0	2	2
Blum	1- 4	0- 0	1	2	2
Esters	0- 1	0- 1	2	1	0
Team			3		
Totals	37-65	19-27	46	20	93

Half time: UCLA 51-46. Attendance: 10,515.

1965

SEMIFINALS
At Portland, Oregon
March 19, 1965

CHAMPIONSHIP
At Portland, Oregon
March 20, 1965

Wichita	fg-fga	ft-fta	rb	pf	tp
Smith	4-11	0- 1	2	3	8
Thompson	13-19	10-11	6	2	36
Leach	6-14	0- 1	10	3	12
Pete	6-11	5- 5	6	5	17
Criss	4-13	0- 0	4	4	8
Reed	2- 3	1- 1	4	4	5
Davis	1- 2	0- 0	1	0	2
Trope	0- 1	0- 0	0	0	0
Nosich	0- 0	1- 3	0	0	1
Reimond	0- 1	0- 0	1	0	0
Team			4		
Totals	36-75	17-22	38	21	89

UCLA	fg-fga	ft-fta	rb	pf	tp
Lacey	9-13	6-10	2	13	24
Erickson	1- 6	0- 0	2	5	2
McIntosh	4- 5	3- 4	2	4	11
Goodrich	11-21	6- 8	2	5	28
Goss	8-13	3- 3	2	9	19
Washington	4-13	2- 4	1	7	10
Lynn	5- 9	0- 0	1	8	10
Chambers	0- 5	0- 0	1	2	0
Lyons	2- 3	0- 0	2	1	4
Levins	0- 1	0- 0	1	1	0
Galbraith	0- 0	0- 0	1	0	0
Hoffman	0- 0	0- 0	0	0	0
Totals	44-89	20-29	17	55	108

Half time: UCLA 65-38. Officials: Mihalik and Honzo. Attendance: 13,197.

UCLA	fg-fga	ft-fta	rb	pf	tp
Erickson	1- 1	1- 2	1	1	3
Lacey	5- 7	1- 2	7	3	11
McIntosh	1- 2	1- 2	0	2	3
Goodrich	12-22	18-20	4	4	42
Goss	4-12	0- 0	3	1	8
Washington	7- 9	3- 4	5	2	17
Lynn	2- 3	1- 2	6	1	5
Lyons	0- 0	0- 0	0	1	0
Galbraith	0- 0	0- 0	0	0	0
Hoffman	1- 1	0- 0	1	0	2
Levin	0- 1	0- 0	1	0	0
Chambers	0- 0	0- 1	0	0	0
Team			6		
Totals	33-58	25-33	34	15	91

Michigan	fg-fga	ft-fta	rb	pf	tp
Darden	8-10	1- 1	4	5	17
Pomey	2- 5	0- 0	2	2	4
Buntin	6-14	2- 4	6	5	14
Russell	10-16	8-10	5	2	28
Tregoning	2- 7	1- 1	5	5	5
Myers	0- 4	0- 0	3	2	0
Brown	0- 0	0- 0	0	0	0
Ludwig	1- 2	0- 0	0	0	2
Thompson	0- 0	0- 0	0	0	0
Bankey	0- 0	0- 0	0	0	0
Clawson	3- 4	0- 0	0	2	6
Dill	1- 2	2- 2	1	1	4
Team			7		
Totals	33-64	14-18	33	24	80

Half time: UCLA 47-34. Officials: Mihalik and Honzo. Attendance: 13,204.

1967

<table>
<tr><td colspan="6">SECOND ROUND
At Corvallis, Oregon
March 17, 1967</td></tr>
<tr><td>UCLA</td><td>fg-fga</td><td>ft-fta</td><td>rb</td><td>pf</td><td>tp</td></tr>
<tr><td>Heitz ....</td><td>3- 3</td><td>0- 0</td><td>0</td><td>5</td><td>6</td></tr>
<tr><td>Shackelford ...</td><td>5- 8</td><td>0- 0</td><td>7</td><td>2</td><td>10</td></tr>
<tr><td>Alcindor ......</td><td>12-17</td><td>5- 5</td><td>10</td><td>1</td><td>29</td></tr>
<tr><td>Allen ....</td><td>6-11</td><td>3- 3</td><td>5</td><td>1</td><td>15</td></tr>
<tr><td>Warren.......</td><td>4-11</td><td>2- 4</td><td>5</td><td>0</td><td>10</td></tr>
<tr><td>Chrisman .....</td><td>2- 2</td><td>2- 3</td><td>0</td><td>3</td><td>6</td></tr>
<tr><td>Nielsen ....</td><td>4- 6</td><td>0- 0</td><td>5</td><td>1</td><td>8</td></tr>
<tr><td>Saner ....</td><td>2- 3</td><td>0- 0</td><td>4</td><td>1</td><td>4</td></tr>
<tr><td>Sweek ....</td><td>4- 6</td><td>0- 2</td><td>5</td><td>2</td><td>8</td></tr>
<tr><td>Lynn ....</td><td>0- 1</td><td>0- 0</td><td>0</td><td>1</td><td>0</td></tr>
<tr><td>Sutherland ....</td><td>2- 4</td><td>1- 2</td><td>1</td><td>1</td><td>5</td></tr>
<tr><td>Saffer ....</td><td>4- 6</td><td>0- 0</td><td>2</td><td>0</td><td>8</td></tr>
<tr><td>Team ....</td><td></td><td></td><td>1</td><td></td><td></td></tr>
<tr><td>Totals ......</td><td>48-78</td><td>13-19</td><td>45</td><td>18</td><td>109</td></tr>
</table>

<table>
<tr><td>Wyoming</td><td>fg-fga</td><td>ft-fta</td><td>rb</td><td>pf</td><td>tp</td></tr>
<tr><td>Hall ....</td><td>6-16</td><td>7-11</td><td>5</td><td>2</td><td>19</td></tr>
<tr><td>Asbury ....</td><td>8-20</td><td>4- 6</td><td>10</td><td>2</td><td>20</td></tr>
<tr><td>Von Krosigk...</td><td>1- 7</td><td>2- 4</td><td>8</td><td>4</td><td>4</td></tr>
<tr><td>Wilson ....</td><td>2- 6</td><td>1- 1</td><td>3</td><td>3</td><td>5</td></tr>
<tr><td>Eberle........</td><td>6-12</td><td>0- 1</td><td>5</td><td>4</td><td>12</td></tr>
<tr><td>Nelson ....</td><td>0- 2</td><td>0- 0</td><td>2</td><td>1</td><td>0</td></tr>
<tr><td>Team ....</td><td></td><td></td><td>7</td><td></td><td></td></tr>
<tr><td>Totals ......</td><td>23-63</td><td>14-23</td><td>40</td><td>16</td><td>60</td></tr>
</table>

Half time: UCLA 55-18. Attendance: 8,177.

<table>
<tr><td colspan="6">REGIONAL CHAMPIONSHIP
At Corvallis, Oregon
March 17, 1967</td></tr>
<tr><td>UCLA</td><td>fg-fga</td><td>ft-fta</td><td>rb</td><td>pf</td><td>tp</td></tr>
<tr><td>Heitz ....</td><td>4- 6</td><td>1- 1</td><td>3</td><td>3</td><td>9</td></tr>
<tr><td>Shackelford ...</td><td>3-12</td><td>0- 1</td><td>4</td><td>2</td><td>6</td></tr>
<tr><td>Alcindor ......</td><td>13-20</td><td>12-14</td><td>14</td><td>4</td><td>38</td></tr>
<tr><td>Allen.........</td><td>5- 8</td><td>3- 6</td><td>6</td><td>3</td><td>13</td></tr>
<tr><td>Warren.......</td><td>4- 8</td><td>4- 6</td><td>2</td><td>1</td><td>12</td></tr>
<tr><td>Sweek ....</td><td>1- 4</td><td>0- 0</td><td>0</td><td>4</td><td>2</td></tr>
<tr><td>Saffer ....</td><td>0- 0</td><td>0- 0</td><td>0</td><td>0</td><td>0</td></tr>
<tr><td>Team ....</td><td></td><td></td><td>7</td><td></td><td></td></tr>
<tr><td>Totals ......</td><td>30-58</td><td>20-28</td><td>36</td><td>17</td><td>80</td></tr>
</table>

<table>
<tr><td>Pacific</td><td>fg-fga</td><td>ft-fta</td><td>rb</td><td>pf</td><td>tp</td></tr>
<tr><td>Krulish ......</td><td>5-12</td><td>2- 2</td><td>7</td><td>3</td><td>12</td></tr>
<tr><td>Jones.........</td><td>0- 1</td><td>0- 0</td><td>0</td><td>1</td><td>0</td></tr>
<tr><td>Swagerty ......</td><td>5-12</td><td>1- 5</td><td>8</td><td>4</td><td>11</td></tr>
<tr><td>Fox ....</td><td>6-18</td><td>5- 7</td><td>6</td><td>4</td><td>17</td></tr>
<tr><td>Parsons ....</td><td>1- 3</td><td>5- 6</td><td>6</td><td>2</td><td>7</td></tr>
<tr><td>DeWitt ......</td><td>3- 9</td><td>0- 3</td><td>13</td><td>2</td><td>6</td></tr>
<tr><td>Ferguson .....</td><td>1- 3</td><td>0- 0</td><td>0</td><td>1</td><td>2</td></tr>
<tr><td>Foley ....</td><td>4- 6</td><td>1- 2</td><td>4</td><td>4</td><td>9</td></tr>
<tr><td>Team ....</td><td></td><td></td><td>6</td><td></td><td></td></tr>
<tr><td>Totals ......</td><td>25-64</td><td>14-25</td><td>50</td><td>21</td><td>64</td></tr>
</table>

Half time: Pacific 21-17. Attendance: 8,628.

254

1967

SEMIFINALS	CHAMPIONSHIP
At Louisville, Kentucky	At Louisville, Kentucky
March 24, 1967	March 25, 1967

UCLA	fg-fga	ft-fta	rb	pf	tp
Heitz	0- 0	1- 1	0	1	1
Shackelford	11-19	0- 1	8	1	22
Alcindor	6-11	7-13	20	1	19
Allen	6-15	5- 5	9	2	17
Warren	4-10	6- 7	9	0	14
Nielsen	0- 3	0- 0	3	5	0
Sweek	0- 4	0- 0	1	2	0
Saffer	0- 0	0- 0	0	0	0
Team			1		
Totals	27-62	19-27	51	12	73

Houston	fg-fga	ft-fta	rb	pf	tp
Hayes	12-31	1- 2	24	4	25
Bell	3-11	4- 7	11	4	10
Kruse	2- 5	1- 1	0	2	5
Grider	2- 7	0- 0	2	2	4
Chaney	3-11	0- 2	4	4	6
Lentz	1- 2	0- 3	4	1	2
Spain	1- 5	0- 0	4	2	2
Lewis	0- 0	0- 1	0	1	0
Lee	2- 3	0- 0	1	0	4
Team			1		
Totals	26-75	6-16	51	20	58

Half time: UCLA 39-28. Attendance: 18,889.

UCLA	fg-fga	ft-fta	rb	pf	tp
Heitz	2- 7	0- 0	6	2	4
Shackelford	5-10	0- 2	3	1	10
Alcindor	8-12	4-11	18	0	20
Allen	7-15	5- 8	9	2	19
Warren	8-16	1- 1	7	1	17
Nielsen	0- 1	0- 1	1	3	0
Sweek	1- 1	0- 0	0	1	2
Saffer	2- 5	0- 0	0	1	4
Saner	1- 1	0- 0	2	2	2
Chrisman	0- 0	1- 2	1	2	1
Sutherland	0- 0	0- 0	0	0	0
Lynn	0- 1	0- 0	0	0	0
Team			7		
Totals	34-69	11-25	54	15	79

Dayton	fg-fga	ft-fta	rb	pf	tp
May	9-23	3- 4	17	4	21
Sadlier	2- 5	1- 2	7	5	5
Obrovac	0- 2	0- 0	2	1	0
Klaus	4- 7	0- 0	0	1	8
Hooper	2- 7	2- 4	5	2	6
Torain	3-14	0- 0	4	3	6
Waterman	4-11	2- 3	1	3	10
Sharpenter	2- 5	4- 5	5	1	8
Samanich	0- 2	0- 0	2	0	0
Beckman	0- 0	0- 0	0	0	0
Inderrieden	0- 0	0- 0	0	0	0
Wannemacher	0- 0	0- 0	0	0	0
Team			8		
Totals	26-76	12-18	51	20	64

Half time: UCLA 38-20. Attendance: 18,892.

255

1968

<table>
<tr><td colspan="2">

WEST REGIONAL
At Albuquerque, New Mexico
March 15, 1968
</td></tr>
</table>

UCLA	fg-fga	ft-fta	rb	pf	tp
Lew Alcindor	9-13	10-16	23	3	28
Mike Lynn	2- 7	0- 0	4	3	4
Lucius Allen	3-11	0- 0	3	5	6
Mike Warren	4- 6	2- 2	3	1	10
Lynn Shackelford	2- 7	3- 3	6	3	7
Kenny Heitz	1- 7	1- 3	2	4	3
Jim Nielsen	0- 1	0- 0	0	0	0
Bill Sweek	0- 0	0- 0	0	1	0
Team			9		
Totals	21-52	16-24	50	20	58

New Mexico St.	fg-fga	ft-fta	rb	pf	tp
Robert Evans	4-13	6-10	3	4	14
Jimmy Collins	7-16	2- 5	6	1	16
John Burgess	2- 5	0- 3	5	4	4
Richard Collins	2- 6	1- 2	11	5	5
Sam Lacey	3-12	0- 0	5	5	6
Hardy Murphy	0- 1	0- 0	0	0	0
Paul Landis	1- 4	2- 4	3	0	4
Wes Morehead	0- 1	0- 1	1	0	0
Tom Las	0- 0	0- 0	1	2	0
Team			7		
Totals	19-58	11-25	42	21	49

Half time: 28-28. Officials: Jenkins and Smith. Attendance: 15,345.

<table>
<tr><td colspan="2">

WEST REGIONAL
At Albuquerque, New Mexico
March 16, 1968
</td></tr>
</table>

UCLA	fg-fga	ft-fta	rb	pf	tp
Lew Alcindor	6- 8	10-17	18	2	22
Mike Lynn	5- 9	0- 1	5	4	10
Lucius Allen	7-15	7- 7	8	3	21
Mike Warren	6-14	3- 3	5	3	15
Lynn Shackelford	1- 8	2- 2	6	0	4
Kenny Heitz	3- 8	1- 1	3	1	7
Gene Sutherland	0- 3	0- 0	1	0	0
Neville Saner	1- 3	0- 0	1	3	2
Jim Nielsen	2- 4	0- 0	3	4	4
Bill Sweek	1- 2	0- 0	1	3	2
Team			6		
Totals	32-74	23-31	57	23	87

Santa Clara	fg-fga	ft-fta	rb	pf	tp
Terry O'Brien	3- 6	1- 1	2	3	7
Bob Heaney	2-10	0- 1	1	2	4
Bud Ogden	4- 7	5-10	9	3	13
Joe Diffley	0- 3	2- 2	0	2	2
Dennis Awtrey	7-12	3- 4	10	4	17
Kevin Eagleson	0- 1	2- 3	0	4	2
Bob Stuckey	1- 5	3- 4	2	0	5
Kevin Donahue	0- 0	0- 0	1	0	0
Keith Paulson	0- 3	0- 0	1	1	0
Chris Dempsey	0- 4	1- 2	4	1	1
Ralph Ogden	5-11	1- 1	3	2	11
Ray Thomas	2- 3	0- 1	2	2	4
Team			10		
Totals	24-65	18-29	45	24	66

Half time: UCLA 51-34. Officials: Overby and Jenkins. Attendance: 15,010.

256

1968

SEMIFINALS	CHAMPIONSHIP
At Los Angeles, California	At Los Angeles, California
March 22, 1968	March 23, 1968

Houston	fg-fga	ft-fta	rb	pf	tp
Theodis Lee	2-15	0- 0	4	4	4
Elvin Hayes	3-10	4- 7	5	4	10
Ken Spain	4-12	7-10	13	1	15
Don Chaney	5-13	5- 7	7	2	15
Vern Lewis	2- 8	2- 2	5	0	6
Neimer Hamood	3- 5	4- 6	0	2	10
Tom Gribben	0- 5	0- 1	5	1	0
Carlos Bell	3- 8	3- 4	5	0	9
Kent Taylor	0- 0	0- 0	0	0	0
Larry Cooper	0- 2	0- 0	1	0	0
Team			9		
Totals	22-78	25-37	54	14	69

UCLA	fg-fga	ft-fta	rb	pf	tp
Lynn Shackelford	6-10	5- 5	3	4	17
Mike Lynn	8-10	3- 3	8	4	19
Lew Alcindor	7-14	5- 6	18	3	19
Mike Warren	7-18	0- 0	5	3	14
Lucius Allen	9-18	1- 2	9	1	19
Jim Nielsen	2- 3	0- 0	1	4	4
Kenny Heitz	3- 6	1- 1	1	1	7
Bill Sweek	1- 1	0- 1	0	0	2
Gene Sutherland	0- 1	0- 0	0	1	0
Neville Saner	0- 2	0- 0	1	2	0
Team			11		
Totals	43-83	15-18	57	23	101

Half time: UCLA 53-31. Officials: Honzo and Fouty. Attendance: 15,742.

UCLA	fg-fga	ft-fta	rb	pf	tp
Lynn Shackelford	3- 5	0- 1	2	0	6
Mike Lynn	1- 7	5- 7	6	3	7
Lew Alcindor	15-21	4- 4	16	3	34
Mike Warren	3- 7	1- 1	3	2	7
Lucius Allen	3- 7	5- 7	5	0	11
Jim Nielsen	1- 1	0- 0	1	1	2
Kenny Heitz	3- 6	1- 1	2	3	7
Gene Sutherland	1- 2	0- 0	2	1	2
Bill Sweek	0- 1	0- 0	0	1	0
Neville Saner	1- 3	0- 0	2	2	2
Team			9		
Totals	31-60	16-21	48	16	78

North Carolina	fg-fga	ft-fta	rb	pf	tp
Larry Miller	5-13	4- 6	6	3	14
Bill Bunting	1- 3	1- 2	2	5	3
Rusty Clark	4-12	1- 3	8	3	9
Charlie Scott	6-17	0- 1	3	3	12
Dick Grubar	2- 5	1- 2	0	2	5
Ed Fogler	1- 4	2- 2	0	0	4
Joe Brown	2- 5	2- 2	5	1	6
Gerald Tuttle	0- 0	0- 0	0	0	0
Jim Frye	1- 2	0- 1	1	0	2
Gra Whitehead	0- 0	0- 0	0	0	0
Jim Delany	0- 1	0- 0	0	0	0
Ralph Fletcher	0- 1	0- 0	0	0	0
Team			10		
Totals	22-63	11-19	35	17	55

Half time: UCLA 32-22. Officials: Honzo and Fouty. Attendance: 14,438.

1969

WEST REGIONAL
At Los Angeles, California
March 13, 1969

UCLA	fg-fga	ft-fta	rb	pf	tp
Curtis Rowe	3-12	2- 2	7	2	8
Lynn Shackelford .	4-10	0- 0	3	0	8
Lew Alcindor.....	8-15	0- 5	16	3	16
Kenny Heitz	4- 6	1- 1	4	3	9
John Vallely......	5-12	0- 0	5	1	10
Sidney Wicks	0- 2	0- 0	0	0	0
Bill Sweek	1- 1	0- 2	0	1	2
Steve Patterson ...	0- 0	0- 0	0	1	0
Terry Schofield ...	0- 0	0- 0	0	0	0
Team			7		
Totals	25-58	3-10	42	11	53

New Mexico St.	fg-fga	ft-fta	rb	pf	tp
Jeff Smith	2- 4	3- 3	8	3	7
Chito Reyes......	2- 5	1- 2	2	0	5
Sam Lacey	5-16	1- 1	11	4	11
Jimmy Collins	4-17	3- 3	4	1	11
John Burgess	0- 3	0- 1	2	0	0
Hardy Murphy ...	1- 2	0- 0	1	1	2
Herb Bowen	1- 1	0- 0	0	0	2
Team			5		
Totals	15-48	8-10	33	9	38

Half time: UCLA 21-17. Officials: Wirtz and
Fouty. Attendance: 12,817.

WEST REGIONAL
At Los Angeles, California
March 15, 1969

UCLA	fg-fga	ft-fta	rb	pf	tp
Lynn Shackelford .	3- 7	0- 1	3	1	6
Curtis Rowe	3- 6	1- 2	5	1	7
Lew Alcindor.....	8-14	1- 3	7	2	17
John Vallely......	5- 5	1- 2	3	2	11
Kenny Heitz	3- 6	0- 0	1	2	6
Bill Sweek	4- 7	4- 5	1	1	12
Sidney Wicks	3- 4	5- 8	2	1	11
Steve Patterson ...	4- 6	1- 1	5	4	9
Terry Schofield ...	1- 6	0- 0	2	0	2
John Ecker	2- 2	1- 1	1	0	5
Bill Seibert.......	0- 0	2- 2	3	1	2
George Farmer ...	1- 2	0- 0	0	0	2
Team			6		
Totals	37-65	16-25	39	15	90

Santa Clara	fg-fga	ft-fta	rb	pf	tp
Ralph Ogden.....	1-13	2- 4	7	2	4
Bud Ogden	3-10	3- 3	5	4	9
Dennis Awtrey ...	5- 9	4- 6	8	4	14
Kevin Eagleson ...	0- 0	0- 1	3	3	0
Terry O'Brien ...	0- 2	0- 1	1	2	0
Joe Diffley	1- 4	0- 0	2	2	2
Keith Paulson	2- 4	1- 3	1	0	5
Chris Dempsey ...	2- 3	1- 1	2	2	5
Bob Tobin	1- 2	0- 0	4	2	2
Tom Scherer	2- 5	0- 0	1	0	4
Gary Graves	1- 1	1- 1	1	1	3
Mitch Champi ...	2- 3	0- 0	2	3	4
Team			5		
Totals	20-56	12-20	42	25	52

Half time: UCLA 46-25. Officials: Fouty and
Payak. Attendance: 12,812.

258

1969

Drake	fg-fga	ft-fta	rb	pf	tp
Dolph Pulliam	4-14	4- 5	5	4	12
Al Williams	0- 1	0- 0	1	4	0
Willie Wise	5- 7	3- 4	16	3	13
Willie McCarter ..	10-27	4- 4	1	3	24
Don Draper	5-13	2- 2	1	2	12
Garry Odom	0- 2	0- 1	2	4	0
Rick Wanamaker .	4- 7	1- 1	7	4	9
Gary Zeller	4-12	4- 6	3	3	12
Ron Gwin	0- 0	0- 1	1	3	0
Team			4		
Totals	32-83	18-24	41	30	82

UCLA	fg-fga	ft-fta	rb	pf	tp
Lynn Shackelford .	2- 5	2- 3	2	4	6
Curtis Rowe	6- 9	2- 2	13	2	14
Lew Alcindor.....	8-14	9-16	21	3	25
Kenny Heitz	3- 6	1- 3	1	5	7
John Vallely......	9-11	11-14	6	5	29
Sidney Wicks	0- 2	0- 0	1	1	0
Bill Sweek	0- 0	0- 0	0	1	0
Steve Patterson ...	0- 0	2- 2	0	0	2
Terry Schofield ...	0- 3	2- 4	0	0	2
Team			4		
Totals	28-50	29-44	48	21	85

Half time: UCLA 44-43. Officials: Fouty and DiTomasso. Attendance: 18,435.

UCLA	fg-fga	ft-fta	rb	pf	tp
Lynn Shackelford .	3- 8	5- 8	9	3	11
Curtis Rowe	4-10	4- 4	12	2	12
Lew Alcindor.....	15-20	7- 9	20	2	37
Kenny Heitz	0- 3	0- 1	3	4	0
John Vallely......	4- 9	7-10	4	3	15
Bill Sweek	3- 3	0- 1	1	3	6
Sidney Wicks	0- 1	3- 6	4	1	3
Terry Schofield ...	1- 2	0- 0	0	0	2
Steve Patterson ...	1- 1	2- 2	2	0	4
Bill Seibert.......	0- 0	0- 0	1	0	0
George Farmer ...	0- 0	0- 0	0	1	0
John Ecker	1- 1	0- 0	0	0	2
Team			5		
Totals	32-58	28-41	61	19	92

Purdue	fg-fga	ft-fta	rb	pf	tp
Herman Gilliam ..	2-14	3- 3	11	2	7
George Faerber ..	1- 2	0- 0	3	5	2
Jerry Johnson	4- 9	3- 4	9	2	11
Rick Mount	12-36	4- 5	1	3	28
Bill Keller	4-17	3- 4	4	5	11
Frank Kaufman ...	0- 0	2- 2	5	5	2
Tyrone Bedford ...	3- 8	1- 3	8	3	7
Larry Weather- ford	1- 5	2- 2	1	3	4
Ted Reasoner	0- 1	0- 1	1	2	0
Ralph Taylor	0- 0	0- 0	0	0	0
Team			5		
Totals	27-92	18-24	48	30	72

Half time: UCLA 50-41. Officials: Di-Tomasso and Brown. Attendance: 18,669.

WEST REGIONAL
At Seattle, Washington
March 12, 1970

UCLA	fg-fga	ft-fta	rb	pf	tp
Sidney Wicks	8-14	4- 7	11	3	20
Curtis Rowe	5-11	5- 9	11	1	15
Steve Patterson ...	6-14	1- 1	12	4	13
John Vallely......	6-15	2- 5	5	2	14
Henry Bibby	8-13	4- 5	6	2	20
Kenny Booker	0- 1	0- 0	0	1	0
John Ecker	1- 2	0- 0	1	0	2
Terry Schofield ...	1- 2	0- 0	1	0	2
Bill Siebert.......	0- 1	0- 0	0	0	0
Jon Chapman	1- 1	0- 0	1	0	2
Team			6		
Totals	36-74	16-27	54	13	88

Long Beach St.	fg-fga	ft-fta	rb	pf	tp
Sam Robinson	7-13	4- 6	7	2	18
Billy Jankans	2-10	1- 3	7	5	5
George Trapp	10-18	0- 1	4	3	20
Ray Gritton	0- 2	0- 0	1	1	0
Shawn Johnson ..	5-12	3- 3	4	0	13
Dave McLucas ...	0- 0	0- 0	1	0	0
Dwight Taylor....	1- 7	1- 2	0	3	3
Arthur Montgom-					
ery	3- 4	0- 0	1	5	6
Bernard Williams .	0- 1	0- 0	1	2	0
Team			8		
Totals	28-67	9-15	34	21	65

Half time: UCLA 42-29. Officials: Stout and Huiot. Attendance: 5,500.

WEST REGIONAL
At Seattle, Washington
March 14, 1970

UCLA	fg-fga	ft-fta	rb	pf	tp
Sidney Wicks	10-14	6- 7	8	4	26
Curtis Rowe	9-17	8- 8	16	3	26
Steve Patterson ...	4-12	1- 2	9	2	9
Henry Bibby	4- 8	7- 9	7	4	15
John Vallely......	5-13	4- 7	3	1	14
Kenny Booker	2- 4	0- 1	1	2	4
John Ecker	0- 0	1- 2	2	1	1
Terry Schofield ...	0- 0	0- 0	0	0	0
Jon Chapman	0- 2	0- 0	3	0	0
Bill Seibert.......	1- 1	2- 2	1	1	4
Rick Betchley	1- 2	0- 0	0	0	2
Andy Hill........	0- 0	0- 0	0	0	0
Team			6		
Totals	36-73	29-38	56	18	101

Utah State	fg-fga	ft-fta	rb	pf	tp
Nate Williams	7-24	0- 0	11	4	14
Marv Roberts	14-35	5- 7	15	4	33
Tim Tollestrup ...	1- 4	4- 6	10	4	6
Jeff Tebbs	0- 4	0- 0	2	4	0
Paul Jeppesen ...	4- 6	4- 4	1	4	12
Ed Epps.........	6-13	0- 1	6	3	12
Ron Hatch.......	0- 4	2- 2	2	2	2
John Ericksen	0- 0	0- 0	0	0	0
Terry Wakefield ..	0- 0	0- 0	0	1	0
Dick Wade	0- 1	0- 0	1	0	0
Chris Bean.......	0- 0	0- 0	1	0	0
Team			5		
Totals	32-91	15-20	54	26	79

Half time: UCLA 51-44. Officials: Huiot and White. Attendance: 4,200.

1970

SEMIFINALS	CHAMPIONSHIP
At College Park, Maryland	At College Park, Maryland
March 19, 1970	March 21, 1970

UCLA	fg-fga	ft-fta	rb	pf	tp
Curtis Rowe	4- 7	7-11	15	0	15
Steve Patterson ...	5- 9	2- 2	6	3	12
Sidney Wicks	10-12	2- 5	16	3	22
John Vallely......	7-19	9-10	4	3	23
Henry Bibby	8-13	3- 3	2	5	19
Kenny Booker	0- 1	0- 0	0	2	0
Rick Betchley	0- 0	0- 0	0	0	0
Terry Schofield ...	0- 0	0- 0	0	1	0
John Ecker	0- 0	0- 0	0	0	0
Bill Seibert.......	0- 1	0- 0	1	0	0
Andy Hill........	0- 0	0- 1	0	1	0
Jon Chapman	1- 1	0- 0	1	0	2
Team			0		
Totals.........	35-63	23-32	45	18	93

New Mexico St.	fg-fga	ft-fta	rb	pf	tp
Charley Criss.....	6-16	7- 9	2	5	19
Jimmy Collins	13-23	2- 3	0	3	28
John Burgess	1- 6	0- 0	2	2	2
Jeff Smith	4-11	2- 3	7	5	10
Sam Lacey	3- 9	2- 3	16	3	8
Chito Reyes......	1- 6	0- 0	4	2	2
Roy Neal	2- 4	0- 0	6	2	4
Milton Horne	0- 4	2- 2	1	2	2
Bill Moore	1- 1	0- 0	1	0	2
Lonnie Lefevre ...	0- 0	0- 0	1	0	0
Rudy Franco	0- 0	0- 0	0	0	0
Tom McCarthy ...	0- 0	0- 0	0	0	0
Team			5		
Totals.........	31-80	15-20	45	24	77

Half time: UCLA 48-41. Officials: White and Wirtz. Attendance: 14,380.

Jacksonville	fg-fga	ft-fta	rb	pf	tp
Vaughn Wede-king	6-11	0- 0	2	2	12
Mike Blevins	1- 2	1- 2	0	1	3
Rex Morgan	5-11	0- 0	4	5	10
Pembrook Bur-rows	6- 9	0- 0	6	1	12
Artis Gilmore	9-29	1- 1	16	5	19
Greg Nelson	3- 9	2- 2	5	1	8
Chip Dublin	0- 5	2- 2	1	4	2
Rusty Baldwin	0- 0	0- 0	0	0	0
Rod McIntyre	1- 3	0- 0	3	4	2
Dan Hawkins.....	0- 1	1- 1	1	1	1
Ken Selke........	0- 0	0- 0	0	0	0
Team			2		
Totals.........	31-80	7- 8	40	24	69

UCLA	fg-fga	ft-fta	rb	pf	tp
Curtis Rowe	7-15	5- 5	8	4	19
Steve Patterson ...	8-15	1- 4	11	1	17
Sidney Wicks	5- 9	7-10	18	3	17
John Vallely......	5-10	5- 7	7	2	15
Henry Bibby	2-11	4- 4	4	1	8
Kenny Booker	0- 0	2- 3	0	0	2
Bill Seibert.......	0- 1	0- 0	1	1	0
John Ecker	1- 1	0- 0	0	0	2
Rick Betchley	0- 0	0- 1	0	0	0
Jon Chapman	0- 1	0- 0	1	0	0
Andy Hill........	0- 0	0- 1	0	0	0
Terry Schofield ...	0- 0	0- 0	0	0	0
Team			3		
Totals.........	28-63	24-35	53	12	80

Half time: UCLA 41-36. Officials: Scott and Wirtz. Attendance: 14,380.

1971

WEST REGIONAL
At Salt Lake City, Utah
March 18, 1971

UCLA	fg-fga	ft-fta	rb	pf	tp
Curtis Rowe	5-11	3- 6	9	0	13
Sidney Wicks	6-16	2- 5	20	1	14
Steve Patterson ...	6-13	1- 3	11	4	13
Henry Bibby	6-13	3- 3	9	3	15
Kenny Booker	2- 6	0- 0	1	2	4
Terry Schofield ...	6-13	0- 2	6	3	12
Larry Farmer	5- 9	1- 3	6	0	11
John Ecker	1- 3	0- 0	0	0	2
Rick Betchley	3- 4	1- 1	0	0	7
Team			2		
Totals	40-88	11-23	64	13	91

Brigham

Young	fg-fga	ft-fta	rb	pf	tp
Phil Tollestrup ...	0- 3	1- 2	1	2	1
Steve Kelly	9-16	6- 6	5	1	24
Kresimir Cosic	8-18	2- 2	23	3	18
Bernie Fryer	8-19	2- 6	4	3	18
Jim Miller	4-11	2- 5	5	3	10
Jay Bunker	1- 3	0- 0	5	4	2
Craig Jorgensen ...	0- 1	0- 0	1	0	0
Kalevi Sarkalahti ..	0- 0	0- 0	0	0	0
Dave Bailey	0- 1	0- 0	0	1	0
Team			2		
Totals	30-72	13-21	46	17	73

Half time: UCLA 41-32. Officials: White and Strauthers. Attendance: 15,032.

WEST REGIONAL
At Salt Lake City, Utah
March 20, 1971

Long Beach St.	fg-fga	ft-fta	rb	pf	tp
George Trapp	5-13	5- 6	16	3	15
Chuck Terry	4- 4	3- 4	6	3	11
Bob Lynn........	3-10	1- 3	5	4	7
Bernard Williams .	1- 7	0- 0	4	3	2
Ed Ratleff	8-14	2- 4	4	5	18
Eric McWilliams .	0- 1	0- 0	2	2	0
Dwight Taylor	0- 2	2- 4	2	2	2
Team			2		
Totals	21-51	13-21	41	22	55

UCLA	fg-fga	ft-fta	rb	pf	tp
Curtis Rowe	3- 6	6-12	12	2	12
Sidney Wicks	5-13	8-12	15	4	18
Steve Patterson ...	2- 8	1- 1	5	2	5
Henry Bibby	4-18	3- 3	6	4	11
Kenny Booker	0- 4	0- 0	2	0	0
Terry Schofield ...	3- 9	0- 0	3	1	6
Larry Farmer	0- 3	1- 2	4	2	1
Rick Betchley	1- 1	2- 2	0	0	4
John Ecker	0- 0	0- 0	0	1	0
Team			4		
Totals	18-62	21-32	51	16	57

Half time: Long Beach State 31-27. Attendance: 14,003.

262

1971

<table>
<tr><td colspan="6">SEMIFINALS
At Houston, Texas
March 25, 1971</td><td colspan="6">CHAMPIONSHIP
At Houston, Texas
March 25, 1971</td></tr>
</table>

SEMIFINALS
At Houston, Texas
March 25, 1971

Kansas	fg-fga	ft-fta	rb	pf	tp
Dave Robisch	7-19	3- 6	6	3	17
Pierre Russell.....	5-12	2- 2	4	4	12
Roger Brown	3- 8	1- 3	9	4	7
Bud Stallworth ...	5-10	2- 4	5	5	12
Aubrey Nash	3- 9	1- 2	3	1	7
Bob Kivisto	1- 1	1- 4	1	2	3
Randy Canfield ...	0- 0	0- 0	0	1	0
Mark Williams ...	0- 1	2- 2	0	2	2
Mark Mathews ...	0- 0	0- 0	0	0	0
Greg Douglas	0- 0	0- 0	1	0	0
Team			3		
Totals	24-60	12-23	32	22	60

UCLA	fg-fga	ft-fta	rb	pf	tp
Curtis Rowe	7-10	2- 4	15	2	16
Sidney Wicks	5- 9	11-13	8	2	21
Steve Patterson ...	3-11	0- 0	6	2	6
Henry Bibby	6- 9	6- 6	4	3	18
Kenny Booker	1- 2	1- 2	5	3	3
Terry Schofield ...	1- 3	0- 1	0	3	2
Larry Farmer	0- 2	0- 1	2	1	0
Rick Betchley	0- 0	0- 1	0	0	0
John Ecker	0- 1	2- 2	1	0	2
Andy Hill........	0- 0	0- 0	0	0	0
John Chapman ...	0- 0	0- 0	1	2	0
Team			5		
Totals	23-47	22-30	47	18	68

Half time: UCLA 32-25. Officials: White and Honzo. Attendance: 31,428.

CHAMPIONSHIP
At Houston, Texas
March 25, 1971

Villanova	fg-fga	ft-fta	rb	pf	tp
Clarence Smith ...	4-11	1- 1	2	4	9
Howard Porter....	10-21	5- 6	8	1	25
H. Siemiontkowski	9-16	1- 2	6	3	19
Tom Ingelsby	3- 9	1- 1	4	2	7
Chris Ford.......	0- 4	2- 3	5	4	2
Joe McDowell	0- 1	0- 0	2	0	0
John Fox	0- 0	0- 0	0	0	0
Team			4		
Totals	26-62	10-13	31	14	62

UCLA	fg-fga	ft-fta	rb	pf	tp
Curtis Rowe	2- 3	4- 5	8	0	8
Sidney Wicks	3- 7	1- 1	9	2	7
Steve Patterson ...	13-18	3- 5	8	1	29
Henry Bibby	6-12	5- 5	2	1	17
Kenny Booker	0- 0	0- 0	0	0	0
Terry Schofield ...	3- 9	0- 0	1	4	6
Rick Betchley	0- 0	1- 2	1	1	1
Team			5		
Totals	27-49	14-18	34	9	68

Half time: UCLA 45-37. Officials: Bain and Brown. Attendance: 31,765.

263

1972

WEST REGIONAL
At Provo, Utah
March 16, 1972

Weber State	fg-fga	ft-fta	rb	pf	tp
Bob Davis	4-14	8-13	6	4	16
Wes VanDyke....	2-11	0- 1	1	3	4
Richard Cooper...	2-10	4- 6	12	4	8
Brady Small	1-12	2- 3	2	0	4
Jonnie Knoble	3- 8	3- 8	9	4	9
Riley Wimberley ..	7-15	0- 0	5	0	14
Ken Gubler	1- 2	0- 0	1	2	2
Greg Soter	0- 0	1- 2	0	0	1
Ralph Williams ...	0- 1	0- 0	0	0	0
Team			18		
Totals.........	20-73	18-33	54	17	58

UCLA	fg-fga	ft-fta	rb	pf	tp
Larry Farmer	7-15	1- 1	7	1	15
Keith Wilkes	4-12	2- 2	13	4	10
Bill Walton	1- 1	2- 5	12	4	4
Greg Lee	3- 8	0- 0	4	1	6
Henry Bibby	7-18	2- 2	3	2	16
Tommy Curtis....	3- 7	1- 1	3	2	7
Larry Hollyfield ..	2- 9	0- 0	5	2	4
Swen Nater	5- 9	2- 4	8	2	12
Vince Carson	0- 3	0- 1	5	2	0
Jon Chapman	1- 1	0- 1	2	1	2
Andy Hill........	3- 4	4- 4	1	2	10
Gary Franklin	2- 2	0- 0	2	0	4
Team			11		
Totals.........	38-89	14-21	76	23	90

Half time: UCLA 42-25. Officials: Copeland and Fouty. Attendance: 15,247.

WEST REGIONAL
At Provo, Utah
March 18, 1972

Long Beach St.	fg-fga	ft-fta	rb	pf	tp
Chuck Terry	2- 6	2- 2	4	4	6
Leonard Gray	2- 5	3- 4	3	4	7
Eric McWilliams .	2- 4	3- 3	5	4	7
Glenn McDonald .	3- 3	2- 2	5	0	8
Ed Ratleff	7-19	3- 6	3	3	17
Bob Lynn........	2- 6	2- 2	8	2	6
Nate Stephens	1- 5	0- 0	3	1	2
Lamont King	2- 2	0- 0	0	3	4
Team			2		
Totals.........	21-50	15-19	33	21	57

UCLA	fg-fga	ft-fta	rb	pf	tp
Keith Wilkes	4-10	6- 7	6	3	14
Larry Farmer	2- 7	1- 3	3	3	5
Bill Walton	7-10	5- 7	11	3	19
Greg Lee	2- 6	2- 3	3	0	6
Henry Bibby	10-17	3- 4	4	2	23
Larry Hollyfield ..	0- 1	0- 0	0	2	0
Swen Nater	2- 2	1- 2	1	0	5
Tommy Curtis....	0- 0	0- 0	0	1	0
Vince Carson	0- 0	0- 0	1	1	0
Andy Hill........	0- 0	1- 3	0	0	1
Team			7		
Totals.........	27-53	19-29	36	15	73

Half time: UCLA 34-23. Officials: Copeland and Wortman. Attendance: 15,152.

1972

SEMIFINALS
At Los Angeles, California
March 23, 1972

Louisville	fg-fga	ft-fta	rb	pf	tp
Mike Lawhon	0- 7	1- 2	3	3	1
Ron Thomas	2- 4	0- 0	3	5	4
Al Vilcheck	3- 6	0- 0	1	5	6
Jim Price	11-23	8- 9	5	3	30
Henry Bacon	5-11	5- 7	4	0	15
Larry Carter	4- 8	0- 0	2	0	8
Bill Bunton	1- 5	1- 1	4	1	3
Ken Bradley......	1- 3	0- 0	2	1	2
Ron Stallings	1- 2	0- 1	1	2	2
Tim Cooper......	0- 1	2- 2	1	1	2
Paul Pry	2- 3	0- 0	1	1	4
Joe Meiman	0- 1	0- 0	1	0	0
Team			4		
Totals	30-74	17-22	32	22	77

UCLA	fg-fga	ft-fta	rb	pf	tp
Keith Wilkes	5-11	2- 2	6	0	12
Larry Farmer	6-12	3- 5	4	2	15
Bill Walton	11-13	11-12	21	2	33
Greg Lee	3- 6	4- 6	4	1	10
Henry Bibby	1- 5	0- 0	3	5	2
Tommy Curtis....	4- 5	0- 0	2	2	8
Larry Hollyfield ...	3- 6	0- 0	4	1	6
Vince Carson	1- 1	0- 0	0	1	2
Swen Nater	0- 0	2- 4	1	1	2
Andy Hill........	1- 1	4- 4	0	1	6
Jon Chapman	0- 0	0- 1	1	0	0
Gary Franklin	0- 1	0- 0	2	0	0
Team			3		
Totals	35-61	26-34	51	16	96

Half time: UCLA 39-31. Officials: Hernjack and Copeland. Attendance: 15,189.

CHAMPIONSHIP
At Los Angeles, California
March 25, 1972

Florida State	fg-fga	ft-fta	rb	pf	tp
Rowland Garrett ..	1- 9	1- 1	5	1	3
Ron King	12-20	3- 3	6	1	27
Reggie Royals	5- 7	5- 6	10	5	15
Lawrence McCray	3- 6	2- 5	6	4	8
Greg Samuel	3-10	0- 0	1	1	6
Ron Harris	7-13	2- 3	6	1	16
Otto Petty	0- 0	1- 1	0	1	1
Otis Cole	0- 2	0- 0	2	1	0
Team			6		
Totals	31-67	14-19	42	15	76

UCLA	fg-fga	ft-fta	rb	pf	tp
Keith Wilkes	11-16	1- 2	10	4	23
Larry Farmer	2- 6	0- 0	6	2	4
Bill Walton	9-17	6-11	20	4	24
Greg Lee	0- 0	0- 0	2	0	0
Henry Bibby	8-17	2- 3	3	2	18
Tommy Curtis....	4-14	0- 1	4	1	8
Larry Hollyfield ...	1- 6	0- 0	2	2	2
Swen Nater	1- 2	0- 1	1	0	2
Team			2		
Totals	36-78	9-18	50	15	81

Half time: UCLA 50-39. Officials: Brown and Scott. Attendance: 15,063.

1973

UCLA	fg-fga	ft-fta	rb	pf	tp
Keith Wilkes	6-14	0- 0	10	2	12
Larry Farmer	5-10	0- 0	4	2	10
Bill Walton	13-18	2- 2	14	3	28
Larry Hollyfield	9-16	2- 2	5	3	20
Greg Lee	1- 2	1- 1	0	0	3
Tommy Curtis	2- 3	3- 3	1	2	7
Dave Meyers	2- 3	2- 3	5	1	6
Swen Nater	2- 5	0- 2	2	2	4
Vince Carson	0- 0	0- 2	1	0	0
Gary Franklin	1- 2	0- 0	2	0	2
Pete Trgovich	2- 5	0- 0	2	0	4
Bob Webb	0- 2	0- 0	0	2	0
Casey Corliss	0- 0	2- 2	0	1	2
Ralph Drollinger	0- 0	0- 0	0	1	0
Team			5		
Totals	43-80	12-17	51	19	98

Arizona State	fg-fga	ft-fta	rb	pf	tp
Ken Gray	2- 4	0- 1	2	0	4
Mark Wasley	3- 8	0- 0	10	1	6
Ron Kennedy	2- 7	5- 6	8	5	9
Mike Contreras	9-20	0- 0	4	3	18
Jim Owens	8-20	6- 8	4	2	22
Rudy White	3- 6	0- 0	2	0	6
Gary Jackson	3- 8	4- 6	4	3	10
Jim Brown	2- 6	2- 3	6	2	6
Jack Schrader	0- 1	0- 0	3	1	0
Mike Moon	0- 2	0- 0	1	0	0
Team			4		
Totals	32-82	17-24	48	17	81

Half time: UCLA 51-37. Officials: Copeland and Fouty. Attendance: 12,671.

San Francisco	fg-fga	ft-fta	rb	pf	tp
Kevin Restani	4-11	0- 0	9	0	8
Phil Smith	8-13	1- 1	3	0	17
Eric Fernsten	2- 5	0- 0	8	3	4
Mike Quick	4- 9	0- 0	2	1	8
John Boro	0- 3	2- 2	0	3	2
Team			4		
Totals	18-41	3- 3	26	7	39

UCLA	fg-fga	ft-fta	rb	pf	tp
Keith Wilkes	6-13	0- 0	1	0	12
Larry Farmer	5-10	3- 3	4	0	13
Bill Walton	4- 7	1- 2	14	0	9
Larry Hollyfield	0- 3	0- 0	1	0	0
Greg Lee	1- 4	0- 0	1	0	2
Dave Meyers	1- 3	0- 0	3	3	2
Tommy Curtis	6- 9	0- 1	1	1	12
Swen Nater	0- 2	0- 0	1	0	0
Gary Franklin	1- 2	0- 0	2	0	2
Vince Carson	0- 0	0- 0	1	1	0
Bob Webb	0- 1	0- 0	0	1	0
Pete Trgovich	1- 2	0- 0	0	0	2
Team			1		
Totals	25-56	4- 6	30	6	54

Half time: UCLA 23-22. Officials: White and Copeland. Attendance: 12,705.

1973

SEMIFINALS
At St. Louis, Missouri
March 24, 1973

UCLA	fg-fga	ft-fta	rb	pf	tp
Keith Wilkes	5-10	3- 4	6	3	13
Larry Farmer	3- 6	1- 2	3	4	7
Bill Walton	7-12	0- 0	17	4	14
Greg Lee	0- 1	0- 0	0	0	0
Larry Hollyfield ...	5- 6	0- 0	2	1	10
Tommy Curtis....	9-15	4- 7	2	2	22
Dave Meyers	2- 3	0- 0	5	1	4
Swen Nater	0- 0	0- 0	0	1	0
Team			3		
Totals	31-53	8-13	38	16	70

Indiana	fg-fga	ft-fta	rb	pf	tp
Quinn Buckner ...	3-10	0- 1	5	2	6
Jim Crews	4-10	0- 0	2	3	8
Steve Downing ...	12-20	2- 4	5	5	26
Steve Green......	1- 7	0- 0	5	2	2
John Ritter	6-10	1- 1	2	3	13
John Laskowski ...	1- 8	0- 0	4	0	2
Tom Abernethy...	0- 1	0- 0	1	1	0
Trent Smock	0- 0	0- 0	0	0	0
Don Noort.......	0- 0	0- 0	1	0	0
Frank Wilson	0- 0	0- 0	0	0	0
Craig Morris	0- 0	0- 0	0	0	0
Steve Ahlfield	0- 0	0- 0	0	0	0
Doug Allen	1- 1	0- 0	0	0	2
Jerry Memering ...	0- 0	0- 0	0	0	0
Team			4		
Totals	28-67	3- 6	29	16	59

Half time: UCLA 40-22. Officials: Shosid and Howell. Attendance: 19,029.

CHAMPIONSHIP
At St. Louis, Missouri
March 26, 1973

UCLA	fg-fga	ft-fta	rb	pf	tp
Keith Wilkes	8-14	0- 0	7	2	16
Larry Farmer	1- 4	0- 0	2	2	2
Bill Walton	21-22	2- 5	13	4	44
Greg Lee	1- 1	3- 3	3	2	5
Larry Hollyfield ...	4- 7	0- 0	3	4	8
Tommy Curtis....	1- 4	2- 2	3	1	4
Dave Meyers	2- 7	0- 0	3	1	4
Swen Nater	1- 1	0- 0	3	2	2
Gary Franklin	1- 2	0- 1	1	0	2
Vince Carson	0- 0	0- 0	0	0	0
Bob Webb.......	0- 0	0- 0	0	0	0
Team			2		
Totals	40-62	7-11	40	18	87

Memphis State	fg-fga	ft-fta	rb	pf	tp
Billy Buford	3- 7	1- 2	3	1	7
Larry Kenon	8-16	4- 4	8	3	20
Ron Robinson ...	3- 6	0- 1	7	4	6
Bill Laurie	0- 1	0- 0	0	0	0
Larry Finch	9-21	11-13	1	2	29
Wes Westfall	0- 1	0- 0	0	5	0
Bill Cook	1- 4	2- 2	0	1	4
Doug McKinney ..	0- 0	0- 0	0	0	0
Clarence Jones ...	0- 0	0- 0	0	0	0
Jerry Tetzlaff	0- 0	0- 2	2	0	1
Jim Liss	0- 1	0- 0	0	0	0
Ken Andrews.....	0- 0	0- 0	0	0	0
Team			2		
Totals	24-57	18-24	21	17	66

Half time: 39-39. Officials: Howell and Shosid. Attendance: 19,301.

1975

WEST FIRST ROUND
At Pullman, Washington
March 15, 1975

UCLA	fg-fga	ft-fta	rb	pf	tp
Rich Washington .	11-14	0- 1	17	4	22
Dave Myers	9-18	8-10	12	4	26
Jim Spillane	2- 7	0- 0	1	1	4
Andre McCarter . .	0- 7	4- 5	2	2	4
Wilbert Olinde . . .	0- 0	0- 0	0	1	0
Raymond Town-					
send	0- 1	0- 0	1	0	0
Pete Trgovich	8-16	1- 2	3	4	17
Ralph Drollinger . .	3- 3	2- 4	3	0	8
Marques Johnson .	9-20	4- 4	13	4	22
Team			7		
Totals	42-86	19-26	59	20	103

Michigan	fg-fga	ft-fta	rb	pf	tp
Joe Johnson	3-12	5- 7	1	4	11
Dave Baxter	0- 1	0- 0	0	0	0
Steve Grote	7-15	0- 0	9	5	14
Wayman Britt	3- 6	2- 2	5	5	8
Rick White	3- 7	0- 1	6	2	6
C. J. Kupec	13-25	2- 4	5	3	28
John Robinson . . .	9-16	6- 6	7	4	24
Team			8		
Totals	38-82	15-20	41	23	91

Half time: Michigan 50-46. Regulation Score: 87-87. Officials: Sherwood and Stern. Attendance: 10,150.

WEST REGIONAL
At Portland, Oregon
March 20, 1975

Montana	fg-fga	ft-fta	rb	pf	tp
Eric Hays	13-16	6- 7	7	2	32
Mike Richardson . .	1- 5	0- 0	4	4	2
Ben DeMers	0- 2	0- 0	0	1	0
Tom Peck	0- 1	0- 0	4	1	0
Larry Smedley	5-12	0- 0	5	2	10
Ken McKenzie . . .	9-22	2- 6	10	3	20
Tim Stambaugh . .	0- 2	0- 0	2	0	0
Team			4		
Totals	28-60	8-13	36	13	64

UCLA	fg-fga	ft-fta	rb	pf	tp
Raymond Town-					
send	1- 1	0- 0	1	0	2
Pete Trgovich	6-11	4- 6	3	3	16
Rich Washington .	7-17	2- 2	11	3	16
Dave Meyers	6-14	0- 0	5	1	12
Ralph Drollinger . .	3- 5	2- 4	9	3	8
Casey Corliss	0- 1	0- 0	0	1	0
Jim Spillane	0- 1	0- 0	0	2	0
Andre McCarter . .	3- 8	0- 2	1	1	6
Marques Johnson .	3- 7	1- 2	6	1	7
Gavin Smith	0- 0	0- 0	0	0	0
Team			4		
Totals	29-65	9-16	40	15	67

Half time: UCLA 34-33. Officials: Workman and Fouty. Attendance: 9,797.

268

1975

WEST REGIONAL
At Portland, Oregon
March 27, 1975

Arizona State	fg-fga	ft-fta	rb	pf	tp
James Holliman ...	1- 5	1- 2	7	3	3
Mike Moon	2- 5	0- 0	0	1	4
Rudy White	6-13	3- 4	5	5	15
Lionel Hollins	8-22	0- 1	0	4	16
Jack Schrader.....	4-12	1- 2	12	4	9
Ken Wright	2- 4	0- 1	3	0	4
Scott Lloyd	8-13	4- 8	9	4	20
Greg White	0- 0	0- 0	0	0	0
Gary Jackson	2- 4	0- 0	2	2	4
Team			2		
Totals	33-78	9-18	40	23	75

UCLA	fg-fga	ft-fta	rb	pf	tp
Pete Trgovich	4-14	0- 1	4	3	8
Rich Washington .	8-13	0- 0	12	5	16
Dave Meyers	4-15	3- 4	13	3	11
Ralph Drollinger ..	3- 4	3- 3	3	5	9
Andre McCarter ..	2- 5	5- 8	5	1	9
Wilbert Olinde ...	0- 0	1- 2	1	1	1
Marques Johnson .	14-20	7- 8	12	1	35
Team			3		
Totals	35-71	19-26	53	19	89

Half time: UCLA 46-36. Officials: Workman and Fouty. Attendance: 8,534.

SEMIFINALS
At San Diego, California
March 29, 1975

Louisville	fg-fga	ft-fta	rb	pf	tp
Allen Murphy	14-28	5- 7	2	2	33
Wesley Cox	5- 8	4-11	16	2	14
William Bunton ..	3- 4	1- 2	7	2	7
Junior Bridgeman .	4-15	4- 4	15	4	12
Phillip Bond	2- 6	2- 2	3	1	6
Ike Whitfield.....	0- 0	0- 0	1	1	0
Ricky Gallon	0- 3	0- 0	2	2	0
Danny Brown	1- 1	0- 0	1	0	2
Rick Wilson	0- 0	0- 0	0	0	0
Terry Howard	0- 0	0- 1	0	0	0
Team			2		
Totals	29-65	16-27	49	14	74

UCLA	fg-fga	ft-fta	rb	pf	tp
Dave Meyers	6-16	4- 6	7	3	16
Marques Johnson .	5-10	0- 0	11	2	10
Rich Washington .	11-19	4- 6	8	4	26
Pete Trgovich	6-12	0- 0	2	5	12
Andre McCarter ..	3-12	0- 0	2	2	6
Ralph Drollinger ..	1- 2	1- 2	4	5	3
Wilbert Olinde ...	0- 0	0- 0	0	0	0
Jim Spillane	1- 2	0- 0	1	1	2
Team			1		
Totals	33-73	9-14	36	22	75

Half time: Louisville 37-33. Regulation Score: 65-65. Officials: Wortman and Nichols. Attendance: 15,151.

1975

CHAMPIONSHIP
At San Diego, California
March 29, 1975

UCLA	fg-fga	ft-fta	rb	pf	tp
Dave Meyers	9-18	6- 7	11	4	24
Marques Johnson .	3- 9	0- 1	7	2	6
Rich Washington .	12-23	4- 5	12	4	28
Pete Trgovich	7-16	2- 4	5	4	16
Andre McCarter ..	3- 6	2- 3	2	1	8
Ralph Drollinger ..	4- 6	2- 5	13	4	10
Team			5		
Totals	38-78	16-25	55	19	92

Kentucky	fg-fga	ft-fta	rb	pf	tp
Kevin Grevey.....	13-30	8-10	5	4	34
Bob Guyette	7-11	2- 2	7	3	16
Rick Robey	1- 3	0- 0	9	5	2
Jimmy Dan Con- ner	4-12	1- 2	5	1	9
Mike Flynn	3- 9	4- 5	3	4	10
Jack Givens	3-10	2- 3	6	3	8
Larry Johnson	0- 3	0- 0	3	3	0
Mike Phillips	1- 7	2- 3	6	4	4
Dan Hall	1- 1	0- 0	1	0	2
James Lee	0- 0	0- 0	0	1	0
Team			4		
Totals	33-86	19-25	49	28	85

Half time: UCLA 43-40. Officials: Nichols and Workman. Attendance: 15,151.

Acknowledgments

MY THANKS to Jack Tobin, who worked with me to construct this narrative from literally hundreds of hours of interviews. I am also deeply grateful to the following individuals, who at some point in time contributed to the finished product: J. D. Morgan, Jean Dunne, Stan Troutman, Norm Schindler, Vic Kelley, Frank Stewart, Peggy Fauquier, Betty Martin, Peggy Veselka, and especially to our editor, Ilyce Glink, and Contemporary Books, who brought *They Call Me Coach* back to life.

About Jack Tobin

IN HIS FIFTY-PLUS YEARS as journalist, Jack Tobin has covered every facet of news from homicides to presidential elections, Super Bowls to sandlot football games, tree plantings to a two-year investigation of James R. Hoffa and the Teamsters' Union pension fund. He has free-lanced for such magazines as *Time*, *Life*, *Look*, *Saturday Evening Post*, *Fortune*, and *Sports Illustrated*. Since 1962, he has been *Sports Illustrated* correspondent for Southern California, handling story suggestions and assignment of photographers, artists, and writers—one of the largest

271

geographic responsibilities in the magazine's system of correspondents.

Jack's love for writing dates from a December Saturday in 1930, when at age ten he first saw the Los Angeles Memorial Coliseum, a Notre Dame football team, and a legend of the era named Knute Rockne. That night, flat on the floor of his Long Beach home, Jack tried to join such famed Los Angeles sportswriters as the late Mark Kelly and the late Bill Henry in reporting on Notre Dame's stunning 27–0 upset of USC.

That desire soon reached reality for Jack. Ever since joining the *Long Beach Press-Telegram* as a teenager, he has used words as a way of life and livelihood, except for three years active duty on a Navy attack transport during World War II. From the *Press-Telegram*, he became part of the original staff of the *Los Angeles Mirror* (later the *Mirror-News*) in 1948, and in 1961 joined the *Los Angeles Times*.

Tobin has also held a number of executive positions. In 1962 he began a four and a half year stint as director of public relations, promotions, and advertising for the Memorial Coliseum Commission in Los Angeles, where he handled two of the largest spectator facilities in the nation, the Memorial Coliseum and the Memorial Sports Arena. In 1966, he was appointed executive vice president of the Los Angeles Toros in the newly born National Professional Soccer League. Following the sale and transfer of that franchise, he became vice president and director of marketing for Computicket Corporation, a computerized ticket and reservation system.

Tobin holds two degrees in journalism, the B.A. from Notre Dame University (1943) and the M.S. from UCLA (1959). He and his wife, Virginia, reside in Playa del Rey, California. Their son, Timothy, is a UCLA theater arts graduate and a film editor today on major feature productions.